THE NORTH POLE

THE FIVE FLAGS AT THE POLE

LEFT TO RIGHT

1. Navy League—Ooqueah   3. Polar Flag Carried 15 Years—Henson
2. D. K. E. Fraternity—Ootah   4. D. A. R. Peace Flag—Egingwah
                    5. Red Cross Flag—Seegloo

THE NORTH POLE

ITS DISCOVERY IN 1909 UNDER THE AUSPICES OF THE PEARY ARCTIC CLUB

BY

ROBERT E. PEARY

FOREWORD BY
THEODORE ROOSEVELT

NEW INTRODUCTION BY
ROBERT M. BRYCE

WITH EIGHT FULL-PAGE ILLUSTRATIONS REPRODUCING PHOTOGRAPHIC
ENLARGEMENTS; ONE-HUNDRED ILLUSTRATIONS FROM PHOTOGRAPHS;
AND WITH A MAP BY GILBERT H. GROSVENOR

Cooper Square Press

First Cooper Square Press Edition 2001

This Cooper Square Press paperback edition of *The North Pole* is an unabridged republication of the edition first published in New York in 1910, with the deletion of one map, the reproduction in black and white of eight photos (originally colored by hand), and the addition of a new introduction by Robert M. Bryce.

New introduction copyright © 2001 by Robert M. Bryce

Published by Cooper Square Press
An Imprint of the Rowman & Littlefield Publishing Group
150 Fifth Avenue, Suite 911
New York, New York 10011

Distributed by National Book Network

Library of Congress Cataloging-in-Publication Data
This book was previously cataloged by the Library of Congress as follows:

Peary, Robert E. (Robert Edwin)
   The North pole, its discovery in 1909 under the auspices of the Peary Arctic club, by Robert E. Peary; with an introduction by Theodore Roosevelt and a foreword by Gilbert H. Grosvenor ... with eight full-page illustrations reproducing photographic enlargements colored by hand; one hundred illustrations in black-and-white, from photographs; and with a map in colors by Gilbert H. Grosvenor./ Robert Edwin Peary.
      p. cm.
1. North Pole. 2. Arctic regions. I. Title

G670 1909.P6

10–022101

ISBN 0-8154-1138-3 (pbk.: alk. paper)

⊖™ The paper used in this publication meets the minimum requirements of American National Standard for Information Sciences— Permanence of Paper for Printed Library Materials, ANSI/NISO Z39.48–1992.
Manufactured in the United States of America.

INTRODUCTION TO THE COOPER SQUARE PRESS EDITION

ROBERT Edwin Peary was described by his first biographer as "The Man Who Refused to Fail." This seemed a logical sobriquet based on nothing more than the apparent single-mindedness of his career.

Although Peary was born in Cresson, Pennsylvania, on May 6, 1856, his parents had only come there to find work. After his father Charles died, when Bert was not quite three years old, his mother immediately moved the family back to Maine. As a child, Bert had a shy and sensitive nature, but he overcame this as well as his mother's smothering love. She tried to raise him as if he were a girl, but Bert proved to be a very mischievous boy. When his classmates made fun of his overly long locks and slight lisp, he defended himself with his fists, and he found an antidote to his mother's overprotectiveness in the freedom of the Maine woods and in the pages of books about explorers in the frozen north. His success in academic and athletic pursuits earned him a scholarship to Bowdoin College, where he graduated second in his class with a degree in civil engineering in 1877. After a couple of years as a surveyor in Maine and several more as a draftsman for the Coast and Geodetic Survey in Washington, D.C., he took a competitive exam and was commissioned as a civil engineer in the U.S. Navy.

Early on he had told his mother of his fondest ambition: "I *must* have fame & I cannot reconcile myself to years of commonplace drudgery & a name late in life when I see an opportunity to gain it now & sip the delicious draught while yet I have youth & strength & capacity to enjoy it to the utmost." Yet, ironically, the opportunity to gain the fame he dreamt of so ardently took twenty-three years of drudgery, though hardly of the commonplace kind, and he made a name for himself with barely ten years left to enjoy. No sooner was it gained than it began to ebb away in whispers of doubt that he had actually accomplished that for which he was most famous.

The route to fame that Peary chose lay over the tortured surface of the Arctic Ocean, to the mathematical point known as the North Pole. But to Peary and many others it was much more than that. By the turn of the twentieth century the North Pole had become the Holy Grail of exploration, worthy of the sacrifices once demanded only of a knightly quest. When he first set out on this quest, Peary admitted he felt "a constant intoxication in such work, in the thought 'my eyes are the first that have ever looked upon this scene, mine the touch that has wakened the sleeping princess.'" A modest, self-financed reconnaissance of Greenland's icecap in 1886 led to a full-fledged expedition in 1891, sponsored by the Academy of Natural Sciences of Philadelphia.

This expedition was a brilliant success, and Peary's claim to have proved the insularity of Greenland, combined with a strenuous lecture tour, provided him the means to return the next year to continue his explorations.

With this third expedition, he hoped to extend his discoveries in Northern Greenland, perhaps even to find land reaching to the Pole itself. But he accomplished none of this; instead, he barely escaped with his life. Indeed, Peary met with so many setbacks that, when he returned in 1895, he believed himself, at age thirty-nine, too old for Arctic work. "I shall never see the North Pole unless someone brings it here," he declared. "I am done with it."

He had little to show for his efforts beyond two large meteorites he had recovered from Cape York. But by loaning these to the American Museum of Natural History in New York, Peary gained powerful friends for the future, including the millionaire philanthropist Morris Jesup. Jesup led the formation of the Peary Arctic Club in 1898, whose avowed purpose was to aid Peary in reaching the North Pole. With such encouragement, Peary decided to try again.

His first attempt at the ultimate prize was aborted in 1899 when Peary lost seven of his toes (an eighth was later removed stateside) to frostbite during a desperate attempt to beat an imagined rival to a forward base for his projected polar journey. His consequent physical impairment caused his next serious attempt to be postponed until 1902. When fifteen days of backbreaking struggle netted him nearly nothing in the way of progress toward the Pole, Peary, at low ebb, wrote in his diary: "Soon they will call me a fake, say I am just hoarding what I can mint from the public's credulity. . . . I have made the best fight, I knew. I believe it has been a good one. But I cannot accomplish the impossible." The romance of the work had all but faded away, but as before, Peary was not "done with it." In fact, once back in civilization, it seemed to him more apparent than ever that reaching the Pole was the thing "which it is intended that I should do, and the thing that I must do."

Peary returned to the Arctic in 1905. But even with the unlimited resources of the millionaires who made up the Peary Arctic Club and with the custom-built ice-ship, that they provided, the *Roosevelt*, Peary failed again in 1906. Even so he claimed to have discovered the most northerly land on earth, "Crocker Land," and to have gone thirty-two miles nearer the Pole than the previous "Farthest North" record.

Although Peary had announced before his departure that this would be his final attempt, he immediately began preparations for another. Unable to repair his ship in time for the planned departure date of July 1907, he had to wait until the summer of 1908. He was fifty-two years old. *The North Pole*, first published by Frederick A. Stokes & Co. in September 1910, purports to be the record of his success, one he attributed to experience above all else and to the indomitable will of "The Man Who Refused to Fail." However, the majority of scholars who have studied *The North Pole* and the vast collection of Peary's personal papers containing the records of his expeditions have concluded that his "discovery" of the North Pole on April 6, 1909, was one of the greatest scientific hoaxes of all time.

Although this consensus of informed judgment has been a long time in coming, suspicions gathered early over his claim as a result of Peary's attempts to discredit his rival, Dr. Frederick A. Cook. When Peary returned from the North on September 5, 1909, he found himself four days behind Cook's announcement of his own polar

conquest and the resultant rapturous reception in Copenhagen, Denmark, where Cook first reached civilization
after staying more than two years in the Arctic. By September 8, Peary intimated his rival was lying, and two
days later bluntly wired the *New York Herald*: "Cook has
simply handed the public a gold brick. He's not been at
the pole April 21, 1908, or any other time."

That charge began the celebrated "Polar Controversy," which reigned on the front pages of newspapers
for nearly four months. Even today, a small group of ar-
dent advocates of each man still insists they champion
the true discoverer. Originally, Cook won public favor because of his gentlemanly response to Peary's bitter attacks. These same attacks had a negative effect on the
way that Peary's own success was perceived. But then a
skillful press campaign mounted by Peary's backers
began to undermine Cook's credibility.

First, members of Peary's expedition swore they had
interviewed Cook's Inuit companions while still in Greenland. The Inuit hunters were said to have denied that they
had ever been out of sight of land on Cook's recent attempt and therefore never came closer than hundreds of
miles to the Pole. Next, the only witness to Cook's Alaskan feat swore out an affidavit stating that the doctor's
claimed ascent of McKinley was merely a hoax arranged
by Cook with his complicity. Finally, two men came forward to swear additional affidavits saying that Cook had
hired them to manufacture a set of faked astronomical
observations in proof of his having been at the Pole.
When Cook's polar "proofs" were examined by a University of Copenhagen committee, to whom he had promised
them while in Denmark, it found no trace of the allegedly

forged observations among them. But it also could not find in them "any proof whatsoever of Dr. Cook having reached the North Pole."

The negative verdict of the committee—judges whom Cook had chosen himself—instantaneously branded him in the press as the "American Munchausen," and a "monster of duplicity." This, coupled with Cook's apparent flight from the country, was taken as an admission of guilt and convinced many that their recent hero was nothing more than a contemptible cheat. At the same time, it allowed Peary to step forward unopposed to claim the prize he had sought for so long: the everlasting fame that belonged to the discoverer of the North Pole.

However, the suspicion unleashed by Peary over his fellow explorer's claims immediately settled on his own. No proofs had ever been demanded of a returning explorer before Peary demanded them of Cook, but now proof was asked of Peary as well. He was very reluctant to put his proofs forward nonetheless. He delayed doing so for two months before offering them to a committee of the National Geographic Society. In its report, the committee stated that it had "carefully examined" Peary's diary and navigational instruments and was "unanimously of the opinion that Commander Peary reached the North Pole April 6, 1909." To the public, it seemed Peary had passed the scientific test that his rival had so ingloriously failed. However, the matter was far from settled.

A number of bills had been introduced into both houses of Congress: to retire Peary with the rank of rear admiral at the highest pay grade, to vote him the Thanks of Congress for discovering the North Pole, and to award him a gold medal. The bill passed the U.S. Senate without question, but just when it seemed that Peary was about to receive the rewards and honors that his friends thought he so richly deserved, things suddenly turned sour.

Although the Peary interests flooded Congress with pro-Peary propaganda, including pamphlets comparing his expedition to a masterful military campaign, and lauding the expedition as the "perfect exploration machine," the Peary bills faced resistance in the House of Representatives.

Peary's actions toward Cook during the months after his return from the Arctic had made him many bitter enemies. Even though his supporters used the collapse of Cook's claim to justify Peary's attitude during the controversy, many simply saw him, as one newspaper put it, as a "coarse-grained and ill-tempered boor," and Cook's Copenhagen fiasco had made some congressmen cautious about any polar claim.

In March 1910, Peary's representatives at a congressional hearing said Peary could not present his proofs to the committee without compromising the literary contracts that he had signed for a series of magazine articles and a book detailing his triumph. Without the documents, hearings on Peary's retirement were put on indefinite hold.

Early in 1911, Peary was compelled to appear in person before the committee. At the hearings it came out that the "careful examination" by the National Geographic Society was, as the report of the congressional committee put it, "anything but minute, careful and rigorous." In fact, it seemed little more than a rubber stamp by a jury of Peary's friends.

The publication of *The North Pole* the previous September had cleared away all the objections that had been made to presenting the committee with his original observations and journal, but, even so, Peary refused to leave his records with the committee for a thorough examination. The committee members had to examine them on the spot. Even then, they noticed a number of physical features that seemed peculiar.

The celestial observations to determine the expedition's position en route to the Pole were not in sequence in the journal but were taken on loose slips of paper [reproduced in appendix II]. Representative Ernest W. Roberts noticed that the crucial memorandum given to Peary by Captain Bob Bartlett certifying that he had left his commander 133 nautical miles from the Pole (all distances are in nautical miles, which are 15% longer than the statute mile commonly used on road maps) seemed to be written in three different kinds of pencil, as if portions of it had been filled in after the fact [pp. 360–61]. When the congressmen examined the journal of the polar trip, they noticed that the return date had been recorded, but the point achieved had simply been left blank. Its cover was inscribed: "No. 1 Roosevelt to ————— and return, February 22 to April [28 crossed out] 27, R. E. Peary, United States Navy." The pages for April 7 and 8, 1909, days when Peary claimed to have been at or near the Pole, were blank, and April 6, the day of the discovery, had the crucial event written on a loose slip of paper and inserted—though there was also a regular entry for the day itself in the diary. The sharp-eyed Roberts also noticed that although Peary had described in *The North Pole* how difficult it was to write in a diary while on the trail [p. 160], this diary was filled with perfectly even lines of script. Not only was the writing neat, the book itself was free from any mark of the oily food consumed by polar explorers. As Roberts noted: "It shows no finger marks or rough usage; a very cleanly kept book."

Despite all this, and despite Peary's apparent reluctance to tell anyone but Bartlett upon his return to the *Roosevelt* whether or not he had reached the North Pole, most of the committee was favorably disposed to take Peary's word that he had. As Representative Butler put it, "We have your word for it, and we have these observations to show that you were at the North Pole. That is the plain way of putting it—your word and your proofs. To me, as a member of this committee, I accept your word; but your proofs, I know nothing at all about."

Still, there were some not willing to accept Peary's bare word. When questioned about his alleged speed, he stated that he had traveled fifty miles, estimated, on his best day. One skeptical committee member contrasted this with Peary's recent performance in a physical test required for promotion by the Navy.

In that test, Peary had taken fifteen hours and thirty-nine minutes to walk the equivalent of a bit more than forty-seven nautical miles on the paved roads of Washington, D.C., spread over three consecutive days, and separated by two nights of sleep. Yet Peary had said he had done better than that on his one best day of the polar journey without any rest. Furthermore, he made his Arctic miles on foot, he insisted, and did not ride the sledges. Sympathetic committee members tried to justify such speed by comparing records made by mail carriers and dog-sled racers in Alaska, which antagonistic members pointed out had no relevance to a journey over the jumbled, treacherous, and ever-moving polar pack ice.

Further questioning revealed that Peary had not taken any longitude sights or made any checks to correct his magnetic compass on the entire journey; even so, he insisted that he stayed on the 70th meridian all the way to the Pole. All of the sights taken for latitude up to the time that he parted from Captain Bartlett were single sun shots taken at noon, made by one of his subordinates and assuming 70th meridian time, which precluded any independent checking of any of his reported positions. Actually, Peary took no sights at all himself until the one by which he determined he had reached the North Pole.

The evidence given by Peary before the committee was characterized by an antagonistic congressman as, "the best information, or so-called proofs, that they could get from the alleged discoverer, when summed up, were a lot of guesses, speculations, assumptions, estimates, and evasions . . . contradicted by a combination of every reasonable physical and scientific impossibility."

Even though Peary's testimony raised serious doubts, the Peary bill passed the House of Representatives by a vote of 154 to 34 and he was retired with the rank of rear admiral. However, the final wording of the bill had been amended to read: "That the Thanks of Congress be, and the same are hereby, tendered to Robert E. Peary, United States Navy, for his Arctic explorations resulting in reaching the North Pole." All references to "discovery" or "discoverer" were deleted. Even so, R. B. Macon, Peary's most vociferous critic on the committee, was not satisfied. Before the roll call he denounced Peary, according to the newspapers, as a "willful and deliberate liar, dirty little pilferer of words, and contemptible little ass." So bitter were his remarks that they were not even printed in the *Congressional Record.*

Certainly, the book Peary wrote should have been the prime document stating his case and resolving all contradictions surrounding his claims; yet, *The North Pole* has been instead the primary document used to argue against his veracity. The central points of doubt elucidated in his congressional testimony were based directly on Peary's own account in *The North Pole,* and most of the attacks on Peary's credibility since then have been drawn from its pages. These attacks are multifaceted, but center on the book's narrative. The incredulity of those who have studied it may be summed up in the most glaring "physical and scientific impossibility" that Peary claimed: the matter of his sledge speed touched upon by the skeptical congressman. While with scientifically trained witnesses, Peary's party makes a good, though reasonable, daily average of thirteen miles across the tortuous pack ice. But as soon as Peary parts from those witnesses, his speed increases greatly, so much so that no one before or since has ever remotely approached Peary's claimed sustained speed over a comparable period sledging on polar pack ice.

A simple summation of what Peary claimed to have done is this: he says he left Captain Robert Bartlett 133 nautical miles short of the North Pole on April 2 and proceeded north in the company of four Inuit and his assistant Matthew Henson. Peary had 133 miles to go to reach the Pole over an unbroken trail and 133 miles more to travel back just to return to the place where he left

Captain Bartlett, who therefore had a 266-mile head start in returning to the ship. And although Peary claimed a strong North wind died away before he started out, according to Bartlett's sledge log, the wind blew smartly from the North from April 2–5. This aided Bartlett's return, but should have retarded Peary's progress toward the Pole. Such a wind, in Peary's words, would have "stolen some of our miles, for it will close up everything behind us" as it pushed the floating ice that he was traveling over southward. Nonetheless, Peary claimed that he reached the North Pole five days after he left Bartlett. In addition, Peary said he spent thirty hours at the Pole and, while there, traveled thirty-six additional miles "quartering" the Pole to check his position. Having done all of this, he also stopped five miles south of the Pole to take a sounding. And yet he claims that he arrived back at the place he left Bartlett on April 9—less than three days after leaving the Pole and less than eight after leaving Bartlett.

Peary claimed he covered the entire 413 miles from the Pole (allowing nothing for necessary detours because of ice conditions) in a mere sixteen days. The outward journey had taken thirty-seven days, all but the last five with the trail across the worst obstacles broken for him. Bartlett, who had every incentive to make the best time possible, and who traveled every day without any significant delays, took eighteen days. Oddly enough, after returning to the point where he left Bartlett—the place where his speed increased on the northern trip—Peary slowed down again. He took thirteen days to cover the same distance Bartlett did. As it was, Peary regained land less than five days after Bartlett.

Some critics have surmised from Peary's narrative that he had to have traveled in excess of seventy miles on at least one of the days after leaving the Pole. But Peary testified before Congress that his best day was "an estimated distance of about fifty miles." Even this is an utterly fantastic performance, especially for a man who had only the little toe left on each foot and was unable to pick up his feet on a level floor without losing his balance. In his book, Peary describes how he had to give up a hunt over comparatively easy snow slopes because the stumps of his missing toes "were complaining with vehemence" from being stubbed on hidden rocks [p. 148]. Yet this same man said he made record distances struggling with fully loaded sledges over chaotic, rock-hard, slippery hummocks of ice, some reaching thirty-feet high.

The year of the congressional hearings, an anonymous book questioning Peary's claims appeared in England. This was followed in 1915 and 1916 by several scathing speeches placed in the *Congressional Record* by Congressman Henry Helgesen. In his remarks, the congressman included a verbatim copy of the testimony given before the Naval Affairs committee in 1910 and 1911. This testimony had been given little attention; only the favorable report of the full committee had been widely quoted in the press. Thus, Helgesen laid the groundwork for the more detailed attacks that would be made in later years.

The speeches also contained a detailed comparative analysis of Peary's magazine articles and *The North Pole* and made further comparisons with his assistant Matthew Henson's *A Negro Explorer at the North Pole* and fellow expedition member George Borup's *A Tenderfoot with Peary*. Peary's earlier book, *Nearest the Pole*, and the books published by other polar explorers—including Sverdrup, Nansen, and the Duke of Abruzzi—were also combed for compromising evidence. This analysis disclosed numerous discrepancies, contradictions, mistakes, improbabilities, and absurdities, all of which had a cumulative effect of undermining the veracity of Peary's account of his polar journey.

But the most devastating speech was saved for last, in the form of an analysis of Peary's entire career. The attack cited allegedly false or exaggerated claims on Peary's reconnaissance of Greenland in 1886. It pointed out that Peary's observations in 1892 and 1895 were erroneous—and that he had not, in reality, crossed Greenland at all, but only reached the head of a deep fjord. Since the key physical features that he described didn't exist, his widespread claim to having proven the insularity of Greenland at that time was false. It also showed that he had tried, in 1907, to claim the discovery of "Jesup Land," when in reality it was the same island that the Norwegian explorer Otto Sverdrup had named Axel Heiberg Land in 1900. Although Peary made no contemporaneous mention of this discovery at the time, in *Nearest the Pole* he claimed to have seen "Jesup Land" in 1898.

The printed remarks also attempted to show that Peary was a highly inaccurate mapmaker, filling his sketches with fantasies while at the same time eliminating several existing features. Readers were also reminded that Peary's protégé, Donald MacMillan, had shown in 1914 that Peary's "Crocker Land" did not exist. The only claims left standing at the end of Helgesen's remarks were the "Farthest North" of 1906 and the discovery of the most northern cape of Greenland, which, the speech said, needed to be verified in light of Peary's previously demonstrated inaccuracies.

In conclusion, the congressman said: "Peary's claims to exploration and discovery have been given to the world through the mediums of his magazine articles, his books, and (in the case of the North Pole) through his testimony before the Naval Committee of the House. His magazine articles contradict his books, his books contradict each other, and his testimony before the House Committee on Naval Affairs is at variance with both books and magazines. In view of the facts which I have presented, . . . Robert E. Peary's claims to discoveries in the Arctic regions have been proven to rest on fiction and not on geographical facts."

Helgesen's attacks were so cogent that Lucien Alexander, a lawyer who Peary had hired as his personal lobbyist to shepherd his retirement bill through Congress and to counter the efforts being made by Cook's supporters (who supplied Helgesen with the material for his speeches) to discredit him there, came to the conclusion that "it now stands on the face of it as a rather serious indictment of Peary's credibility."

"The numerous Helgesen contentions should not be left as they stand for on their face I am sorry to say they are formidable," he told Peary, "and unanswered they are bound to impress future historians. . . . If your diaries and records have errors we ought to explain how that happened."

But Peary never explained, and his silence haunts his

credibility to this day. Even though Peary's extensive papers have now been open to scholarly research for more than twenty years, no one has yet found any credible evidence that substantively supports Peary's claim to have reached the North Pole. Instead, evidence has emerged from them that indicates that Peary did exaggerate or falsify claims on every one of his former expeditions, just as Congressman Helgesen alleged, establishing ample precedent for a false polar claim in 1909. Even Peary's "Farthest North" of 1906 has been shown to have all of the suspicious elements of his North Pole claim and, indeed, seems to have been a dress rehearsal for the grander hoax to follow.

How could it be that the book that claims to be the record of Peary's ultimate success in the goal of a lifetime has come to be the sourcebook of those who brand him a fraud? The answer may lie in the strange history of this book, which gives every indication that Peary had relatively little to do with the finished narrative that appears on its pages.

Immediately after Cook's announcement of his polar attainment, an enterprising magazine publisher named Benjamin Hampton tried to obtain the explorer's story for serialization. In this he failed, so he turned to Peary, hoping to get at least part of the story that had been the obsession of the nation since it first broke. To this end he sent the poet Elsa Barker (whose ode, *The Frozen Grail*, Peary much admired) along with a young writer named T. Everett Harry to persuade him. After a month of escalating offers, they landed the rights to what was published in *Hampton's Magazine* as "Peary's Own Story" for

$40,000—the equivalent in today's money of half a million dollars.

Barker left a detailed account of her dealings with Peary. She recalled that when she first proposed she write the articles, Peary did not question her suggestion: "Peary, a specialist himself, did not seem surprised at the suggestion that the technique of writing popular magazine articles was another specialty which perhaps he had not acquired." Barker wrote a preliminary article, "Peary: The Man and His Work," signed by herself, to introduce the series. But because Peary was considering a long lecture tour through the Western states, the prospect of incessant travel with a woman collaborator seemed unsuitable for reasons of propriety. Although Hampton still wanted Barker's pen, he assigned Harris Merton Lyon to do the work. Lyon immediately left for Washington, D.C., to gather material for the first article. But Lyon failed.

After talking to Peary about the Arctic and its trials, he couldn't fathom why anyone would want to reach the North Pole. He wasn't interested in the subject, and it showed in the article he submitted. Hampton was so displeased with Lyon's copy that he dropped him and insisted that Barker resume work. "I knew what the magazine was paying for those serial rights," she recalled. "That fact, alone, was an unanswerable argument." Despite misgivings, she went to Washington with Lyon.

When presented with the situation, Peary agreed that Hampton should have the author of his choice. Lyon hired a male stenographer and a room, and thus began "the first of those many long sessions made up of my questions and Peary's answers to my questions, on all the details relative to that part of the narrative which I had determined beforehand should form the substance of the first article," Barker recalled.

The result of the session was a 30,000-word typescript that she took back to New York to work from. Barker said she studied it until she knew it by heart and could quote it verbatim. For weeks she had been studying Peary's former books in preparation for the work, and between the two she wrote the article entirely from memory. Indeed, certain passages of *Nearest the Pole* found their way, nearly intact, into the new book. Each month after that Peary would come to New York to work with Barker and a court stenographer at the *Hampton's Magazine* offices.

Part of the way through the series Barker hired her own stenographer, Lilian Kiel, and dictated the balance of the series to her from memory. Based on this experience, Kiel, an eventual Cook sympathizer, testified before a congressional committee in 1915 that Peary had not written a word of the articles at all, but that, in fact, she had taken them down directly from Barker's own mouth.

Barker dismissed this, saying Kiel was certainly aware of the interviews that she was conducting with Peary and added that although she dictated from memory, she always compared the galley proofs with the stenographic notes to ensure factual accuracy. Barker added that she always sent the revised galley proofs to Peary, and any suggestion he wanted to make was incorporated, though Peary made very few changes. (This is borne out by the copies of the galleys now at the National Archives, which show his slight emendations.) In addition to material taken down at monthly interviews with Peary, Barker said she worked from typed copies of Peary's diaries and copies of the diaries of other expedition members. She also had occasional interviews with Bartlett and the expedition's physician, John Goodsell. According to Kiel, Barker also filled in some details from copies of Cook's syndicated narrative of his claimed polar conquest that had appeared previously in the *New York Herald*, copies of which Barker kept under her kitchen sink. Whatever the source, "Not one word was published in those North Pole articles which had not been passed by Peary and authorized by him," Barker insisted.

Even with all of this material, Barker could quickly see that she had taken on "a gigantic labor" in agreeing to do the Peary series and asked for additional assistance: "I have had so little time during the last seven months to think about myself that I had forgotten that while I may have a man's ability for work and a man's will, I have only a woman's nerves," she wrote to Peary. "Of course I cannot break down before the end of this work, any more than you could have broken down on the road to the Pole. I merely tell you the situation, in order that you might help me all you can."

As the first anniversary of his discovery approached, Barker wrote to Peary hoping to get enough information about his proofs to convince anyone that he had actually found the Pole. Although she had received a copy of his diary covering his time there, it did not contain the information that she needed.

I hope you will have sent me before this reaches
you more of the data which I need for April 6th and

7th. That is the climax of the story, and the possibility
is very great. If we do not have an article, which will
make everybody sit up and take notice, it is our own
fault.

I hope you will have found time to dictate two or
three thousand words relative to those days. Your eyes
being so tired from the observations, there are no entries in the journal. The whole world is intensely interested in what you did during those two days, even to
minute details. You know humanity is simply a many-
headed child, and children all love stories. Even my
associates on the Magazine are as curious about this
as are the little boys in the street. The instinct is universal.

As an illustration of her associates' curiosity, she
attached a memorandum from *Hampton's* editorial staff
indicating the trend of the comments the series was gen-
erating:

The tone of many letters that come to us is that of
impatience. Writers say that Peary has not substantiated his claim to discovery; has not presented any scientific data. . . . Along lines of general criticism of
lack of scientific data in reports published thus far, it
has been questioned that he got any nearer the pole
than Cook did, because his descriptions of the conditions are so similar to those described by Cook. It has
been said of his lectures that they lack detail in the
events of the last few days of the dash to the Pole, and
that he describes too quickly the return journey. I am
convinced that careful attention to detail and putting
into popular form the Commander's scientific observa-

tions are the chief essentials of the July and August articles.

Even so, those articles did not satisfy many readers. Most of the complaints to *Hampton's* came from the heartland, where Cook still had a strong following and where many believed Peary an unworthy hero, even if he had succeeded. In Kansas, the *Emporia Gazette* editorialized that there were "legions of people in the country" who agreed with Congressman Macon:

> He says there is no more proof that Peary discovered the Pole than there was that Cook discovered it, and he is right. When Peary first returned from the Arctic, he declined to make public his alleged proofs, because he wanted to use them in his magazine narrative, and his magazine narrative presents nothing that can be considered proof. Dozens of geographers and other experts have criticized it, and have pointed out that it presents all sorts of inconsistencies. Peary has been asked a hundred times how it was he went to the pole an inch at a time, and returned wearing seven league boots, and he never has explained.
>
> His attitude has been so insolent from the first that the people are tired of him. He has profited by the humiliation of Cook. Because Cook has proved a faker, it has been taken for granted that Peary must be genuine.
>
> The latter has disgusted the people by the mercenary spirit he has shown. While writing about his devotion to science, his chief concern seems to be nailing the money.

Shortly after concluding his deal with Hampton, Peary signed a contract with Frederick A. Stokes to produce his

North Pole narrative in book form at a price rumored to be the highest on record for a single work—$150,000 (nearly $2.5 million in 2001 dollars). Peary immediately asked for "a first-class literary man," who could assist in the preparation of the material for the book: "What I want is someone who has the big, masculine literary instinct," he told Stokes, "as well as literary practice and training, to take hold of and revise material already written, cut out such portions as do not seem desirable, transpose portions and, if necessary, strengthen, under my direction."

Stokes recommended A. E. Thomas, a former reporter for the New York *Sun*, "a man of unusual energy, good judgment and capacity for work." Peary approved the choice, as long as Thomas's contribution was kept entirely confidential, and asked Stokes to set him to work revising the first three *Hampton's Magazine* articles for starters. But Stokes objected that he needed at least an outline of the proposed contents of the whole book before he could really begin. He didn't get it.

Beyond the *Hampton's* material, Thomas had to rely on personal interviews with expedition members Donald MacMillan and Robert Bartlett, although they seemed reluctant, Thomas thought, to say anything that Peary might not like. Peary specifically forbade him to interview Matthew Henson, the only other civilized expedition member to reach the Pole. For many details he was forced to draw upon the voluminous diaries of John Goodsell, which Peary furnished. Peary, himself, it seemed, was too preoccupied with trying to get his retirement bill through Congress to be of much help.

Stokes was as frustrated as Barker when it came to obtaining Peary's polar proofs and wrote to the commander, who was about to start a triumphal tour of Europe: "Mr. Thomas is becoming disturbed about the possibility of completing his work or even doing a satisfactory amount of it before the time of your departure for Europe. He has been able to do nothing for a week for lack of copy."

In the 1920s, Thomas told the writer William Shea that he had written 80 percent of *The North Pole* and that "certainly, Mrs. Elsa Barker had nothing to do with the writing of the book." That may be true in the literal sense, but a direct comparison of Peary's book with the *Hampton's Magazine* articles authored by Barker shows that at least 80 percent of the book's material is *absolutely identical* to the articles, and the great majority of what is not identical could be termed no more than editorial changes, many of them slight. A number of other passages were lifted directly from Goodsell's diary. The publishing of passages of Goodsell's work verbatim as Peary's own so compromised the commercial value of Goodsell's manuscript that he alone, of all of its members, was unable to publish a book containing an account of the expedition during his lifetime.

Considering this history, how A. E. Thomas could claim *The North Pole*'s authorship is puzzling—unless he wrote the magazine articles, and there is no evidence of that whatsoever. Thomas was not proud of the work that he did do, in any case. He blamed this on Peary, whom he described as "a damned dull human being," incapable of providing exciting narrative material.

Despite generally good reviews, *The North Pole* was not a financial success. Stokes's salesmen in many parts of the country reported resistance by store owners to carrying it. One from the South wrote, "The feeling that he has not proved his case seems to be universal." In the East, store owners were more pragmatic. One noted that sales of *Hampton's Magazine* had dropped 50 percent when it ran Peary's story and considered the book a bad risk; another said he still had copies of *Nearest the Pole* on hand that he couldn't sell.

The same criticisms expressed to the *Hampton's Magazine* editorial department could be made of *The North Pole*, since the text is largely identical. Indeed, Peary's German publisher sued him, contending that the book's miniscule sales in Germany were due to the fact that it contained no proof that Peary was ever at the Pole.

Nevertheless, *The North Pole* retains its importance as the source document around which the arguments both for and against Peary's conquest of the Pole still swirl. It is required reading for those interested in this historical question, as well as the larger questions of individual and group psychology that keep the dispute alive. Its republication also gives another opportunity to discover the clues necessary to weigh the question of whether the fame and honorable name Peary so desired was truly deserved or falsely obtained.

Robert Peary died in 1920, and "Discoverer of North Pole" was inscribed on his grave monument, but his claim to that title was already in dispute. In 1917, Thomas Hall published *Has the North Pole Been Discovered?*, a massive examination of the evidence available at the time. It convinced many that if the Pole had been found, Peary was not the discoverer. Since then, five major books have devoted themselves to showing that

Peary's narrative does not hold up on its own internal evidence. Although one may differ on their authors' individual points, it is difficult to deny their common conclusion. One said he came as close as fifty miles, another no nearer than 300, but all agreed that Robert E. Peary did not reach the North Pole.

Even so, is it possible that Peary actually achieved his life's ambition? Was he "The Man Who Refused to Fail"? These two questions can never be answered to everyone's satisfaction, because some people will always believe what they wish to believe, even if it is against all evidence. All evidence, beyond Peary's bare word, indicates that Peary did in fact fail. What he refused to do was admit it.

ROBERT M. BRYCE
Monrovia, Maryland
August 2000

In the wake of the 1997 publication of his monumental study, *Cook & Peary, the Polar Controversy Resolved*, **ROBERT M. BRYCE** is widely regarded as the leading authority on the controversy surrounding the rival claims of Frederick Cook and Robert Peary to have been the first man to have reached the North Pole. He has been a scholar of the subject for more than twenty-five years and has studied extensively the original diaries and personal papers of both explorers. His discovery of a copy of Cook's original polar notebook in Denmark was a major blow to Cook's credibility, as it contained important evidence that his claim to have reached the North Pole on

April 21, 1908, was a hoax. His recovery of an original print of the photograph claimed by Cook to have been made at the summit of Mt. McKinley in 1906 made national news in 1998. The picture proved to be a deception, taken nearly twenty miles from the mountain's summit, adding immeasurably to the overwhelming evidence that Cook's assertion to have been first to summit the highest peak in North America was another of his fantasies. Likewise, his examination of Peary's papers brought much new evidence to light that supports the widening consensus that Peary's claim to have discovered the North Pole on April 6, 1909, was also a hoax.

TO
MY WIFE

CONTENTS

CONTENTS

ILLUSTRATIONS

FULL-PAGE PLATES REPRODUCING
PHOTOGRAPHIC ENLARGEMENTS

BLACK AND WHITE ILLUSTRATIONS FROM PHOTOGRAPHS

ILLUSTRATION XXXV

NOTE. — The general plan of illustration is based on an unusually close adherence to the negatives, as giving more interesting and valuable results. Many of the most important pictures are from photographs not retouched in the least, e.g., those facing pages 270, 284, 290, etc. In others the sky-line has been indicated, e.g., those facing pages 208, 271, 299 (top), etc.; but change of no other sort has been made except to remove specks and other similar mechanical defects not widely extended.

THE PUBLISHERS

FOREWORD

SOME *years ago I met at a dinner in Washington the famous Norwegian arctic explorer, Nansen, himself one of the heroes of polar adventure; and he remarked to me, "Peary is your best man; in fact I think he is on the whole the best of the men now trying to reach the Pole, and there is a good chance that he will be the one to succeed." I cannot give the exact words; but they were to the above effect; and they made a strong impression on me. I thought of them when in the summer of 1908 I, as President of the United States, went aboard Peary's ship to bid him Godspeed on the eve of what proved to be his final effort to reach the Pole. A year later, when I was camped on the northern foothills of Mt. Kenia, directly under the equator, I received by a native runner the news that he had succeeded, and that thanks to him the discovery of the North Pole was to go on the honor roll of those feats in which we take a peculiar pride because they have been performed by our fellow countrymen.*

Probably few outsiders realize the well-nigh incredible toil and hardship entailed in such an achievement as Peary's; and fewer still understand how many years of careful training and preparation there must be before the feat can be even attempted with any chance of success. A "dash for the pole" can be successful only if there have been many preliminary years of painstaking, patient toil. Great physical hardihood and endurance, an iron will and unflinching courage, the power of command, the thirst

*for adventure, and a keen and farsighted intelligence —
all these must go to the make-up of the successful arctic
explorer; and these, and more than these, have gone to
the make-up of the chief of successful arctic explorers, of
the man who succeeded where hitherto even the best and the
bravest had failed.*

*Commander Peary has made all dwellers in the civi-
lized world his debtors; but, above all, we, his fellow Ameri-
cans, are his debtors. He has performed one of the great
feats of our time; he has won high honor for himself and
for his country; and we welcome his own story of the
triumph which he won in the immense solitudes of the
wintry North.*

THEODORE ROOSEVELT.

THE WHITE NILE, *March 12, 1910.*

PORTRAIT OF ROBERT E. PEARY, IN HIS ACTUAL NORTH POLE COSTUME

PREFACE

THE struggle for the North Pole began nearly one hundred years before the landing of the Pilgrim Fathers at Plymouth Rock, being inaugurated (1527) by that king of many distinctions, Henry VIII of England.

In 1588 John Davis rounded Cape Farewell, the southern end of Greenland, and followed the coast for eight hundred miles to Sanderson Hope. He discovered the strait which bears his name, and gained for Great Britain what was then the record for the farthest north, 72° 12′, a point 1128 miles from the geographical North Pole. Scores of hardy navigators, British, French, Dutch, German, Scandinavian, and Russian, followed Davis, all seeking to hew across the Pole the much-coveted short route to China and the Indies. The rivalry was keen and costly in lives, ships, and treasure, but from the time of Henry VIII for three and one-half centuries, or until 1882 (with the exception of 1594–1606, when, through Wm. Barents, the Dutch held the record), Great Britain's flag was always waving nearest the top of the globe.

The same year that Jamestown was founded, Henry Hudson (1607), also seeking the route to the Indies, discovered Jan Mayen, circumnavigated Spitzbergen, and advanced the eye of man to 80° 23′. Most valu-

able of all, Hudson brought back accounts of great
multitudes of whales and walruses, with the result
that for the succeeding years these new waters were
thronged with fleets of whaling ships from every mari-
time nation. The Dutch specially profited by Hudson's discovery. During the 17th and 18th centuries
they sent no less than 300 ships and 15,000 men each
summer to these arctic fisheries and established on
Spitzbergen, within the Arctic Circle, one of the most
remarkable summer towns the world has ever known,
where stores and warehouses and reducing stations
and cooperages and many kindred industries flourished
during the fishing season. With the approach of
winter all buildings were shut up and the population,
numbering several thousand, all returned home.

Hudson's record remained unequaled for 165 years,
or until 1773, when J. C. Phipps surpassed his farthest
north by twenty-five miles. To-day the most interesting fact connected with the Phipps expedition is
that Nelson, the hero of Trafalgar and of the Battle of
the Nile, then a lad of fifteen, was a member of the
party. Thus the boldest and strongest spirits of the
most adventurous and hardy profession of those days
sought employment in the contest against the frozen
wilderness of the north.

The first half of the 19th century witnessed many
brave ships and gallant men sent to the arctic regions.
While most of these expeditions were not directed
against the Pole so much as sent in an endeavor to
find a route to the Indies round North America —
the Northwest Passage — and around Asia — the
Northeast Passage — many of them are intimately

interwoven with the conquest of the Pole, and were a necessary part of its ultimate discovery. England hurled expedition after expedition, manned by the best talent and energy of her navy, against the ice which seemingly blocked every channel to her ambitions for an arctic route to the Orient.

In 1819 Parry penetrated many intricate passages and overcame one-half of the distance between Greenland and Bering Sea, winning a prize of £5000, offered by Parliament to the first navigator to pass the 110th meridian west of Greenwich. He was also the first navigator to pass directly north of the magnetic North Pole, which he located approximately, and thus the first to report the strange experience of seeing the compass needle pointing due south.

So great was Parry's success that the British government sent him out in command of two other expeditions in search of the Northwest Passage. In explorations and discoveries the results of these two later expeditions were not so rich, but the experience in ice work so obtained gave Parry conclusions which revolutionized all methods in arctic navigation.

Hitherto all attempts to approach the Pole had been in ships. In 1827 Parry suggested the plan of a dash to the Pole on foot, from a base on land. He obtained the assistance of the government, which for the fourth time sent him to the Arctic provided with well-equipped ships and able officers and men. He carried a number of reindeer with him to his base in Spitzbergen, purposing to use these animals to drag his sledges. The scheme proved impracticable, however, and he was compelled to depend on the muscles of his men to haul his two heavy sledges, which were in reality boats on steel runners. Leaving Spitzbergen on June 23 with twenty-eight men, he pushed northward. But the summer sun had broken up the ice floes, and the party repeatedly found it necessary to take the runners off their boats in order to ferry across the stretches of open water. After thirty days' incessant toil Parry had reached 82° 45', about 150 miles north of his base and 435 geographical miles from the Pole. Here he found that, while his party rested, the drift of the ice was carrying him daily back, almost as much as they were able to make in the day's work. Retreat was therefore begun.

Parry's accomplishments, marking a new era in polar explorations, created a tremendous sensation. Knighthood was immediately bestowed upon him by the King, while the British people heaped upon him all the honors and applause with which they have invariably crowned every explorer returning from the north with even a measure of success. In originality of plan and equipment Parry has been equaled and surpassed only by Nansen and Peary.

In those early days, few men being rich enough to pay for expeditions to the north out of their own pockets, practically every explorer was financed by the government under whose orders he acted. In 1829, however, Felix Booth, sheriff of London, gave Captain John Ross, an English naval officer, who had achieved only moderate success in a previous expedition, a small paddle-wheel steamer, the *Victory*, and entered him in the race for the Northwest Passage. Ross was assisted, as mate, by his nephew, James

Clark Ross, who was young and energetic, and who was later to win laurels at the opposite end of the globe. This first attempt to use steam for ice navigation failed, owing to a poor engine or incompetent engineers, but in all other respects the Rosses achieved gloriously. During their five years' absence, 1829–1834, they made important discoveries around Boothia Felix, but most valuable was their definite location of the magnetic North Pole and the remarkable series of magnetic and meteorological observations which they brought back with them.

No band of men ever set out for the unknown with brighter hopes or more just anticipation of success than Sir John Franklin's expedition of 1845. The frightful tragedy which overwhelmed them, together with the mystery of their disappearance, which baffled the world for years and is not yet entirely explained, forms the most terrible narrative in arctic history. Franklin had been knighted in 1827, at the same time as Parry, for the valuable and very extensive explorations which he had conducted by snowshoes and canoe on the North American coast between the Coppermine and Great Fish rivers, during the same years that Parry had been gaining fame in the north. In the interval Franklin had served as Governor of Tasmania for seven years. His splendid reputation and ability as an organizer made him, though now fifty-nine years of age, the unanimous choice of the government for the most elaborate arctic expedition it had prepared in many years. Franklin's fame and experience, and that of Crozier and his other lieutenants, who had seen much service in the north, his able ships, the *Terror* and the

Erebus, which had just returned from a voyage of unusual success to the Antarctic, and his magnificent equipment, aroused the enthusiasm of the British to the highest pitch and justified them in their hopes for bringing the wearying struggle for the Northwest Passage to an immediate conclusion.

For more than a year everything prospered with the party. By September, 1846, Franklin had navigated the vessels almost within sight of the coast which he had explored twenty years previously, and beyond which the route to Bering Sea was well known. The prize was nearly won when the ships became imprisoned by the ice for the winter, a few miles north of King William Land. The following June Franklin died; the ice continued impenetrable, and did not loosen its grip all that year. In July, 1848, Crozier, who had succeeded to the command, was compelled to abandon the ships, and, with the 105 survivors who were all enfeebled by the three successive winters in the Arctic, started on foot for Back River. How far they got we shall probably never know.

Meanwhile, when Franklin failed to return in 1848 — he was provisioned for only three years — England became alarmed and despatched relief expeditions by sea from the Bering Sea and the Atlantic and by land north from Canada, but all efforts failed to gather news of Franklin till 1854, when Rae fell in with some Eskimo hunters near King William Land, who told him of two ships that were beset some years previous, and of the death of all the party from starvation.

In 1857 Lady Franklin, not content with this bare and indirect report of her husband's fate, sacrificed

a fortune to equip a searching party to be commanded
by Leopold McClintock, one of the ablest and tough-
est travelers over the ice the world has ever known.
In 1859 McClintock verified the Eskimos' sad story
by the discovery on King William Land of a record
dated April, 1848, which told of Franklin's death and
of the abandonment of the ships. He also found
among the Eskimos silver plate and other relics of
the party; elsewhere he saw one of Franklin's boats on
a sledge, with two skeletons inside and clothing and
chocolate; in another place he found tents and flags;
and elsewhere he made the yet more ghastly discovery of a bleached human skeleton prone on its face, as
though attesting the truthfulness of an Eskimo woman
who, claiming to have seen forty of the survivors late
in 1848, said "they fell down and died as they
walked."

The distinction of being the first to make the
Northwest Passage, which Franklin so narrowly missed,
fell to Robert McClure (1850–53) and Richard Collinson (1850–55),who commanded the two ships sent north
through Bering Strait to search for Franklin.   McClure
accomplished the passage on foot after losing his ship
in the ice in Barrow Strait, but Collinson brought his
vessel safely through to England.   The Northwest
Passage was not again made until Roald Amundsen
navigated the tiny *Gjoa*, a sailing sloop with gasoline
engine, from the Atlantic to the Pacific, 1903–06.

Yankee whalers each year had been venturing
further north in Davis Strait and Baffin Bay and Bering Sea, but America had taken no active part in polar
exploration until the sympathy aroused by the tragic

disappearance of Franklin induced Henry Grinnell and George Peabody to send out the *Advance* in charge of Elisha Kent Kane to search for Franklin north of Smith Sound. In spite of inexperience, which resulted in scurvy, fatal accidents, privations, and the loss of his ship, Kane's achievements (1853–55) were very brilliant. He discovered and entered Kane Basin, which forms the beginning of the passage to the polar ocean, explored both shores of the new sea, and outlined what has since been called the American route to the Pole.

Sixteen years later (1871) another American, Charles Francis Hall, who had gained much arctic experience by a successful search for additional traces and relics of Franklin (1862–69), sailed the *Polaris* through Kane Basin and Kennedy Channel, also through Hall Basin and Robeson Channel, which he discovered, into the polar ocean itself, thus completing the exploration of the outlet which Kane had begun. He took his vessel to the then unprecedented (for a ship) latitude of 82° 11'. But Hall's explorations, begun so auspiciously, were suddenly terminated by his tragic death in November from over-exertion caused by a long sledge journey.

When the ice began to move the ensuing year, his party sought to return, but the *Polaris* was caught in the deadly grip of an impassable ice pack. After two months of drifting, part of the crew, with some Eskimo men and women, alarmed by the groaning and crashing of the ice during a furious autumn storm, camped on an ice floe which shortly afterwards separated from the ship. For five months, December to April, they lived on this cold and desolate raft, which

carried them safely 1300 miles to Labrador, where
they were picked up by the *Tigress*. During the winter one of the Eskimo women presented the party
with a baby, so that their number had increased during the arduous experience. Meanwhile the *Polaris*
had been beached on the Greenland shore, and those
remaining on the ship were eventually also rescued.

In 1875 Great Britain began an elaborate attack
on the Pole *viâ* what was now known as the American
route, two ships most lavishly equipped being despatched under command of George Nares. He succeeded in navigating the *Alert* fourteen miles further
north than the *Polaris* had penetrated four years previous. Before the winter set in, Aldrich on land
reached 82° 48', which was three miles nearer the Pole
than Parry's mark made forty-eight years before, and
the following spring Markham gained 83° 20' on the
polar ocean. Other parties explored several hundred
miles of coast line. But Nares was unable to cope
with the scurvy, which disabled thirty-six of his men,
or with the severe frosts, which cost the life of one
man and seriously injured others.

The next expedition to this region was that sent
out under the auspices of the United States government and commanded by Lieutenant — now Major-
General — A. W. Greely, U. S. A., to establish at
Lady Franklin Bay the American circumpolar station (1881). Greely during the two years at Fort
Conger carried on extensive explorations of Ellesmere
Land and the Greenland coast, and by the assistance
of his two lieutenants, Lockwood and Brainard,
wrested from Great Britain the record which she had

held for 300 years. Greely's mark was 83° 24′, which bettered the British by four miles. As the relief ship, promised for 1883, failed to reach him or to land supplies at the prearranged point south of Fort Conger, the winter of 1883–84 was passed in great misery and horror. When help finally came to the camp at Cape Sabine, seven men only were alive.

While these important events were occurring in the vicinity of Greenland, interesting developments were also taking place in that half of the polar area north of Siberia. When in 1867 an American whaler, Thomas Long, reported new land, Wrangell Land, about 500 miles northwest of Bering Strait, many hailed the discovery as that of the edge of a supposed continent extending from Asia across the Pole to Greenland, for the natives around Bering Strait had long excited explorers by their traditions of an icebound big land beyond the horizon. Such extravagant claims were made for the new land that Commander De Long, U. S. N., determined to explore it and use it as a base for gaining the Pole. But his ship, the *Jeannette*, was caught in the ice (September, 1879) and carried right through the place where the new continent was supposed to be. For nearly two years De Long's party remained helpless prisoners until in June, 1881, the ship was crushed and sank, forcing the men to take refuge on the ice floes in mid ocean, 150 miles from the New Siberian Islands. They saved several boats and sledges and a small supply of provisions and water. After incredible hardships and suffering, G. W. Melville, the chief engineer, who was in charge of one of the boats, with nine men, reached, on September

26, a Russian village on the Lena. All the others perished, some being lost at sea, by the foundering of the boats, while others, including De Long, had starved to death after reaching the desolate Siberian coast.

Three years later some Eskimos found washed ashore on the southeast coast of Greenland several broken biscuit boxes and lists of stores, which are said to be in De Long's handwriting. The startling circumstance that these relics in their long drift from where the ship sank had necessarily passed across or very near to the Pole aroused great speculation as to the probable currents in the polar area. Nansen, who had already made the first crossing of Greenland's ice cap, argued that the same current which had guided the relics on their long journey would similarly conduct a ship. He therefore constructed a unique craft, the *Fram*, so designed that when hugged by the ice pack she would not be crushed, but would be lifted up and rest on the ice; he provisioned the vessel for five years and allowed her to be frozen in the ice near where the *Jeannette* had sunk, 78° 50′ N., 134° E. (September 25, 1893). When at the end of eighteen months the ship had approached 314 miles nearer to the Pole, Nansen and one companion, Johansen, with kayaks, dogs, sledges, and three months' provisions, deliberately left the ship and plunged northward toward the Pole, March 14, 1895. In twenty-three days the two men had overcome one-third of the distance to the Pole, reaching 86° 12′. To continue onward would have meant certain death, so they turned back. When their watches ran down Providence guided them, and the marvelous physique of both sustained them through fog and storm and threatened starvation until they reached Franz Josef Land, late in August. There they built a hut of stones and killed bears for meat for the winter. In May, 1896, they resumed their southward journey, when fortunately they met the Englishman Jackson, who was exploring the Archipelago.

Meanwhile the *Fram*, after Nansen left her, continued her tortuous drifting across the upper world. Once she approached as near as 85° 57′ to the Pole — only fifteen miles less than Nansen's farthest. At last, in August, 1896, with the help of dynamite, she was freed from the grip of the ice and hurried home, arriving in time to participate in the welcome of Nansen, who had landed a few days earlier.

Franz Josef Land, where Nansen was rescued by Jackson, has served as the base of many dashes for the Pole. It was from its northernmost point that the illustrious young member of the royal family of Italy, the Duke of the Abruzzi, launched the party captained by Cagni that won from Nansen for the Latin race the honor of the farthest north, 86° 34′, in 1901.

This land, which consists of numerous islands, had been named after the Emperor of Austria-Hungary by Weyprecht and Payer, leaders of the Austrian-Hungarian polar expedition of 1872–74, who discovered and first explored the Archipelago.

It was from Spitzbergen that Andree, with two companions, sailed in his balloon toward the Pole, in July, 1897, never to be heard from again, except for three message buoys dropped in the sea a few miles from the starting-point.

The Northeast Passage was first achieved in 1878–

1879 by Adolph Erik Nordenskjold. Step by step energetic explorers, principally Russian, had been mapping
the arctic coasts of Europe and Siberia until practically all the headlands and islands were well defined.

Nordenskjold, whose name was already renowned
for important researches in Greenland, Nova Zembla,
and northern Asia, in less than two months guided
the steam whaler *Vega* from Tromsoe, Norway, to the
most easterly peninsula of Asia. But when barely
more than 100 miles from Bering Strait, intervening
ice blocked his hopes of passing from the Atlantic to
the Pacific in a single season and held him fast for
ten months.

No résumé of polar exploration is complete without
mention of Wm. Barents (1594–96) who, for the Dutch
of Amsterdam, made three attempts to accomplish
the Northeast Passage around Nova Zembla; Wm.
Baffin, who discovered Baffin Bay and Smith Sound
(1616); Wm. Scoresby, Sr., who reached by ship 81°
30′ N., 19′ E. (1806), a record till Parry eclipsed it;
Wm. Scoresby, Jr., who changed all ideas of East
Greenland (1822) and made valuable scientific observations, and the German North Polar expedition of
1869–70. One of the ships of the latter was crushed in
the ice and sank. The crew escaped to an ice floe on
which they drifted in the darkness of an arctic winter
for 1300 miles along the coast of Greenland to Fred-
eriksthaal.

The preceding brief summary gives only an inade-
quate conception of the immense treasures of money
and lives expended by the nations to explore the northern ice world and to attain the apex of the earth.

All efforts to reach the Pole had failed, notwithstanding the unlimited sacrifice of gold and energy and blood which had been poured out without stint for nearly four centuries.   But the sacrifice had not been without compensation.   Those who had ventured their lives in the contest had not been actuated solely by the ambition to win a race — to breast the tape first — but to contribute, in Sir John Franklin's words, "to the extension of the bounds of science."   The scores of expeditions, in addition to new geographical discoveries, had brought back a wealth of information about the animals and vegetable life, the winds and currents, deep sea temperatures, soundings, the magnetism of the earth, fossils and rock specimens, tidal data, etc., which have enriched many branches of science and greatly increased the sum of human knowledge.

A brief summer excursion to Greenland in 1886 aroused Robert E. Peary, a civil engineer in the United States Navy, to an interest in the polar problem. Peary a few years previously had been graduated from Bowdoin College second in his class, a position which means unusual mental vigor in an institution which is noted for the fine scholarship and intellect of its alumni.   He realized at once that the goal which had eluded so many hundreds of ambitious and dauntless men could be won only by a new method of attack.

The first arctic problem with which Peary grappled was considered at that time in importance second only to the conquest of the Pole; namely, to determine the insularity of Greenland and the extent of its projection northward.   At the very beginning of his first expedition to Greenland, in 1891, he suffered an accident which sorely taxed his patience as well as his body, and which is mentioned here as it illustrates the grit and stamina of his moral and physical make-up. As his ship, the *Kite*, was working its way through the ice fields off the Greenland shore, a cake of ice became wedged in the rudder, causing the wheel to reverse. One of the spokes jammed Peary's leg against the casement, making it impossible to extricate himself until both bones of the leg were broken. The party urged him to return to the United States for the winter and to resume his exploration the following year. But Peary insisted on being landed as originally planned at McCormick Bay, stating that the money of his friends had been invested in the project and that he must "make good" to them. The assiduous nursing of Mrs. Peary, aided by the bracing air, so speedily restored his strength that at the ensuing Christmas festivities which he arranged for the Eskimos, he outraced on snowshoes all the natives and his own men!

In the following May, with one companion, Astrup, he ascended to the summit of the great ice cap which covers the interior of Greenland, 5000 to 8000 feet in elevation, and pushed northward for 500 miles over a region where the foot of man had never trod before, in temperatures ranging from 10° to 50° below zero, to Independence Bay, which he discovered and named, July 4, 1892. Imagine his surprise on descending from the tableland to enter a little valley radiant with gorgeous flowers and alive with murmuring bees, where musk oxen were lazily browsing.

This sledding journey, which he duplicated by another equally remarkable crossing of the ice cap three years later, defined the northern extension of Greenland and conclusively proved that it is an island instead of a continent extending to the Pole. In boldness of conception and brilliancy of results these two crossings of Greenland are unsurpassed in arctic history. The magnitude of Peary's feat is better appreciated when it is recalled that Nansen's historic crossing of the island was below the Arctic Circle, 1000 miles south of Peary's latitude, where Greenland is some 250 miles wide.

Peary now turned his attention to the Pole, which lay 396 geographical miles farther north than any man had penetrated on the western hemisphere. To get there by the American route he must break a virgin trail every mile north from Greely's 83° 24'. No one had pioneered so great a distance northward. Markham and others had attained enduring fame by advancing the flag considerably less than 100 miles, Parry had pioneered 150 miles, and Nansen 128 from his ship.

His experiences in Greenland had convinced Peary, if possible more firmly than before, that the only way of surmounting this last and most formidable barrier was to adopt the manner of life, the food, the snowhouses, and the clothing of the Eskimos, who by centuries of experience had learned the most effective method of combating the rigors of arctic weather; to utilize the game of the northland, the arctic reindeer, musk ox, etc., which his explorations had proved comparatively abundant, thus with fresh meat keeping his men fit and good-tempered through the depressing winter night; and lastly to train the Eskimo to become his sledging crew.

In his first north polar expedition, which lasted for

four years, 1898–1902, Peary failed to get nearer than 343 miles to the Pole. Each successive year dense packs of ice blocked the passage to the polar ocean, compelling him to make his base approximately 700 miles from the Pole, or 200 miles south of the head-quarters of Nares, too great a distance from the Pole to be overcome in one short season. During this trying period, by sledging feats which in distance and physical obstacles overcome exceeded the extraordinary records made in Greenland, he explored and mapped hundreds of miles of coast line of Greenland and of the islands west and north of Greenland.

On the next attempt, Peary insured reaching the polar ocean by designing and constructing the *Roosevelt*, whose resistless frame crushed its way to the desired haven on the shores of the polar sea. From here he made that wonderful march of 1906 to 87° 6', a new world's record. Winds of unusual fury, by opening big leads, robbed him of the Pole and nearly of his life.

The story of the last Peary expedition, which resulted in the discovery of the Pole and of the deep ocean surrounding it, is told in the present volume by Commander Peary. The 396 miles from Greely's farthest had been vanquished as follows: 1900, 30 miles; 1902, 23 miles; 1906, 169 miles; 1909, 174 miles.

No better proof of the minute care with which every campaign was prearranged can be given than the fact that, though Peary has taken hundreds of men north with him on his various expeditions, he has brought them all back, and in good health, with the exception of two, who lost their lives in accidents for which the leader was in no wise responsible. What a contrast this record is to the long list of fatalities from disease, frost, shipwreck, and starvation which in the popular mind has made the word arctic synonymous with tragedy and death.

Thus Robert E. Peary has crowned a life devoted to the exploration of the icy north and to the advancement of science by the hard-won discovery of the North Pole. The prize of four centuries of striving yielded at last to the most persistent and scientific attack ever waged against it. Peary's success was made possible by long experience, which gave him a thorough knowledge of the difficulties to be overcome, and by an unusual combination of mental and physical power — a resourcefulness which enabled him to find a way to surmount all obstacles, a tenacity and courage which knew no defeat, and a physical endowment such as nature gives to few men.

It has been well said that the glory of Peary's achievement belongs to the world and is shared by all mankind. But we, his fellow-countrymen, who have known how he has struggled these many years against discouragement and scoffing and how he has persevered under financial burdens that would have crushed less stalwart shoulders, specially rejoice that he has "made good at last," and that an American has become the peer of Hudson, Magellan, and Columbus.

GILBERT H. GROSVENOR.

National Geographic Society,
    Washington, D. C., U. S. A.
        August 30, 1910.

STELLAR PROJECTION, SHOWING THE RELATION OF THE POLAR SEA TO THE
VARIOUS CONTINENTS

THE NORTH POLE

CHAPTER I

THE PLAN

IT may not be inapt to liken the attainment of
the North Pole to the winning of a game of
chess, in which all the various moves leading to a
favorable conclusion had been planned in advance,
long before the actual game began. It was an old
game for me — a game which I had been playing for
twenty-three years, with varying fortunes. Always,
it is true, I had been beaten, but with every defeat
came fresh knowledge of the game, its intricacies, its
difficulties, its subtleties, and with every fresh attempt
success came a trifle nearer; what had before appeared
either impossible, or, at the best, extremely dubious,
began to take on an aspect of possibility, and, at last,
even of probability. Every defeat was analyzed as
to its causes in all their bearings, until it became possible to believe that those causes could in future be
guarded against and that, with a fair amount of good
fortune, the losing game of nearly a quarter of a century
could be turned into one final, complete success.

It is true that with this conclusion many well informed and intelligent persons saw fit to differ. But
many others shared my views and gave without stint
their sympathy and their help, and now, in the end,

1

one of my greatest unalloyed pleasures is to know that their confidence, subjected as it was to many trials, was not misplaced, that their trust, their belief in me and in the mission to which the best years of my life have been given, have been abundantly justified.

But while it is true that so far as plan and method are concerned the discovery of the North Pole may fairly be likened to a game of chess, there is, of course, this obvious difference: in chess, brains are matched against brains. In the quest of the Pole it was a struggle of human brains and persistence against the blind, brute forces of the elements of primeval matter, acting often under laws and impulses almost unknown or but little understood by us, and thus many times seemingly capricious, freaky, not to be foretold with any degree of certainty. For this reason, while it was possible to plan, before the hour of sailing from New York, the principal moves of the attack upon the frozen North, it was not possible to anticipate all of the moves of the adversary. Had this been possible, my expedition of 1905–1906, which established the then "farthest north" record of 87° 6′, would have reached the Pole. But everybody familiar with the records of that expedition knows that its complete success was frustrated by one of those unforeseen moves of our great adversary — in that a season of unusually violent and continued winds disrupted the polar pack, separating me from my supporting parties, with insufficient supplies, so that, when almost within striking distance of the goal, it was necessary to turn back because of the imminent peril of starvation.

When victory seemed at last almost within reach, I was blocked by a move which could not possibly have been foreseen, and which, when I encountered it, I was helpless to meet. And, as is well known, I and those with me were not only checkmated but very nearly lost our lives as well.

But all that is now as a tale that is told. This time it is a different and perhaps a more inspiring story, though the records of gallant defeat are not without their inspiration. And the point which it seems fit to make in the beginning is that success crowned the efforts of years because strength came from repeated defeats, wisdom from earlier error, experience from inexperience, and determination from them all.

Perhaps, in view of the striking manner in which the final event bore out the prophecies that I had made, it may be of interest to compare in some detail the plan of campaign that was announced, over two months before the *Roosevelt* sailed from New York on her final voyage to the North, with the manner in which that campaign was actually executed.

Early in May, 1908, in a published statement I sketched the following plan:

"I shall use the same ship, the *Roosevelt;* shall leave New York early in July; shall follow the same route north, via Sydney, C. B., Strait of Belle Isle, Davis Strait, Baffin Bay, and Smith Sound; shall use the same methods, equipments, and supplies; shall have a minimum party of white men, supplemented with Eskimos; shall take on these Eskimos and dogs in the Whale Sound region as before, and shall endeavor to force my ship to the same or similar winter quar-

ters on the north shore of Grant Land as in the winter
of 1905–1906.

"The sledge march will begin as before in February, but my route will be modified as follows: First,
I shall follow the north coast of Grant Land as far
west as Cape Columbia, and possibly beyond, instead
of leaving this land at Point Moss as I did before.

"Second, leaving the land, my course will be more
west of north than before, in order to counteract or
allow for the easterly set of the ice between the north
coast of Grant Land and the Pole, discovered on my
last expedition. Another essential modification will
be a more rigid massing of my sledge divisions en route,
in order to prevent the possibility of a portion of the
party being separated from the rest by the movement
of the ice, with insufficient supplies for a protracted
advance, as happened on the last expedition.

"There is no doubt in my mind that this 'big lead'
(a lane of open water), encountered in both my
upward and return marches in my last expedition, is
an essentially permanent feature of this part of the
Arctic Ocean. I have little doubt of my ability to
make this 'lead,' instead of the north coast of Grant
Land, my point of departure with fully loaded sledges.
If this is done it will shorten the route to the Pole by
nearly one hundred miles and distinctly simplify the
proposition.

"On the return march in the next expedition I shall
probably do voluntarily what I did involuntarily last
time; that is, retreat upon the north coast of Greenland (a course diagonally *with* the set of the ice) instead
of attempting to come back to the north coast of Grant

Land (diagonally *against* the set of the ice). An adjunct of this program will probably be the establishment of a depot well up the north coast of Greenland by the first of the supporting parties returning to the ship."

The main features of this program I summarized as follows:

"First, the utilization of the Smith Sound or 'American' route. This must be accepted to-day as the best of all possible routes for a determined, aggressive attack upon the Pole. Its advantages are a land base one hundred miles nearer the Pole than is to be found at any other point of the entire periphery of the Arctic Ocean, a long stretch of coast line upon which to return, and a safe and (to me) well-known line of retreat independent of assistance, in the event of any mishap to the ship.

"Second, the selection of a winter base which commands a wider range of the central polar sea and its surrounding coasts than any other possible base in the Arctic regions. Cape Sheridan is practically equidistant from Crocker Land, from the remaining unknown portion of the northeast coast of Greenland, and from my 'Nearest the Pole' of 1906.

"Third, the use of sledges and Eskimo dogs. Man and the Eskimo dog are the only two machines capable of such adjustment as to meet the wide demands and contingencies of Arctic travel. Airships, motor cars, trained polar bears, etc., are all premature, except as a means of attracting public attention.

"Fourth, the use of the hyperborean aborigine (the Whale Sound Eskimo) for the rank and file of the sledge party. It seems unnecessary to enlarge upon the fact that the men whose heritage is life and work in that very region must present the best obtainable material for the personnel of a serious Arctic party. This is my program. The object of the work is the clearing up, or at least the fixing in their general proportions, of the remaining large problems in the American segment of the polar regions and the securing for the United States of that great world trophy which has been the object of effort and emulation among practically all the civilized nations of the world for the last three centuries."

The details of this plan have been here set forth so explicitly because the faithfulness with which they were carried out constitutes a record which is perhaps unique in the annals of Arctic exploration. Compare this scheme, if you please, with the manner of its execution. As had been planned, the expedition sailed from New York early in July, 1908, July 6, to be exact. It sailed from Sydney July 17, from Etah August 18, and arrived at Cape Sheridan, the winter quarters of the *Roosevelt*, on September 5, within a quarter of an hour of the same time it had arrived at the same spot three years before. The winter was occupied in hunting, in various side journeys, in making our sledging equipment, and in moving supplies from the *Roosevelt* along the northern shore of Grant Land to Cape Columbia, which was to be our point of departure from the land on our drive for the Pole itself.

The sledge divisions left the *Roosevelt* from February 15 to 22, 1909, rendezvoused at Cape Columbia, and on March 1 the expedition left Cape Columbia, heading across the Polar Ocean for the Pole. The 84th parallel was crossed on March 18, the 86th on March 23, the Italian record was passed the next day, the 88th parallel on April 2, the 89th on April 4, and the North Pole was reached on April 6 at ten o'clock in the morning. I spent thirty hours at the Pole with Matt Henson, Ootah, the faithful Eskimo who had gone with me in 1906 to 87° 6', the then "farthest north," and three other Eskimos who had also been with me on previous expeditions. The six of us left the much desired "ninety north" on April 7 on the return journey and reached land at Cape Columbia again on April 23.

It will be noted that while the journey from Cape Columbia to the Pole consumed thirty-seven days, (though only twenty-seven marches) we returned from the Pole to Cape Columbia in only sixteen days. The extraordinary speed of the return journey is to be accounted for by the fact that we merely had to retrace our old trail instead of making a new one, and because we were fortunate in encountering no delays. Excellent conditions of ice and weather also contributed, not to mention the fact that the exhilaration of success lent wings to our sorely battered feet. But Ootah, the Eskimo, had his own explanation. Said he: "The devil is asleep or having trouble with his wife, or we should never have come back so easily."

It will be noted in this comparison, that practically the only feature of the plan from which essential deviation was made was in returning to Cape Columbia on the coast of Grant Land instead of further east-

ward to the northern coast of Greenland as I had done
in 1906. This change was made for excellent reasons,
which will be made clear in their proper place. Upon
this record there is only one shadow — a tragic one
indeed. I refer, of course, to the lamentable death
of Prof. Ross G. Marvin, who was drowned on April
10, four days after the Pole had been reached, forty-
five miles north of Cape Columbia, while returning
from 86° 38′ north, in command of one of the supporting parties. With this sad exception, the history
of the expedition is flawless. We returned as we
went, in our own ship, battered but unharmed, in
excellent health and with a record of complete
success.

There is a lesson in all this — a lesson so obvious
that it is perhaps superfluous to point it out. The
plan, so carefully made and executed with such faithfulness to detail, was composed of a number of elements,
the absence of any one of which might have been fatal
to success. We could scarcely have succeeded without the help of our faithful Eskimos; nor even with
them, had it not been for our knowledge of their
capacities for work and endurance, and for the confidence which years of acquaintance had taught them
to repose in me. We could certainly not have succeeded without the Eskimo dogs which furnished the
traction power for our sledges, and so enabled us to
carry our supplies where no other power on earth
could have moved them with the requisite speed and
certainty. It may be that we could not have succeeded without the improved form of sledge which I
was able to construct and which, combining in its

construction, strength, lightness, and ease of traction, made the heavy task of the dogs far easier than it would otherwise have been. It may even be that we should have failed had it not been for so simple a thing as an improved form of water boiler which I was fortunate enough to have hit upon. By its aid we were able to melt ice and make tea in ten minutes. On our previous journeys this process had taken an hour. Tea is an imperative necessity on such a driving journey, and this little invention saved one and one-half hours in each day while we were struggling toward the Pole on that journey when time was the very essence of success.

Success crowned the work, it is true, but, for all that, it is a genuine pleasure to reflect that even had we failed, I should have had nothing to reproach myself with in the way of neglect. Every possible contingency that years of experience had taught me to expect was provided for, every weak spot guarded, every precaution taken. I had spent a quarter of a century playing the Arctic game. I was fifty-three years old, an age beyond which, perhaps, with the one exception of Sir John Franklin, no man had ever attempted to prosecute work in the Arctic regions. I was a little past the zenith of my strength, a little lacking, perhaps, in the exuberant elasticity and élan of more youthful years, a little past the time when most men begin to leave the strenuous things to the younger generation; but these drawbacks were fully balanced perhaps by a trained and hardened endurance, a perfect knowledge of myself, and of how to conserve my strength. I knew it was my last game upon the great

Arctic chess-board. It was win this time or be forever defeated.

The lure of the North! It is a strange and a powerful thing. More than once I have come back from
the great frozen spaces, battered and worn and baffled,
sometimes maimed, telling myself that I had made my
last journey thither, eager for the society of my kind,
the comforts of civilization and the peace and serenity
of home. But somehow, it was never many months
before the old restless feeling came over me. Civilization began to lose its zest for me. I began to long
for the great white desolation, the battles with the ice
and the gales, the long, long arctic night, the long,
long arctic day, the handful of odd but faithful Eskimos
who had been my friends for years, the silence and
the vastness of the great, white lonely North. And
back I went accordingly, time after time, until, at
last, my dream of years came true.

CHAPTER II

A GREAT many persons have asked when I first conceived the idea of trying to reach the North Pole. That question is hard to answer. It is impossible to point to any day or month and to say, "Then the idea first came to me." The North Pole dream was a gradual and almost involuntary evolution from earlier work in which it had no part. My interest in arctic work dates back to 1885, when as a young man my imagination was stirred by reading accounts of explorations by Nordenskjöld in the interior of Greenland. These studies took full possession of my mind and led to my undertaking, entirely alone, a summer trip to Greenland in the following year. Somewhere in my subconscious self, even so long ago as that, there may have been gradually dawning a hope that I might some day reach the Pole itself. Certain it is, the lure of the North, the "arctic fever," as it has been called, entered my veins then, and I came to have a feeling of fatality, a feeling that the reason and intent of my existence was the solution of the mystery of the frozen fastnesses of the Arctic.

But the actual naming of the Pole as the object of an expedition did not materialize until 1898, when the first expedition of the Peary Arctic Club went north with the avowed intention of reaching ninety north — if it were possible. Since then I have made six different attempts, in six different years, to reach the coveted point. The sledging season, when such a "dash" is possible, extends from about the middle of February until the middle of June. Before the middle of February there is not sufficient light, and after the middle of June there is likely to be too much open water.

During these six former attempts made by me to win the prize, the successive latitudes of 83° 52′, 84° 17′, and 87° 6′ were attained, the last giving back to the United States the record of "farthest north," which had for a time been wrested from it by Nansen, and from him in turn by the Duke of the Abruzzi.

In writing the story of this last and successful expedition, it is necessary to go back to my return from the former expedition of 1905–6. Before the *Roosevelt* entered port, and before I reached New York, I was planning for another journey into the North, which, if I could obtain the essential funds — and retained my health — I intended to get under way as soon as possible. It is a principle in physics that a ponderable body moves along the line of least resistance; but that principle does not seem to apply to the will of man. Every obstacle which has ever been placed in my way, whether physical or mental, whether an open "lead" or the opposition of human circumstances, has ultimately acted as a spur to the determination to accomplish the fixed purpose of my life—if I lived long enough.

On my return in 1906, great encouragement was received from Mr. Jesup, the president of the Peary

Arctic Club, who had contributed so generously to my former expeditions, and in whose honor I had named the northernmost point of land in the world, latitude 83° 39', Cape Morris K. Jesup. He said, in so many words, that he would "see me through" on another journey north. His promise meant that I should not have to beg all the money in small sums from a more or less reluctant world.

The winter of 1906–7 and the spring of 1907 were devoted to presenting to the world the results of the previous undertaking, and to the work of interesting friends as far as possible in another expedition. We had the ship, which had cost about $100,000 in 1905; but $75,000 more was needed for new boilers and other changes, for equipment and for operating expenses. While the bulk of the necessary funds was furnished by the members and friends of the Peary Arctic Club, a very considerable amount came from all parts of the country in contributions ranging from $100 to $5 and even $1. These donations were not less appreciated than the big ones, because they showed the friendliness and the interest of the givers, and demonstrated to me the general recognition of the fact that while the expedition was financed by private individuals, it was in spirit a national affair.

At last the funds, actual and promised, were in such amount as to authorize our contracting for new boilers for the *Roosevelt*, and ordering certain modifications in her structure which would fit her more effectively for another voyage: such as enlarging the quarters forward for the crew, adding a lug sail to the foremast, and changing the interior arrangements somewhat. The general features of the ship had already proved themselves so well adapted for the purpose for which she was intended that no alteration in them was required.

Experience had taught me how to figure on delays in the North; but the exasperating delays of ship contractors at home had not yet entered into my scheme of reckoning. Contracts for this work on the *Roosevelt* were signed in the winter, and called for the completion of the ship by July 1, 1907. Repeated oral promises were added to contractual agreements that the work should certainly be done on that date; but, as a matter of fact, the new boilers were not completed and installed until September, thus absolutely negativing any possibility of going north in the summer of 1907.

The failure of the contractors to live up to their word, with the consequent delay of a year, was a serious blow to me. It meant that I must attack the problem one year older; it placed the initiation of the expedition further in the future, with all the possible contingencies that might occur within a year; and it meant the bitterness of hope deferred.

On the day when it became lamentably clear that I positively *could not* sail north that year, I felt much as I had felt when I had been obliged to turn back from 87° 6′, with only the empty bauble "farthest north," instead of the great prize which I had almost strained my life out to achieve. Fortunately I did not know that Fate was even then clenching her fist for yet another and more crushing blow.

While trying to possess my soul in patience despite the unjustified delay, there came the heaviest calamity encountered in all my arctic work — the death of my friend, Morris K. Jesup. Without his promised help the future expedition seemed impossible. It may be said with perfect truth that to him, more than to any other one man, had been due the inception and the continuance of the Peary Arctic Club, and the success of the work thus far. In him we lost not only a man who was financially a tower of strength in the work, but I lost an intimate personal friend in whom I had absolute trust. For a time it seemed as if this were the end of everything; that all the effort and money put into the project had been wasted. Mr. Jesup's death, added to the delay caused by the default of the contractors, seemed at first an absolutely paralyzing defeat.

Nor was it much help that there was no lack of well-meaning persons who were willing to assure me that the year's delay and Mr. Jesup's death were warnings indicating that I should never find the Pole.

Yet, when I gathered myself together and faced the situation squarely, I realized that the project was something too big to die; that it never, in the great scheme of things, would be allowed to fall through. This feeling carried me past many a dead center of fatigue and utter ignorance as to where the rest of the money for the expedition was to be obtained. The end of the winter and the beginning of the spring of 1908 were marked by more than one blue day for everybody concerned in the success of the expedition.

Repairs and changes in the *Roosevelt* had exhausted all the funds in the Club's treasury. We still needed the money for purchase of supplies and equipment, pay of crew, and running expenses. Mr. Jesup was gone; the country had not recovered from the financial crash of the previous fall; every one was poor.

Then from this lowest ebb the tide turned. Mrs. Jesup, in the midst of her distracting grief, sent a munificent check which enabled us to order essential items of special supplies and equipment which required time for preparation.

General Thomas H. Hubbard accepted the presidency of the Club, and added a second large check to his already generous contribution. Henry Parish, Anton A. Raven, Herbert L. Bridgman — the "Old Guard" of the Club — who had stood shoulder to shoulder with Mr. Jesup from the inception of the organization, stood firm now to keep the organization of the Club intact; other men came forward, and the crisis was past. But the money still came hard. It was the subject of my every waking thought; and even in sleep it would not let me rest, but followed with mocking and elusive dreams. It was a dogged, dull, desperate time, with the hopes of my whole life rising and falling day by day.

Then came an unexpected rift in the clouds, the receipt of a very friendly letter from Mr. Zenas Crane, the great paper manufacturer, of Massachusetts, who had contributed to a previous expedition, but whom I had never met. Mr. Crane wrote that he was deeply interested; that the project was one which should have the support of every one who cared for big things and

THOMAS GUSHUE, MATE

CHARLES PERCY, STEWARD

GEORGE A. WARDWELL
CHIEF ENGINEER

ROBERT A. BARTLETT, MASTER

BANKS SCOTT
SECOND ENGINEER

PROFESSOR ROSS G. MARVIN
ASSISTANT

GEORGE BORUP, ASSISTANT

DONALD B. MACMILLAN
ASSISTANT

DR. J. W. GOODSELL, SURGEON

for the prestige of the country, and he asked me to come to see him, if I could make it convenient. I could. I did. He gave a check for $10,000 and promised to give more if it should be required. The promise was kept, and a little later he accepted the vice-presidency of the Club. What this $10,000 meant to me at that time would need the pen of Shakespere to make entirely clear.

From this time on the funds came in slowly but steadily, to an amount that, combined with rigid economy and thorough knowledge of what was and what was not needed, permitted the purchase of the necessary supplies and equipment.

During all this time of waiting, a small flood of "crank" letters poured in from all over the country. There was an incredibly large number of persons who were simply oozing with inventions and schemes, the adoption of which would absolutely insure the discovery of the Pole. Naturally, in view of the contemporaneous drift of inventive thought, flying machines occupied a high place on the list. Motor cars, guaranteed to run over any kind of ice, came next. One man had a submarine boat that he was sure would do the trick, though he did not explain how we were to get up through the ice after we had traveled to the Pole beneath it.

Still another chap wanted to sell us a portable sawmill. It was his enterprising idea that this should be set up on the shore of the central polar sea and that I was to use it for shaping lumber with which to build a wooden tunnel over the ice of the polar sea all the way to the Pole. Another chap proposed that a central soup station be installed where the other man would have set up his sawmill, and that a series of hose lines be run thence over the ice so that the outlying parties struggling over the ice to the Pole could be warmed and invigorated with hot soup from the central station.

Perhaps the gem of the whole collection was furnished by an inventor who desired me to play the part of the "human cannon-ball." He would not disclose the details of his invention, apparently lest I should steal it, but it amounted to this: If I could get the machine up there, and could get it pointed in exactly the right direction, and could hold on long enough, it would shoot me to the Pole without fail. This was surely a man of one idea. He was so intent on getting me shot to the Pole that he seemed to be utterly careless of what happened to me in the process of landing there or of how I should get back.

Many friends of the expedition who could not send cash sent useful articles of equipment, for the comfort or amusement of the men. Among such articles were a billiard table, various games, and innumerable books. A member of the expedition having said to a newspaper man, a short time before the *Roosevelt* sailed, that we had not much reading matter, the ship was deluged with books, magazines, and newspapers, which came literally in wagon loads. They were strewn in every cabin, in every locker, on the mess tables, on the deck, — everywhere. But the generosity of the public was very gratifying, and there was much good reading among the books and magazines.

When the time came for the *Roosevelt* to sail, we had everything which we absolutely needed in the way of equipment, including boxes of Christmas candy, one for every man on board, a gift from Mrs. Peary.

It is a great satisfaction to me that this whole expedition, together with the ship, was American from start to finish. We did not purchase a Newfoundland or Norwegian sealer and fix it over for our purposes, as in the case of other expeditions. The *Roosevelt* was built of American timber in an American shipyard, engined by an American firm with American metal, and constructed on American designs. Even the most trivial items of supplies were of American manufacture. As regards personnel almost the same can be said. Though Captain Bartlett and the crew were Newfoundlanders, the Newfoundlanders are our next-door neighbors and essentially our first cousins. This expedition went north in an American-built ship, by the American route, in command of an American, to secure if possible an American trophy. The *Roosevelt* was built with a knowledge of the requirements of arctic navigation, gained by the experience of an American on six former voyages into the Arctic.

I was extremely fortunate in the personnel of this last and successful expedition, for in choosing the men I had the membership of the previous expedition to draw from. A season in the Arctic is a great test of character. One may know a man better after six months with him beyond the Arctic circle than after a lifetime of acquaintance in cities. There is a something — I know not what to call it — in those frozen spaces, that brings a man face to face with himself and with his companions; if he is a man, the man comes out; and, if he is a cur, the cur shows as quickly.

First and most valuable of all was Bartlett, master of the *Roosevelt*, whose ability had been proved on the expedition of 1905–6. Robert A. Bartlett, "Captain Bob," as we affectionately call him, comes from a family of hardy Newfoundland navigators, long associated with arctic work. He was thirty-three when we last sailed north. Blue-eyed, brown-haired, stocky, and steel-muscled Bartlett, whether at the wheel of the *Roosevelt* hammering a passage through the floes, or tramping and stumbling over the ice pack, with the sledges, or smoothing away the troubles of the crew, was always the same — tireless, faithful, enthusiastic, true as the compass.

Matthew A. Henson, my negro assistant, has been with me in one capacity or another since my second trip to Nicaragua, in 1887. I have taken him with me on each and all of my northern expeditions, except the first, in 1886, and almost without exception on each of my "farthest" sledge trips. This position I have given him, primarily because of his adaptability and fitness for the work; secondly on account of his loyalty. He has shared all the physical hardships of my arctic work. He is now about forty years old, and can handle a sledge better, and is probably a better dog-driver, than any other man living, except some of the best of the Eskimo hunters themselves.

Ross G. Marvin, my secretary and assistant, who lost his life on the expedition; George A. Wardwell, chief engineer; Percy, the steward; and Murphy, the boatswain, had all been with me before. Dr. Wolf, who was the surgeon of the expedition of 1905–6, had made professional arrangements which prevented him from going north again, and his place was taken by Dr. J. W. Goodsell, of New Kensington, Pa.

Dr. Goodsell is a descendant of an old English family that has had representatives in America for two hundred and fifty years. His great grandfather was a soldier in Washington's army when Cornwallis surrendered, and his father, George H. Goodsell, spent many adventurous years at sea and fought through the Civil War in the Union army. Dr. Goodsell was born near Leechburg, Pa., in 1873. He received his medical degree from Pulte Medical College, Cincinnati, O., and has since practised medicine at New Kensington, Pa., specializing in clinical microscopy. He is a member of the Homeopathic Medical Society of Pennsylvania and of the American Medical Association. At the time of his departure on the expedition he was president of the Alleghany Valley Medical Society. His publications include "Direct Microscopic Examination as Applied to Preventive Medicine and the Newer Therapy" and "Tuberculosis and Its Diagnosis."

As the scope of this expedition was wider than that of the previous ones, contemplating more extensive tidal observations for the United States Coast and Geodetic Survey, and, if conditions permitted, lateral sledge trips east to Cape Morris K. Jesup and west to Cape Thomas Hubbard, I enlarged my field party, as it may be called, and added to the expedition Mr. Donald B. MacMillan, of Worcester Academy, and Mr. George Borup, of New York City.

MacMillan is the son of a sea captain and was born at Provincetown, Mass., in 1874. His father's ship sailed from Boston nearly thirty years ago and was never heard from again. His mother died the next year, leaving the son with four other young children. When MacMillan was fifteen years old he went to live with his sister at Freeport, Me., where he was prepared in the local high school to enter Bowdoin College, being graduated from my alma mater in 1898. Like Borup, MacMillan excelled in undergraduate athletics, played half-back on the Bowdoin 'varsity eleven and won a place on the track team. From 1898 to 1900 he was principal of the Levi Hall School at North Gorham, Me., going thence to become head master of the Latin Department at Swarthmore Preparatory School of Swarthmore, Pa. Here he remained until 1903 when he became instructor in Mathematics and Physical Training at Worcester Academy, Mass., where he remained until he went north with the expedition. He holds the Humane Society's certificate for saving a number of lives some years ago, an exploit which it is difficult to induce him to talk about.

George Borup was born at Sing Sing, N. Y., Sept. 2, 1885. He prepared for Yale at Groton School, where he spent the years from 1889 to 1903, and was graduated from Yale in 1907. At college he was prominent in athletics, was a member of the Yale track and golf teams, and made a reputation as a wrestler. After his graduation he spent a year as a special apprentice in the machine shops of the Pennsylvania Railroad Company at Altoona, Pa.

To Captain Bartlett I left the selection of his officers and men, with the single exception of the chief engineer.

The personnel of the expedition, as finally completed when the *Roosevelt* left Sydney on the 17th of July, 1908, included twenty-two men, as follows: Robert E. Peary, commanding expedition; Robert A. Bartlett, master of the *Roosevelt;* George A. Wardwell, chief engineer; Dr. J. W. Goodsell, surgeon; Prof. Ross G. Marvin, assistant; Donald B. MacMillan, assistant; George Borup, assistant; Matthew A. Henson, assistant; Thomas Gushue, mate; John Murphy, boatswain; Banks Scott, second engineer; Charles Percy, steward; William Pritchard, cabin boy; John Connors, John Coady, John Barnes, Denis Murphy, George Percy, seamen; James Bently, Patrick Joyce, Patrick Skeans, John Wiseman, firemen.

The supplies for the expedition were abundant in quantity, but not numerous in variety. Years of experience had given me the knowledge of exactly what I wanted and how much of it. The absolutely essential supplies for a serious arctic expedition are few, but they should be of the best quality. Luxuries have no place in arctic work.

Supplies for an arctic expedition naturally divide themselves into two classes: those for the sledge work in the field; those for the ship, going and returning, and in winter quarters. The supplies for sledge work are of a special character, and have to be prepared and packed in such a way as to secure the maximum of nourishment with the minimum of weight, of bulk, and of tare (that is, the weight of the packing). The essentials, and the only essentials, needed in a serious arctic sledge journey, no matter what the season, the temperature, or the duration of the journey

— whether one month or six — are four: pemmican, tea, ship's biscuit, condensed milk. Pemmican is a prepared and condensed food, made from beef, fat and dried fruits. It may be regarded as the most concentrated and satisfying of all meat foods, and is absolutely indispensable in protracted arctic sledge journeys.

The food for use on shipboard and in winter quarters comprises standard commercial supplies. My expeditions have been perhaps peculiar in omitting one item — and that is meat. For this important addition to arctic food I have always depended on the country itself. Meat is the object of the hunting expeditions of the winter months — not sport, as some have fancied.

Here are a few of the items and figures on our list of supplies for the last expedition: Flour, 16,000 pounds; coffee, 1,000 pounds; tea, 800 pounds; sugar, 10,000 pounds; kerosene, 3,500 gallons; bacon, 7,000 pounds; biscuit, 10,000 pounds; condensed milk, 100 cases; pemmican, 30,000 pounds; dried fish, 3,000 pounds; smoking tobacco, 1,000 pounds.

CHAPTER III

FROM her berth beside the recreation pier at the foot of East Twenty-fourth Street, New York, the *Roosevelt* steamed north on the last expedition, about one o'clock in the afternoon of July 6, 1908. As the ship backed out into the river, a cheer that echoed over Blackwell's Island went up from the thousands who had gathered on the piers to see us off; while the yacht fleet, the tugboats and the ferryboats tooted their good wishes. It was an interesting coincidence that the day on which we started for the coldest spot on earth was about the hottest which New York had known for years. There were thirteen deaths from heat and seventy-two heat prostrations recorded in Greater New York for that day, while we were bound for a region where sixty below zero is not an exceptional temperature.

We started with about one hundred guests of the Peary Arctic Club on board the *Roosevelt*, and several members of the Club, including the president, General Thomas H. Hubbard; the vice-president, Zenas Crane; and the secretary and treasurer, Herbert L. Bridgman.

As we steamed up the river the din grew louder and louder, the whistles of the power-houses and the factories adding their salutations to the tooting of the river craft. At Blackwell's Island many of the inmates were out in force to wave us their good-bys, and their farewells were not the less appreciated because given by men whom society had placed under restraint for society's good. Anyhow, they wished us well. I hope they are all enjoying liberty now, and, what is better, deserving it. Near Fort Totten we passed President Roosevelt's naval yacht, the *Mayflower*, and her small gun roared out a parting salute, while the officers and men waved and cheered. Surely no ship ever started for the end of the earth with more heart-stirring farewells than those which followed the *Roosevelt*.

Just before we reached the Stepping Stone Light, Mrs. Peary, the members and guests of the Peary Arctic Club, and myself were transferred to the tug *Narkeeta* and returned to New York. The ship went on to Oyster Bay, Long Island, the summer home of President Roosevelt, where Mrs. Peary and I were to lunch with the President and Mrs. Roosevelt the following day.

Theodore Roosevelt is to me the most intensely vital man, and the biggest man, America has ever produced. He has that vibrant energy and enthusiasm which is the basis of all real power and accomplishment. When it came to christening the ship by whose aid it was hoped to fight our way toward the most inaccessible spot on earth, the name of *Roosevelt* seemed to be the one and inevitable choice. It held up as ideals before the expedition those very qualities of strength, insistence, persistence, and triumph over obstacles, which have made the twenty-sixth President of the United States so great.

In the course of that last luncheon at Sagamore Hill, President Roosevelt reiterated what he had said to me so many times before, that he was earnestly and profoundly interested in my work, and that he believed I would succeed if success were possible.

After luncheon the President and Mrs. Roosevelt, with their three sons, came on board the ship with Mrs. Peary and me. Mr. Bridgman was on deck, to welcome them in the name of the Peary Arctic Club. The Roosevelt party remained on board about an hour; the President inspected every part of the ship, shook hands with every member of the expedition present, including the crew, and even made the acquaintance of my Eskimo dogs, North Star and the others, which had been brought down from one of my islands in Casco Bay, on the coast of Maine. As he was going over the rail, I said to him: "Mr. President, I shall put into this effort everything there is in me — physical, mental, and moral." And he replied, "I believe in you, Peary, and I believe in your success — if it is within the possibility of man."

The *Roosevelt* stopped at New Bedford for the whale-boats, and also made a short stop at Eagle Island, our summer home on the coast of Maine, to take aboard the massive, steel-bound spare rudder, which we carried as a precaution against disaster in the coming battle royal with the ice. On the former expedition, when we had no extra rudder, we could have used two. But, as things turned out this time, when we had the extra rudder we had no occasion to use it.

Our departure from Eagle Island was timed so that Mrs. Peary and I should arrive by train at Sydney, Cape Breton, the same day as the ship. I have a very tender feeling for the picturesque little town of Sydney. Eight times have I headed north from there on my arctic quest. My recollections of the town date back to 1886, when I went there with Captain Jackman in the whaler *Eagle*, and lay at the coal wharves for a day or two filling the ship with coal for my very first northern voyage, the summer cruise to Greenland, during which journey the "arctic fever" got a grip upon me from which I have never recovered.

Since that time the town has grown from a little settlement of one decent hotel and a few houses, to a prosperous city with seventeen thousand inhabitants, many industries, and one of the largest steel plants in the western hemisphere. My reason for choosing Sydney as a starting point was because of the coal mines there. It is the place nearest to the arctic regions where a ship can fill with coal.

My feelings, on leaving Sydney this last time, though difficult to describe, were different from those at the start of any previous expedition. I felt no uneasiness once the lines were cast off, for I knew that everything had been done which could be done to insure success, and that every essential item of supplies was on board. On former journeys I had sometimes felt anxiety, but through the whole of this last expedition I allowed nothing to worry me. Perhaps this feeling of surety was because every possible contingency had been discounted, perhaps because the setbacks and knock-out blows received in the past had dulled my sense of danger.

The *Roosevelt* having coaled at Sydney, we crossed the bay to North Sydney to take on some last items of supplies. When we started to leave the wharf over there we discovered that we were aground, and had to wait an hour or so for the tide to rise. In our efforts to move the ship, one of the whale-boats was crushed between the davits and the side of the pier; but after eight arctic campaigns one does not regard a little accident like that as a bad omen.

We got away from North Sydney about half past three in the afternoon of July 17, in glittering golden sunshine. As we passed the signal station, they signaled us, "Good-by and a prosperous voyage"; we replied, "Thank you," and dipped our colors.

A little tug, which we had chartered to take our guests back to Sydney, followed the *Roosevelt* as far as Low Point Light, outside the harbor; there she ran alongside, and Mrs. Peary and the children, and Colonel Borup, with two or three other friends, transferred to her. As my five-year-old son, Robert, kissed me good-by, he said, "Come back soon, dad." With reluctant eyes I watched the little tug grow smaller and smaller in the blue distance. Another farewell — and there had been so many! Brave, noble little woman! You have borne with me the brunt of all my arctic work. But, somehow, this parting was less sad than any which had gone before. I think that we both felt it was the last.

By the time the stars came out, the last items of supplies taken on at North Sydney were stowed, and

the decks at least were unusually free for an arctic
ship just starting northward — all but the quarter-
deck, which was piled high with bags of coal.

Inside the cabins, however, all was litter and con-
fusion. My room was filled so full of things — instruments, books, furniture, presents from friends, supplies, et cetera — that there was no space for me.
Since my return some one has asked me if I played on
the pianola in my cabin that first day at sea. I did
not, for the excellent reason that I could not get near
it. The thrilling experiences of those first few hours
were mainly connected with excavating a space some
six feet long by two feet broad in the region of my
bunk, where I could lay myself down to sleep when the
time came.

I have a special affection for my little cabin on
the *Roosevelt*. Its size and the comfort of the bathroom adjoining were the only luxuries which I allowed
myself. The cabin is plain, of matched yellow pine,
painted white. Its conveniences are the evolution
of long experience in the arctic regions. It has a
wide built-in bunk, an ordinary writing desk, several
book units, a wicker chair, an office chair, and a chest
of drawers, these latter items of furniture being Mrs.
Peary's contributions to my comfort. Hanging over
the pianola was a photograph of Mr. Jesup, and on
the side wall was one of President Roosevelt, auto-
graphed. Then there were the flags, the silk one made
by Mrs. Peary, which I had carried for years, the
flag of my college fraternity, Delta Kappa Epsilon,
the flag of the Navy League, and the peace flag of
the Daughters of the American Revolution. There

was also a photograph of our home on Eagle Island, and a fragrant pillow made by my daughter Marie from the pine needles of that island.

The pianola, a gift from my friend H. H. Benedict, had been my pleasant companion on my previous voyage, and again on this it proved one of our greatest sources of pleasure. There were at least two hundred pieces of music in my collection, but the strains of "Faust" rolled out over the Arctic Ocean more often than any other. Marches and songs were also popular, with the "Blue Danube" waltz; and sometimes, when the spirits of my party were at rather a low ebb, we had ragtime pieces, which they especially enjoyed.

There was also in my cabin a fairly complete, arctic library — absolutely complete in regard to all the later voyages. These books, with a large assortment of novels and magazines, could be depended upon to relieve the tedium of the long arctic night, and very useful they were found for that purpose. Sitting up late at night means something when the night is some months long.

On the second day out the carpenter began the repairs on the crushed whale-boat, using lumber which we carried for such purposes. The sea was rough, and the waist of the ship was awash nearly all day. My companions were gradually getting settled in their cabins; and if any man had qualms of homesickness, he kept them to himself.

Our living quarters were in the after deckhouse, which extends the full width of the *Roosevelt* from a little aft of the mainmast to the mizzenmast. In the center is the engine-room, with the skylight and the uptake from the boilers, and on either side are the cabins and the messrooms. My own cabin occupied the starboard corner aft; forward from this was Henson's room, the starboard messroom, and in the forward starboard corner Surgeon Goodsell's room. On the port side aft was Captain Bartlett's room, occupied by himself and Marvin, and forward from this in succession the cabin of the chief engineer and his assistant, the cabin of Percy, the steward, and the cabin of MacMillan and Borup; then the mate and the boatswain were in the forward port corner of the deckhouse, next the port messroom of the junior officers. The starboard mess comprised Bartlett, Dr. Goodsell, Marvin, MacMillan, Borup, and myself.

I shall not dwell at great length upon the first stage of the journey from Sydney to Cape York, Greenland, for the reason that is only a pleasant summer cruise at that season of the year, such as any fair-sized yacht may undertake without peril or adventure; and there are more interesting and unusual things to write about. In passing through the Straits of Belle Isle, "the graveyard of ships," where there is always danger of encountering icebergs in the fog, or being swung upon the shore by the strong and capricious currents, I remained up all night, as any man would who had care for his ship. But I could not help contrasting that easy summer passage with our return in November, 1906, when the *Roosevelt* was standing on end half the time, and the rest of the time was rolling the rail under water, losing two rudders, being smashed by the sea, creeping along the Labrador coast in the berg season, through dense fog, and picking up Point Amour Light only when within a stone's throw of the shore, guided only by the sirens at Point Amour and Bald Head, and the whistles of the big steamships lying at the entrance of the strait, afraid to attempt the passage.

CHAPTER IV

O N Sunday, July 19, we sent a boat ashore at Point Amour Light with telegrams back home — the last. I wondered what my first despatch would be the following year.

At Cape St. Charles we dropped anchor in front of the whaling station. Two whales had been captured there the day before, and I immediately bought one of them as food for the dogs. This meat was stowed on the quarter-deck of the *Roosevelt*. There are several of these "whale factories" on the Labrador coast. They send out a fast steel steamer, with a harpoon gun at the bow. When a whale is sighted they give chase, and when near enough discharge into the monster a harpoon with an explosive bomb attached. The explosion kills him. Then he is lashed alongside, towed into the station, hauled out on the timberways, and there cut up, every part of the enormous carcass being utilized for some commercial purpose.

We stopped again at Hawks Harbor, where the *Erik*, our auxiliary supply steamer, was awaiting us with some twenty-five tons of whale meat on board; and an hour or two later, a beautiful white yacht followed us in. I recognized her as Harkness's *Wakiva* of the New York Yacht Club. Twice during the winter she had lain close to the *Roosevelt* in New York, at the East Twenty-fourth Street pier, coaling between her voyages; and now, by a strange chance, the two vessels lay side by side again in this little out-of-the-way harbor on the Labrador coast. No two ships could be more unlike than these two: one white as snow, her brasswork glittering in the sun, speedy, light as an arrow; the other black, slow, heavy, almost as solid as a rock — each built for a special purpose and adapted to that purpose.

Mr. Harkness and a party of friends, including several ladies, came on board the *Roosevelt*, and the dainty dresses of our feminine guests further accentuated the blackness, the strength, and the not over cleanly condition of our ship.

We stopped once more at Turnavik Island, a fishing station belonging to Captain Bartlett's father, and took on a consignment of Labrador skin boots, for which we should have use in the North. Just before reaching the Island we encountered a furious thunderstorm. It was the most northerly thunderstorm which I remember having experienced.

I recall, however, that on our upward voyage in 1905 we ran into very heavy thunderstorms with electrical displays quite as sharp as any encountered in Gulf storms on voyages in southern waters, though the storms of 1905 were met in the neighborhood of Cabot Strait, far south of those of 1908.

Our voyage to Cape York was a peaceful one, lacking even the small excitement of the same journey three years before, when, not far from Cape St. George, all hands were startled by an alarm of fire which started in one of the main deck beams from the uptake of

the boilers. Nor were we so plagued with fog in
the early stages of our journey as we were in 1905.
In fact, every omen was auspicious from the very
start, so auspicious indeed that perhaps the more
superstitious of the sailors thought our luck was too
good to last, while one member of our expedition was
continually "knocking on wood," just as a precaution,
as he expressed it. It would be rash to say that his
forethought had much to do with our success, but it
eased his mind, at all events.

As we steamed steadily northward the nights grew
shorter and shorter, and lighter and lighter, so that
when we crossed the Arctic Circle, soon after midnight
on July 26, we were in perpetual daylight. I have
crossed the Circle some twenty times, going and coming, so the fine edge of that experience has been somewhat dulled for me; but the arctic "tenderfeet" among
my party, Dr. Goodsell, MacMillan, and Borup, were
appropriately impressed. They felt as one feels in
crossing the equator the first time — that it is an
event.

The *Roosevelt*, steaming ever northward, was now
well on her way to one of the most interesting of all
arctic localities. It is the little oasis amid a wilderness of ice and snow along the west coast of northern
Greenland midway between Kane Basin on the north
and Melville Bay on the south. Here, in striking
contrast to the surrounding country, is animal and
vegetable life in plenty, and in the course of the last
hundred years some half dozen arctic expeditions
have wintered here. Here, too, is the home of a little
tribe of Eskimos.

SNOWY OWL, CAPE SHERIDAN

BRANT-GOOSE

SABINE'S GULL

RED-THROATED DIVER, MALE AND
FEMALE

KING EIDER, DRAKE

This little refuge is about a 3,000 mile sail from New York and about 2,000 miles as the bird flies. It is about 600 miles north of the Arctic Circle and about half way from that great latitudinal mark to the Pole itself. Here the great arctic night averages one hundred and ten days in winter, during which time no ray of light falls upon the sight, save that of the moon and the stars, while in summer the sun is visible every moment for an equal number of days. Within the limits of this little country is found the favorite haunt of the reindeer, which find sufficient pasturage. But we are interested for the present in this unique spot only in passing and for the reason that here we picked up the little denizens of the frigid zone who were to help us in our struggle farther north.

Before we reached this odd little oasis, but several hundred miles beyond the Arctic Circle, we came to a most significant point in our upward journey, marking as it did the grimness of the task before us. No civilized man can die in this savage Northland without his grave having a deep meaning for those who come afterwards; and constantly, as we sailed on, these voiceless reminders of heroic bones told their silent but powerful story.

At the southern limit of Melville Bay we passed the Duck Islands, where is the little graveyard of the Scotch whalers who were the pioneers in forcing the passage of Melville Bay and who died there, waiting for the ice to open. These graves date back to the beginning of the nineteenth century. From this point on, the arctic highway is marked by the graves of those who have fallen in the terrible fight with cold and hunger. These rude rock piles bring home to any thoughtful person the meaning of arctic exploration. The men who lie there were not less courageous, not less intelligent, than the members of my own party; they were simply less fortunate.

Let us look along that highway for a moment and consider these memorials. At North Star Bay are one or two graves of men from the British ship *North Star*, which wintered there in 1850. Out on the Cary Islands is the nameless grave of one of the ill-fated Kallistenius Expedition. Still farther north, at Etah, is the grave of Sontag, the astronomer of Hayes's Expedition; and a little above it, that of Ohlsen of Kane's party. On the opposite side are the unmarked places where sixteen of Greely's ill-fated party died. Still farther north, on the eastern or Greenland side, is the grave of Hall, the American commander of the Polaris Expedition. On the western, or Grant Land side, are the graves of two or three sailors of the British Arctic Expedition of 1876. And right on the shore of the central Polar Sea, near Cape Sheridan, is the grave of the Dane, Petersen, the interpreter of the British Arctic Expedition of 1876. These graves stand as mute records of former efforts to win the prize, and they give a slight indication of the number of brave but less fortunate men who have given the last possession of mortal life in their pursuit of the arctic goal.

The first time I saw the graves of the whalers on Duck Islands I sat there, in the arctic sunlight, looking at those headboards, sobered with a realization of what they meant. When I first saw Sontag's grave, at Etah, I carefully replaced the stones around it, as a tribute to a brave man. At Cape Sabine, where Greely's party died, I was the first man to step into the ruins of the stone hut after the seven survivors were taken away years before — the first man, and I stepped into those ruins in a blinding snowstorm late in August, and saw there the mementos of those unfortunates.

Passing the Duck Islands on the upward voyage, approaching Cape York in 1908, and thinking of the graves there, I little dreamed that a loved member of my own party, Professor Ross G. Marvin, who ate at my table and acted as my secretary, was fated to add his name to this long list of arctic victims, and that his grave, in uncounted fathoms of black water, was to be the most northerly grave on this earth.

We reached Cape York on the first day of August. Cape York is the bold, bluff headland which marks the southern point of the stretch of arctic coast inhabited by my Eskimos, the most northerly human beings in the world. It is the headland whose snowy cap I have seen so many times rising in the distance above the horizon line of Melville Bay as my ships have steamed north. At the base of the headland nestles the most southerly of all the Eskimo villages, and it has marked the point of meeting, year after year, between the members of this tribe and myself.

At Cape York we were on the threshold of the actual work. I had on board the ship when I arrived there all the equipment and assistance which the civilized world could yield. Beginning there, I was to take on the tools, the material, the personnel, that the arctic regions themselves were to furnish for their own conquest. Cape York, or Melville Bay, is the dividing line between the civilized world on the one side and the arctic world on the other — the arctic world with its equipment of Eskimos, dogs, walrus, seal, fur clothing, and aboriginal experience.

Behind me lay the civilized world, which was now absolutely useless, and which could give me nothing more. Ahead of me lay that trackless waste through which I must literally cut my way to the goal. Even the ship's journey from Cape York to winter quarters on the north coast of Grant Land is not "plain sailing"; in fact, it is not sailing at all during the later stages; it is jamming and butting and dodging and hammering the ice, with always the possibility that the antagonist will hit back a body blow. It is like the work of a skilled heavy-weight pugilist, or the work of an old Roman fighter with the cestus.

Beyond Melville Bay the world, or what we know as the world, is left behind. On leaving Cape York, we had exchanged the multifarious purposes of civilization for the two purposes for which there is room in those wide wastes: food for man and dog, and the covering of miles of distance.

Behind me now lay everything that was mine, everything that a man personally loves, family, friends, home, and all those human associations which linked me with my kind. Ahead of me lay — my dream, the goal of that irresistible impulse which had driven me for twenty-three years to measure myself, time after time, against the frigid *No* of the Great North.

Should I succeed? Should I return? Success in the attainment of 90° North would not inevitably carry with it the safe return. We had learned *that* on recrossing the "big lead" in 1906. In the Arctic the chances are always against the explorer. The inscrutable guardians of the secret appear to have a well-nigh inexhaustible reserve of trump cards to play against the intruder who insists upon dropping into the game. The life is a dog's life, but the work is a man's work.

As we steamed northward from Cape York, on the first day of August, 1908, I felt that I was now in truth face to face with the final struggle. Everything in my life appeared to have led up to this day. All my years of work and all my former expeditions were merely preparations for this last and supreme effort. It has been said that well-directed labor toward a given end is an excellent kind of prayer for its attainment. If that be so, then prayer has been my portion for many years. Through all the seasons of disappointment and defeat I had never ceased to believe that the great white mystery of the North must eventually succumb to the insistence of human experience and will, and, standing there with my back to the world and my face toward that mystery, I believed that I should win in spite of all the powers of darkness and of desolation.

CHAPTER V

AS we approached Cape York, which is farther from the Pole in actual distance than New York is from Tampa, Florida, it was with a peculiar feeling of satisfaction that I saw the foremost of our Eskimo friends putting out to meet us in their tiny kayaks, or skin canoes. Here is the southernmost of the Eskimo villages, by which a permanent settlement is not meant, for these barbarians are nomads. One year there may be two families there; another year ten; and still another season none at all, for the Eskimos seldom live more than a year or two in one place.

As we neared the Cape, the headland was encircled and guarded by an enormous squadron of floating icebergs which made it difficult for the *Roosevelt* to get near shore; but long before we reached these bergs the hunters of the settlement were seen putting out to greet us. The sight of them skimming the water so easily in their frail kayaks was the most welcome spectacle I had seen since we sailed from Sydney.

It seems fitting to give a good deal of attention at this point to the consideration of this interesting little race, the most northerly people in all the world, for their help is one of the elements without which it is possible that the North Pole might never have been

ESKIMOS COMING OFF TO THE ROOSEVELT IN KAYAKS

THE MIDNIGHT SUN AS SEEN IN THE WHALE SOUND REGION

ESKIMO IN KAYAK

reached. Some years ago, in fact, I had occasion to write of these people a few sentences that, as it has turned out, were so prophetic that it seems appropriate to reproduce them here. Those sentences were:

"I have often been asked: Of what use are Eskimos to the world? They are too far removed to be of value for commercial enterprises and, furthermore, they lack ambition. They have no literature nor, properly speaking, any art. They value life only as does a fox, or a bear, purely by instinct. But let us not forget that these people, trustworthy and hardy, will yet prove their value to mankind. With their help, the world shall discover the Pole."

The hope that had been expressed in this language so long before was in my mind as I saw my old friends coming out to meet us in their tiny kayaks, for I realized that I was once more in contact with these faithful dwellers of the North, who had been my constant companions for so many years, through all the varying circumstances and fortunes of my arctic work, and from whom I was again to select the pick and flower of the hunters of the whole tribe, extending from Cape York to Etah, to assist in this last effort to win the prize.

Since 1891 I had been living and working with these people, gaining their absolute confidence, making them my debtors for things given them, earning their gratitude by saving, time after time, the lives of their wives and children by supplying them with food when they were on the verge of starvation. For eighteen years I had been training them in my methods; or, to put it another way, teaching them how to modify and concentrate their wonderful ice technic and endurance, so as to make them useful for my purposes. I had studied their individual characters, as any man studies the human tools with which he expects to accomplish results, until I knew just which ones to select for a quick, courageous dash, and just which dogged, unswerving ones would, if necessary, walk straight through hell for the object I had placed before them.

I know every man, woman, and child in the tribe, from Cape York to Etah. Prior to 1891 they had never been farther north than their own habitat. Eighteen years ago I went to these people, and my first work was from their country as a base.

Much nonsense has been told by travelers in remote lands about the aborigines' regarding as gods the white men who come to them, but I have never placed much credence in these stories. My own experience has been that the average aborigine is just as content with his own way as we are with ours, just as convinced of his own superior knowledge, and that he adjusts himself with his knowledge in regard to things in the same way that we do. The Eskimos are not brutes; they are just as human as Caucasians. They know that I am their friend, and they have abundantly proved themselves my friends.

When I went ashore at Cape York I found there four or five families, living in their summer tupiks, or skin tents, From them I learned what had happened in the tribe in the last two years; who had died, in what families children had been born, where this family and that family were then living — that is, the distribution of the tribe for that particular summer. I thus learned where to find the other men I wanted.

It was about seven o'clock in the morning when we arrived at Cape York. I selected the few men needed from that place, told them that when the sun reached a certain point in the heavens that evening the ship would sail, and that they and their families and possessions must be aboard the ship. As hunting is the only industry in these Eskimo villages, and as their goods are of an easily portable character, consisting mainly of tents, dogs and sledges, a few skins, pots and pans, they were able to transport themselves to the *Roosevelt* in our boats without much loss of time. As soon as they were on board we started north again.

There was no question of their willingness to follow me; they were only too glad to go. These men knew from past experience that, once enrolled as members of my expedition, there was no danger that their wives or children would suffer from hunger; and they knew also that at the end of the journey, when we brought them back to their homes, I would turn over to them the remaining supplies and equipment of the expedition, which would ensure living for another year in absolute plenty, that, in comparison with the other members of their tribe, they would indeed be multi-millionaires.

An intense and restless curiosity is one of the peculiar characteristics of these people. As an illustration, one winter, years ago, when Mrs. Peary was in Greenland with me, an old woman of the tribe walked a hundred miles from her village to our winter quarters in order that she might see a white woman.

It may perhaps be fairly said that it has been my fortune to utilize the Eskimos for the purpose of discovery to a degree equaled by no other explorer, and for that reason it may not seem amiss to suspend the general narrative long enough to give a little information regarding their characteristics, the more so as without some knowledge of these peculiar people it would be impossible for any one really to understand the workings of my expedition to the North Pole. It has been a fundamental principle of all my arctic work to utilize the Eskimos for the rank and file of my sledge parties. Without the skilful handiwork of the women we should lack the warm fur clothing which is absolutely essential to protect us from the winter cold, while the Eskimo dog is the only tractive force suitable for serious arctic sledge work.

The members of this little tribe or family, inhabiting the western coast of Greenland from Cape York to Etah, are in many ways quite different from the Eskimos of Danish Greenland, or those of any other arctic territory. There are now between two hundred and twenty and two hundred and thirty in the tribe. They are savages, but they are not savage; they are without government, but they are not lawless; they are utterly uneducated according to our standard, yet they exhibit a remarkable degree of intelligence. In temperament like children, with all a child's delight in little things, they are nevertheless enduring as the most mature of civilized men and women, and the best of them are faithful unto death. Without religion and having no idea of God, they will share their last meal with any one who is hungry, while the aged and the helpless among them are taken care of as a matter of course. They are healthy and pure-blooded; they have no vices, no intoxicants, and no bad habits — not even gambling. Altogether, they are a people unique upon the face of the earth. A friend of mine well calls them the philosophic anarchists of the North.

I have been studying the Eskimos for eighteen years and no more effective instruments for arctic work could be imagined than these plump, bronze-skinned, keen-eyed and black-maned children of nature. Their very limitations are their most valuable endowments for the purposes of arctic work. I have a sincere interest in these people, aside from their usefulness to me; and my plan from the beginning has been to give them such aid and instruction as would fit them more effectively to cope with their own austere environment, and to refrain from teaching them anything which would tend to weaken their self-confidence or to make them discontented with their lot.

The suggestions of some well-meaning persons that they be transported to a more hospitable region would, if carried out, cause their extermination in two or three generations. Our variable climate they could not endure, as they are keenly susceptible to pulmonary and bronchial affections. Our civilization, too, would only soften and corrupt them, as their racial inheritance is one of physical hardship; while to our complex environment they could not adjust themselves without losing the very childlike qualities which constitute their chief virtues. To Christianize them would be quite impossible; but the cardinal graces of faith, hope, and charity they seem to have already, for without them

they could never survive the six-months' night and
the many rigors of their home.

Their feeling for me is a blending of gratitude and
confidence. To understand what my gifts have meant
to them, imagine a philanthropic millionaire descending upon an American country town and offering every
man there a brownstone mansion and an unlimited
bank account. But·even this comparison falls short
of the reality, for in the United States even the poorest
boy knows that there is a possibility of his attaining
for himself those things on which he sets his heart, if he
will labor and endure, while to the Eskimos the things
which I have given them are absolutely out of their
world, as far beyond their own unaided efforts as the
moon and Mars are beyond the dwellers on this
planet.

My various expeditions into that region have had
the effect of raising the Eskimos from the most abject
destitution, lacking every appliance and accessory of
civilized life, to a position of relative affluence, with the
best material for their weapons, their harpoons and
lances, the best of wood for their sledges, the best of
cutlery, knives, hatchets, and saws for their work, and
the cooking utensils of civilization. Formerly they were
dependent upon the most primitive hunting weapons;
now they have repeating rifles, breech-loading shotguns,
and an abundance of ammunition. There was not a
rifle in the tribe when I first went there. As they have
no vegetables, and live solely on meat, blood, and blubber, the possession of guns and ammunition has
increased the food-producing capacity of every hunter,
and relieved the whole tribe from the formerly ever-

present danger of starvation for a family, or even an entire village.

There is a theory, first advanced by Sir Clements Markham, ex-president of the Royal Geographical Society of London, that the Eskimos are the remnants of an ancient Siberian tribe, the Onkilon; that the last members of this tribe were driven out on the Arctic Ocean by the fierce waves of Tartar invasion in the Middle Ages, and that they found their way to the New Siberian Islands, thence eastward over lands yet undiscovered to Grinnell Land and Greenland. I am inclined to believe in the truth of this theory for the following reasons:

Some of the Eskimos are of a distinctly Mongolian type, and they display many Oriental characteristics, such as mimicry, ingenuity, and patience in mechanical duplication. There is a strong resemblance between their stone houses and the ruins of the houses found in Siberia. The Eskimo girl brought home by Mrs. Peary, in 1894, was mistaken by Chinamen for one of their own people. It has also been suggested that their invocation of the spirits of their dead may be a survival of Asian ancestor worship.

As a general rule the Eskimos are short in stature, as are the Chinese and Japanese, though I could name several men who stand about five feet ten inches. The women are short and plump. They all have powerful torsos, but their legs are rather slender. The muscular development of the men is astonishing, though their fatty roundness hides the differentiation of the muscles.

These people have no written speech, and their language is agglutinative, with complicated prefixes and suffixes, by which they extend a word to a considerable length from the original stem. The language is relatively easy to acquire, and during my first summer in Greenland I gained a fair knowledge of it. In addition to their ordinary speech, they have an esoteric language known only to the adults of the tribe. I cannot say wherein it differs from the other, having made no attempt to learn it, and I doubt if any white man has been fully taught this secret speech, as the knowledge is carefully guarded by its possessors.

The Eskimos of this region have not, as a rule, applied themselves to the study of English, for they were clever enough to see that we could learn their language more easily than they could learn ours. Occasionally, however, an Eskimo will startle all hands by rolling out an English phrase or sentence, and, like a parrot, he seems to have a special aptitude in picking up from the sailors phrases of slang or profanity.

On the whole, these people are much like children, and should be treated as such. They are easily elated, easily discouraged. They delight in playing tricks on each other and on the sailors, are usually good-natured, and when they are sulky there is no profit in being vexed with them. The methods which children characterize as "jollying" are best for such emergencies. Their mercurial temperament is Nature's provision for carrying them through the long dark night, for if they were morose like the North American Indians, the whole tribe would long ago have lain down and died of discouragement, so rigorous is their lot.

In managing the Eskimos it is necessary to make a psychological study of them, and to consider their peculiar temperament. They are keenly appreciative of kindness, but, like children, they will impose upon a weak or vacillating person. A blending of gentleness and firmness is the only effective method. The fundamental point in all my dealings with them has been always to mean just what I say and to have things done exactly as ordered. For instance, if I tell an Eskimo that if he does a certain thing properly he will get a certain reward, he always gets the reward if he obeys. On the other hand, if I tell him that a certain undesirable thing will happen if he follows a course I have forbidden, that thing invariably happens.

I have made it to their interest to do what I want done. For example, the best all-round man on a long sledge journey got more than the others. A record was always kept of the game secured by each Eskimo, and the best hunter got a special prize. Thus I kept them interested in their work. The man who killed the musk ox with the finest set of horns and the man who killed the deer with the most magnificent antlers were specially rewarded. I have made it a point to be firm with them, but to rule them by love and gratitude rather than by fear and threats. An Eskimo, like an Indian, never forgets a broken promise — nor a fulfilled one.

It would be misleading to infer that almost any man who went to the Eskimos with gifts could obtain from them the kind of service they have given me; for it must be remembered that they have known me personally for nearly twenty years. I have saved whole villages from starvation, and the children are taught by their parents that if they grow up and become good hunters or good seamstresses, as the case may be, "Pearyaksoah" will reward them sometime in the not too distant future. Old Ikwah, for example, who is the father of the girl for whose possession hot-hearted young Ooqueah of my North Pole party fought his way with me to the goal, was the first Eskimo I had, away back in 1891.

This young knight of the Northland is an illustration of the fact that sometimes an Eskimo man or woman may be as intense in his or her affairs of the heart as we are. As a rule, however, they are more like children in their affections, faithful to their mates from a sort of domestic habit, but easily consoled for the loss of them by death or otherwise.

THE ICE CLIFFS OF HUBBARD GLACIER

PEARY DISTRIBUTING UTENSILS TO WIVES OF HIS HUNTERS AT ETAH

DECK SCENE ON THE ROOSEVELT

CHAPTER VI

AN ARCTIC OASIS

IN a little arctic oasis lives the meager and scattered handful of the Eskimo population — a little oasis along the frowning western coast of Northern Greenland 'between Melville Bay and Kane Basin. This region is three thousand miles north of New York City, as a steamer goes; it lies about half way between the Arctic Circle and the Pole, within the confines of the great night. Here, taking the mean latitude, for one hundred and ten days in summer the sun never sets; for one hundred and ten days in winter the sun never rises, and no ray of light save from the icy stars and the dead moon falls on the frozen landscape.

There is a savage grandeur in this coast, carved by eternal conflict with storms and glaciers, bergs and grinding ice-fields; but behind the frowning outer mask nestle in summer many grass-carpeted, flower-sprinkled, sun-kissed nooks. Millions of little auks breed along this shore. Between the towering cliffs are glaciers which launch at intervals their fleets of bergs upon the sea; before these cliffs lies the blue water dotted with masses of glistening ice of all shapes and sizes; behind the cliffs is the great Greenland ice cap, silent, eternal, immeasurable — the abode, say the Eskimos, of evil spirits and the souls of the unhappy dead.

In some places on this coast in summer, the grass is as thick and long as on a New England farm. Here bloom poppies, with dandelions, buttercups, and saxifrage, though to the best of my knowledge the flowers are all devoid of perfume. I have seen bumblebees even north of Whale Sound; there are flies and mosquitoes, and even a few spiders. Among the fauna of this country are the reindeer (the Greenland caribou), the fox — both blue and white — the arctic hare, the Polar bear, and perhaps once in a generation a stray wolf.

But in the long sunless winter this whole region — cliffs, ocean, glaciers — is covered with a pall of snow that shows a ghastly gray in the wan starlight. When the stars are hidden, all is black, void, and soundless. When the wind is blowing, if a man ventures out he seems to be pushed backward by the hands of an invisible enemy, while a vague, unnamable menace lurks before and behind him. It is small wonder the Eskimos believe that evil spirits walk upon the wind.

During the winter these patient and cheerful children of the North live in igloos, or huts, built of stones and earth. It is only when they are traveling, as sometimes during the moonlit period of the month, that they live in the snow igloos, which three good Eskimos can build in an hour or two, and which we built at the end of every day's march on our sledge journey to the Pole. In summer they live in the tupiks, or skin tents. The stone houses are permanent, and a good one will last perhaps a hundred years, with a little repairing of the roof in summer. Igloos are found in groups, or villages, at intervals along the coast from Cape York Bay to Anoratok. As the people are nomadic, these permanent dwellings belong to the tribe, and not to individuals, constituting thus a crude sort of arctic socialism. One year all the houses in a settlement may be occupied; the next year none, or only one or two.

These houses are about six feet high by eight to ten feet wide by ten to twelve feet long, and one may be constructed in a month. An excavation is made in the earth, which forms the floor of the house; then the walls are built up solidly with stones chinked with moss; long, flat stones are laid across the top of the walls; this roof is covered with earth, and the whole house is banked in with snow. The construction of the arched roof is on the plan which engineers know as the cantilever, and not that of the Roman arch. The long, flat stones which form the roof are weighted and counter-weighted at the outer ends, and in all my arctic experience I have never known the stone roof of an igloo to fall upon the inmates. There are never any complaints made to the Building Department. There is no door in the side, but a hole in the floor at the entrance leads to a tunnel, sometimes ten, sometimes fifteen, or even twenty-five, feet in length, through which the tenants crawl into their home. There is always a small window in the front of the igloo. The window space is not glazed, of course, but is covered with the thin, intestinal membrane of seals, skilfully seamed together. To a traveler across the dark and snowy winter waste, the yellow light from the interior lamp is visible, sometimes, a long distance away.

At the farther end of the igloo is the bed platform, raised about a foot and a half above the earthen floor. Usually this platform is not built, but is the natural level of the earth, the standing space being dug before it. In some houses, however, the bed platform is made of long, flat stones raised upon stone supports. When the Eskimos are ready to move into the stone houses in the fall, they cover the bed platform first with grass, which they bring in by the sledge-load; the grass is then covered with sealskins; above these are spread deerskins, or musk-ox skins, — which form the mattress. Deerskins are used for blankets. Pajamas are not in fashion with the Eskimos. They simply remove all their clothes and crawl in between the deerskins.

The lamp, which stands on a large stone at the front of the bed platform on one side, is kept burning all the time, whether the family is asleep or awake. An imaginative person might liken this lamp to an ever-burning sacred flame upon the stone altar of the Eskimo home. It serves also as a stove for heating and cooking, and makes the igloo so warm that the inhabitants wear little clothing when indoors. They sleep with their heads toward the lamp, so the woman may reach out and tend it.

On the other side of the house food is generally stored. When two families occupy one igloo, there may be a second lamp on the other side; and in that case the food must be stored under the bed. The temperature of these houses varies from eighty or ninety degrees Fahrenheit, on the bed platform and near the roof, to something below freezing point at the floor level. There is a little air-hole in the center of the roof, but in the happy home of an Eskimo family, in winter, the atmosphere could almost be handled with a shovel.

Often, in winter traveling, I have been obliged to sleep in one of these hospitable igloos. On such occasions I have made the best of things, as a man would if compelled to sleep in a tenth-rate railroad hotel or a slum lodging-house, but I have tried to forget the experience as soon as possible. It is not well for an arctic explorer to be too fastidious. A night in one of these igloos, with the family at home, is an offense to every civilized sense, especially that of smell; but there are times when a man, after a long sledge journey in the terrible cold and wind, hungry and footsore, will welcome the dim light shining through the translucent window of an igloo as one welcomes the light of home. It means warmth and comfort, supper, and blessed sleep.

There is no blinking the fact that my Eskimo friends are very dirty. When I have them on the ship with me they make heroic efforts to wash themselves occasionally; but in their own homes they practically never do, and in winter they have no water except from melted snow. On rare occasions, when the dirt gets too thick for comfort, they may remove the outer layer with a little oil. I shall never forget the amazement with which they made acquaintance with the white man's use of the tooth-brush.

With the coming of the summer, the stone and earth houses become damp, dark holes, and the roofs are taken off to dry and ventilate the interior. The family then moves outside and sets up the tupik, or skin tent, which is their home from about the first of June till some time in September. The tupik is made of sealskins, with the hair on the inside. Ten or twelve skins, sewed together in one large piece, make a tent. It is stretched on poles, high in front and sloping toward the back, thus offering the least possible resistance to the wind, the edges held down with stones. The earth floor of these tents is six or eight feet wide and eight or ten feet long, according to the size of the family.

In recent years my Eskimos have adopted an improvement upon the building customs of the west coast natives, and many of them have an entrance extension to their tents made of transparent tanned sealskins, thick enough to keep out the rain but not the light. This adds to the roominess and comfort of their summer dwellings. A usual practice among the better class of Eskimos is to use the old tupik of the previous summer for a rain or weather-guard to the new tent. In heavy winds or heavy summer rains, the old tupik is simply spread over the new one, thus giving a double thickness and protection to the owners.

The bed platform in the tupik is now generally made of lumber, which I have furnished, raised on stones, and in pleasant weather the cooking is done outside. Oil is the only fuel for heat, light, and cooking. The Eskimo women trim the lamps so well that there is no smoke from them, unless there is a draft in the tent or igloo. They cut small pieces of blubber, which they lay on moss and ignite, and the heat from the moss tries out the oil, making a surprisingly hot flame. Until I gave them matches, they had only the primitive means of ignition by flint and steel, which they obtained from a vein of pyrites. When I first went up there, all their lamps and rectangular pots were made of soapstone, two or three veins of which are found in that country. Their ability to utilize the soapstone and pyrites is an illustration of their intelligence and ingenuity.

As a rule little clothing is worn in the tupiks in warm weather, as the normal summer temperature is around fifty degrees Fahrenheit, and in the strong sunlight may go as high as eighty-five or even ninety-five.

The trial marriage is an ineradicable custom among the Eskimos. If a young man and woman are not suited with each other, they try again, and sometimes several times; but when they find mates to whom they are adapted, the arrangement is generally permanent. If two men want to marry the same woman, they settle the question by a trial of strength, and the better man has his way. These struggles are not fights, as the disputants are amiable; they are simply tests of wrestling, or sometimes of pounding each other on the arm to see which man can stand the pounding the longer.

Their fundamental acceptance of the proposition that might is right in such matters sometimes extends to a man saying to the husband of a woman: "I am the better man." In such case the husband has either to prove his superiority in strength, or yield the woman to the other. If a man grows tired of his wife, he simply tells her there is not room for her in his igloo.

She may return to her parents, if they are living; she may go to a brother or a sister; or she may send word to some man in the tribe that she is now at liberty and is willing to start life again. In these cases of primitive divorce, the husband keeps one or all of the children if he wants them; if not, the woman takes them with her.

The Eskimos do not have many children, two or three being the usual number. The woman does not take her husband's name in any case. Akatingwah, for instance, will remain Akatingwah, whether she has had one husband or several. Children do not address their parents as father and mother, but call them by their names, though sometimes very small children use a diminutive which corresponds to our "mamma."

Among the Eskimos the woman is as much a part of the man's property as his dog or sledge — except in some rare cases. The cause of the suffragettes has as yet made little headway in this region. I remember one instance in which an Eskimo woman had a difference of opinion with her husband, and proved her right to independence by blackening the old man's eye; but I am afraid that the more conservative members of the tribe attributed this unfeminine behavior to the corrupting influence of contact with civilization.

As there are more men than women among the Eskimos, the girls marry very young, often about the age of twelve. In many cases the marriages are arranged between the parents when the children are quite young; but the boy and girl are not bound, and

ESKIMO MOTHER AND CHILD

ESKIMO CHILDREN

KUDLAH, ALIAS "MISFORTUNE," WITH PUPPIES

when they are old enough they are permitted to decide for themselves. In fact, they can make several such decisions without losing caste. On the last expedition, as on those of former years, I found that a number of matrimonial changes had taken place among my Northern friends since I was last among them.

It would be worse than useless to attempt to engraft our marriage customs upon these naive children of Nature. Should an arctic explorer consider it his duty to tell a young Eskimo that it was not right for him to exchange wives with his friend, it would be well for the explorer to have his supporting argument well prepared beforehand, for the censured one would probably open wide his eyes and inquire, "Why not?"

These people of the ice-land, like all intelligent savages, are remarkably curious. If confronted, say, with a package containing various supplies unknown to them, they will not rest until they have examined every article of the lot, touched it, turned it over, and even tasted it, chattering all the while like a flock of blackbirds. They exhibit, too, in marked degree, all the Oriental capacity for imitation. Out of walrus ivory, in some respects their substitute for steel, — and a surprisingly good substitute it is, — they will construct amazingly good models or copies of various objects, while it does not take them long to master the use of such tools of civilization as may be put into their hands. It will easily be seen how valuable and useful a quality this has proved for the purposes of the arctic explorer. If he could not rely on the Eskimo to do the white man's work with the white man's tools, the labors of the arctic traveler would be tremendously increased and the size of his expedition would have to be enlarged to limits that might be found unwieldy in the extreme.

My own observations of this interesting people have taught me to repose no confidence whatever in the tales of barbaric craft and cruelty which I have heard of them. On the contrary, taking into consideration their uncivilized state, they must be ranked as a humane people. Moreover, they have always been quick to grasp the purposes that I have had in view and to bend their energies toward achieving the ends for which my expeditions have been striving.

Their humanity, as has been indicated, takes a form that would delight a socialist. They are generous and hospitable in a crude way, almost without exception. As a general rule, good and bad fortune are shared. The tribe shares in the proceeds of good luck on the part of the hunters and, as their existence depends on hunting, this accounts in large measure for the preservation of the tribe.

CHAPTER VII

ODD CUSTOMS OF AN ODD PEOPLE

HARD as is the life of the Eskimo, his end is usually as rigorous. All his life he is engaged in constant warfare with the inhospitable elements of his country, and Death, when it arrives, usually comes in some violent form. Old age has few terrors for the Eskimo, for he seldom lives to reach it. He dies, as a rule, in harness, drowned by the capsizing of his skin canoe, caught by the overturning of an iceberg, or crushed by a snow-slide or a rock-slide. It is seldom that an Eskimo lives to be more than sixty years of age.

Strictly speaking, the Eskimos have no religion, in the sense in which we use the word. But they believe in the survival of the person after death, and they believe in spirits — especially evil spirits. It may be that their lack of any idea of a beneficent God, and their intense consciousness of evil influences, result from the terrible hardships of their lives. Having no special blessings for which to be grateful to a kind Creator, they have not evolved a conception of Him, while the constantly recurring menaces of the dark, the bitter cold, the savage wind and gnawing hunger, have led them to people the air with invisible enemies. The beneficent spirits are those of their ancestors (another Oriental touch), while they have a whole legion

of malevolent spirits, led by Tornarsuk, the great
devil himself.

They are constantly trying to propitiate Tornarsuk
by incantations; and when they kill game, an offering is made to him.   The devil is supposed to have a
keen appeciation of these tidbits.   On leaving a snow
igloo the Eskimos are careful to kick the front out
of it, that the evil spirits may not find shelter there,
and when they throw away a worn-out garment it is
never left intact, but is torn in such a way that the
devil may not use it to warm himself. A comfortable
devil is presumably more dangerous than a shiver-
ing one. Any sudden and unexplained barking or howling among the dogs indicates the invisible presence of
Tornarsuk, and the men will run out and crack
their whips or fire their rifles to scare away the
invader. When, on board the *Roosevelt* in winter
quarters, I was suddenly aroused from sleep by the
crack of rifles, I did not think there was a mutiny
aboard — only that Tornarsuk had ridden by upon
the wind.

When the ice presses hard against the ship, an
Eskimo will call on his dead father to push it away;
when the wind blows with special violence, ancestors
are again appealed to.   Passing along a cliff, on a sledge
journey, a man will sometimes stop and listen and then
say: "Did you hear what the devil said just then?"
I have asked the Eskimo to repeat to me the words of
Tornarsuk, up there on the cliff, and I would not dream
of laughing at my faithful friends at such a time; the
messages of Tornarsuk I receive with a respectful
gravity.

There are no chiefs among these people, no men in
authority; but there are medicine men who have some
influence. The angakok is generally not loved — he
knows too many unpleasant things that are going to
happen, so he says. The business of the angakok is
mainly singing incantations and going into trances,
for he has no medicines. If a person is sick, he may
prescribe abstinence from certain foods for a certain
number of moons; for instance, the patient must not
eat seal meat, or deer meat, but only the flesh of the
walrus. Monotonous incantations take the place of the
white man's drugs. The performance of a self-confident
angakok is quite impressive — if one has not witnessed
it too many times before. The chanting, or howling,
is accompanied by contortions of the body and by
sounds from a rude tambourine, made from the throat
membrane of a walrus stretched on a bow of ivory or
bone. The tapping of the rim with another piece of
ivory or bone marks the time. This is the Eskimo's
only attempt at music. Some women are supposed to
possess the power of the angakok — a combination
of the gifts of the fortune teller, the mental healer, and
the psalmodist, one might say.

Once, years ago, my little brown people got tired of
an angakok, one Kyoahpahdo, who had predicted too
many deaths; and they lured him out on a hunting
expedition from which he never returned. But these
executions for the peace of the community are rare.

Their burial customs are rather interesting. When
an Eskimo dies, there is no delay about removing the
body. Just as soon as possible it is wrapped, fully
clothed, in the skins which formed the bed, and some

extra garments are added to insure the comfort of the spirit. Then a strong line is tied round the body, and it is removed, always head first, from the tent or igloo, and dragged head first over the snow or ground to the nearest place where there are enough loose stones to cover it. The Eskimos do not like to touch a dead body, and it is therefore dragged as a sledge would be. Arrived at the place selected for the grave, they cover the corpse with loose stones, to protect it from the dogs, foxes, and ravens, and the burial is complete.

According to Eskimo ideas, the after-world is a distinctly material place. If the deceased is a hunter, his sledge and kayak, with his weapons and implements, are placed close by, and his favorite dogs, harnessed and attached to the sledge, are strangled so that they may accompany him on his journey into the unseen. If the deceased is a woman, her lamp and the little wooden frame on which she has dried the family boots and mittens are placed beside the grave. A little blubber is placed there, too, and a few matches, if they are available, so that the woman may light the lamp and do some cooking in transit; a cup or bowl is also provided, in which she may melt snow for water. Her needle, thimble, and other sewing things are placed with her in the grave.

In former years, if the woman had a small baby in the hood it was strangled to keep her company; but I have, of course, discouraged this practice, and during the last two expeditions I have not heard of any strangled babies. Among the members of my own party I have simply forbidden the practice, and have promised the relatives sufficient condensed milk and other foods to keep the infant alive. If they have reverted to the old custom during my absence, they have not mentioned the fact to me, knowing of my disapproval.

If a death occurs in a tent, the poles are removed, and the tent is left on the ground to rot or blow away. It is never used again. If the death occurs in an igloo, the structure is vacated and not used again for a long time. The relatives of the dead observe certain formalities in regard to food and clothing, and the name of the lost one is never mentioned. If any other members of the tribe have the same name, they must take another until an infant is born to which the proscribed name can be given. This appears to remove the ban.

Eskimos are children in their grief, as in their pleasure; they weep for a dead friend a few days, then they forget. Even a mother who has been inconsolable at the death of her baby soon laughs again and thinks of other things.

In a country where the stars are visible for so many weeks at a time it is not strange perhaps that they receive much attention from the natives. The Eskimos are, within barbaric limits, astronomers. The principal constellations visible in northern latitudes are well known to them and they have given them their own names and descriptions. In the Great Dipper they see a herd of celestial reindeer. The Pleiades are to the Eskimos a team of dogs pursuing a solitary polar bear. Gemini they describe as two stones in the entrance of an igloo. The moon and the sun represent to the Eskimo, as to some of our North American Indian tribes, a fleeing maiden and her pursuing admirer.

Time is, of course, of small value to the Eskimo, so far as he is himself personally concerned, yet after the Eskimo has been trained to the ways of the white man he seems to absorb an excellent notion of the value of punctuality and will carry out orders with a surprising degree of promptness and despatch.

The strength and capacity for enduring hardships exhibited by this people is extraordinary and is not, I believe, exceeded by that shown by any other aboriginal race now in existence. It is true that the average size of the Eskimo is, judged by our own standards, small; but I could give the names of several of them who stand five feet ten inches and weigh 185 pounds. The popular idea that they are clumsily fashioned is not correct. That notion is merely another case of judging a man by the clothes he wears, and an Eskimo's garments are not precisely what we should call of fashionable cut.

To my mind, the skin canoe of these Northern aborigines is, with its hunting implements, one of the most complete and ingenious manifestations of intelligence to be found in any aboriginal tribe. Over a light framework, an almost infinite number of small pieces of wood deftly lashed together with sealskin thongs, is stretched the tanned skin of seals, the seams being neatly sewed by the women, and then rendered watertight by an application of seal oil and soot from the native lamps. The result is a craft of great buoyancy, some grace, and especial fitness and effectiveness for the purposes for which it is intended, that is, to enable the hunter to creep softly and noiselessly upon seal, walrus, or white whale. This canoe, while varying somewhat with the size of the owner and maker, will average between twenty and twenty-four inches in width by sixteen or eighteen feet in length. It carries one man only. I may have helped the Eskimos a little in perfecting it, by giving them more suitable material for the framework, but the canoe is original with them.

It will scarcely be considered strange that I have grown to love this childlike, simple people, as well as to value their many admirable and useful qualities. For it must be borne in mind that for nearly a quarter of a century they have been more thoroughly known to me than any other group of human beings in the world. The present generation of able-bodied Eskimos has practically grown up under my personal observation. Every individual member of the tribe — man, woman, and child — is known to me by name and sight as thoroughly as the patients of an old-fashioned family physician are known to him, and perhaps the feeling existing between us is not so very different. And the knowledge of individuals gained in this intimate way has been priceless in the work of reaching the Pole.

Take, for example, the quartet of young Eskimos who formed a portion of the sledge party that finally reached the long-courted "ninety North." The oldest of the four, Ootah, is about 34 years of age. This young man is one of the sturdiest of the tribe. He stands about 5 feet 8 inches and is a fine hunter. When I first saw him he was a young boy. Egingwah, another of the group, is about 26 years old, a big chap weighing about 175 pounds. Seegloo and Ooqueah are about 24 and 20 respectively. All four of them have been brought up to regard me as the patron, protector, and guide of their people. Their capacities, peculiarities, and individual characteristics were perfectly known to me, and they were chosen out of the whole tribe for the final great effort because I knew them to be most perfectly adapted to the work in hand.

Before taking up the story of our advance from Cape York, a word ought to be said about those remarkable creatures, the Eskimo dogs, for without their help success could never have crowned the efforts of the expedition. They are sturdy, magnificent animals. There may be larger dogs than these, there may be handsomer dogs; but I doubt it. Other dogs may work as well or travel as fast and far when fully fed; but there is no dog in the world that can work so long in the lowest temperatures on practically nothing to eat. The male dogs average in weight from eighty to one hundred pounds, though I had one which weighed one hundred and twenty-five pounds. The females are somewhat smaller. Their special physical characteristics are a pointed muzzle, great breadth between the eyes, sharp-pointed ears, very heavy coat underlaid with a thick, soft fur, powerful, heavy-muscled legs, and a bushy tail or brush similar to that of the fox. There is only one breed of Eskimo dogs, but they are variously marked and of different colors, black, white, gray, yellow, brown, and mottled. Some scientists believe that they are the direct descendants of the Arctic wolf, yet, as a rule, they are as affectionate and obedient to their masters as our own dogs at home. Their food is meat, and meat only. That they cannot

KING ESKIMO DOG

THE DOG MARKET AT CAPE YORK

THE WHALE BOAT RETURNING TO THE SHIP FROM THE WALRUS HUNT

THE CAPE JESUP GRENADIERS

live on any other food I know, for I have made the experiment. For water they eat snow.

The dogs are not housed at any season of the year; but summer and winter they are tied somewhere near the tent or igloo. They are never allowed to roam at large, lest they be lost. Sometimes a special pet, or a female that has young puppies, will be taken into the igloo for a time; but Eskimo puppies only a month old are so hardy that they can stand the severe winter weather.

Enough has been said to give the reader a general idea of these strange people, that have been so valuable to me in my arctic work. But I want to say again, at the risk of being misunderstood, that I hope no efforts will ever be made to civilize them. Such efforts, if successful, would destroy their primitive communism, which is necessary to preserve their existence. Once give them an idea of real-estate interest and personal-property rights in houses and food, and they might become as selfish as civilized beings; whereas now any game larger than a seal is the common property of the tribe and no man starves while his neighbors are gorging themselves. If a man has two sets of hunting implements, he gives one of them to the man who has none. It is this feeling of good-fellowship which alone preserves the race. I have taught them some of the fundamental principles of sanitation and the care of themselves, the treatment of simple diseases, of wounds, and other accidents; but there I think their civilization should stop. This opinion is not based on theory or prejudice, but on eighteen years of intimate study and experience.

CHAPTER VIII

WHEN on August 1 the *Roosevelt* steamed out from Cape York, she had on board several Eskimo families which we had picked up there and at Salvo Island. We also had about one hundred dogs, bought from the Eskimos. When I say "bought," I do not mean paid for with money, as these people have no money and no unit of value. All exchange between them is based on the principle of pure barter. For instance, if one Eskimo has a deerskin which he does not need, and another has something else, they exchange. The Eskimos had dogs which we wanted, and we had many things which they wanted, such as lumber, knives and other cutlery, cooking utensils, ammunition, matches, et cetera. So, as the Yankees say, we traded.

Steaming in a northwesterly course from Cape York, we passed the "Crimson Cliffs," so named by Sir John Ross, the English explorer, in 1818. This vivid name was applied to the cliffs by reason of the quantities of "red snow" which can be seen from a ship miles out at sea. The color is given to the permanent snow by the *Protococcus nivalis*, one of the lowest types of the single, living protoplasmic cell. The nearly transparent gelatinous masses vary from a quarter inch in diameter to the size of a pin-head, and

they draw from the snow and the air the scanty nourishment which they require. Seen from a distance,
the snow looks like blood. This red banner of the
Arctic has greeted me on all my northern journeys.

Sailing by these cliffs, which extend for thirty or
forty miles, my thoughts were busy with the work
before us. First and most necessary of all was the
task of gathering our arctic personnel of Eskimos and
dogs, already begun before we left Cape York.

Our next stop, after Cape York, was on August 3,
at North Star Bay, Oomunnui, as the natives call
it, on Wolstenholm Sound. Here I found the *Erik*,
which had become separated from us in Davis Strait
several days before during heavy weather. At Oomunnui we took on two or three families of Eskimos and
more dogs. Ooqueah, one of my North Pole party,
came aboard at this place; Seegloo had joined us at
Cape York.

On the night of August 5, a clear and sunshiny
night, between Hakluyt and Northumberland Islands
I left the *Roosevelt* and transferred to the *Erik*, taking
Matt Henson with me, for a reconnaissance of the
various Eskimo settlements on Inglefield Gulf and
along the coast. This detour was for the purpose of
picking up more Eskimos and dogs. The *Roosevelt*
was sent ahead to Etah, to get in shape for her coming
battle royal with the ice in Kane Basin and the channels beyond.

There was for me a strange mingling of pleasure
and sadness in this gathering together of our brown-
skinned helpers, for I felt that it was for the last
time. The business consumed several days. I went

first to Karnah, on the Redcliffe Peninsula, thence to
Kangerdlooksoah and Nunatoksoah, near the head of
the gulf. Returning on our course, we came back to
Karnah, then went south to the neighborhood of the
Itiblu Glacier, then northwest again by a devious
course around the islands and the points to Kookan,
in Robertson Bay, then to Nerke, on C. Saumarez,
then on to Etah, where we joined the *Roosevelt*, having obtained all the Eskimos and dogs we needed, —
two hundred and forty-six of the latter, to be exact.

There was no intention of taking to the far North
all the Eskimos taken aboard the *Erik* and the *Roosevelt* — only the best of them. But if any family
wanted transportation from one settlement to another,
we were glad to accommodate them. It is to be
doubted if anywhere on the waters of the Seven Seas
there was ever a more outlandishly picturesque vessel than ours at this time — a sort of free tourist
steamship for traveling Eskimos, with their chattering children, barking dogs, and other goods and
chattels.

Imagine this man-and-dog-bestrewn ship, on a
pleasant, windless summer day in Whale Sound. The
listless sea and the overarching sky are a vivid blue
in the sunlight — more like a scene in the Bay of Naples
than one in the Arctic. There is a crystalline clearness in the pure atmosphere that gives to all colors a
brilliancy seen nowhere else — the glittering white
of the icebergs with the blue veins running through
them; the deep reds, warm grays, and rich browns of
the cliffs, streaked here and there with the yellows
of the sandstone; a little farther away sometimes the

ESKIMO DOGS OF THE EXPEDITION (246 IN ALL) ON SMALL ISLAND, ETAH FJORD

soft green grass of this little arctic oasis; and on the distant horizon the steel-blue of the great inland ice. When the little auks fly high against the sunlit sky, they appear like the leaves of a forest when the early frost has touched them and the first gale of autumn carries them away, circling, drifting, eddying through the air. The desert of northern Africa may be as beautiful as Hichens tells us; the jungles of Asia may wear as vivid coloring; but to my eyes there is nothing so beautiful as the glittering Arctic on a sunlit summer day.

On August 11 the *Erik* reached Etah, where the *Roosevelt* was awaiting her. The dogs were landed on an island, the *Roosevelt* was washed, the boilers were blown down and filled with fresh water, the furnaces cleaned, and the cargo overhauled and re-stowed to put the vessel in fighting trim for her coming encounter with the ice. About three hundred tons of coal were transferred from the *Erik* to the *Roosevelt*, and about fifty tons of walrus and whale meat.

Fifty tons of coal were cached at Etah for the *Roosevelt's* expected return the following year. Two men, boatswain Murphy and Pritchard, the cabin boy, with full provisions for two years, were left in charge. Harry Whitney, a summer passenger on the *Erik*, who was ambitious to obtain musk-oxen and polar bears, asked permission to remain with my two men at Etah. The permission was granted, and Mr. Whitney's belongings were landed.

At Etah, Rudolph Franke, who had come north with Dr. Cook in 1907, came to me and asked permission to go home on the *Erik*. He showed me a letter from Dr. Cook directing him to go home this season on a whaler. An examination by Dr. Goodsell, my surgeon, showed that the man suffered from incipient scurvy, and that he was in a serious mental state, so I had no alternative but to give him passage home on the *Erik*. Boatswain Murphy, whom I was to leave at Etah, was a thoroughly trustworthy man, and I gave him instructions to prevent the Eskimos from looting the supplies and equipment left there by Dr. Cook, and to be prepared to render Dr. Cook any assistance he might require when he returned, as I had no doubt he would as soon as the ice froze over Smith Sound (presumably in January) so as to enable him to cross to Anoratok from Ellesmere Land, where I had no doubt he then was.

On the *Erik* were three other passengers, Mr. C. C. Crafts, who had come north to take a series of magnetic observations for the department of terrestrial magnetism of the Carnegie Institution in Washington, Mr. George S. Norton, of New York, and Mr. Walter A. Larned, the tennis champion. The *Roosevelt's* carpenter, Bob Bartlett, of Newfoundland (not related to Captain Bob Bartlett), and a sailor named Johnson also went back on the *Erik*. That vessel was commanded by Captain Sam Bartlett (Captain Bob's uncle), who had been master of my own ship on several expeditions.

At Etah we took on a few more Eskimos, including Ootah and Egingwah, who were destined to be with me at the Pole; and I left there all the remaining Eskimos that I did not wish to take with me to winter quarters in the North. We retained forty-nine —

twenty-two men, seventeen women, ten children — and two hundred and forty-six dogs. The *Roosevelt*, as usual, was loaded almost to the water's edge with the coal that had been crowded into her, the seventy tons of whale meat which we had bought in Labrador, and the meat and blubber of nearly fifty walruses.

We parted company from the *Erik* and steamed north on the 18th of August, an intensely disagreeable day, with driving snow and rain, and a cutting wind from the southeast which made the sea very rough. As the two ships separated, they signaled "good-by and good luck" with the whistles, and our last link with civilization was broken.

Since my return I have been asked if I did not feel deep emotion on parting with my companions on the *Erik*, and I have truthfully replied that I did not. The reader must remember that this was my eighth expedition into the Arctic, and that I had parted from a supply ship many times before. Constant repetition will take the edge from the most dramatic experience. As we steamed north from the harbor of Etah, my thoughts were on the condition of the ice in Robeson Channel; and the ice in Robeson Channel is more dramatic than any parting — save from one's nearest and dearest, and I had left mine three thousand miles below at Sydney. We had some three hundred and fifty miles of almost solid ice to negotiate before we could reach our hoped-for winter quarters at Cape Sheridan. I knew that beyond Smith Sound we might have to make our slow way rod by rod, and sometimes literally inch by inch, butting and ramming and dodging the mountainous ice; that, if the *Roose-*

velt survived, I should probably not have my clothes off, or be able to snatch more than an hour or two of sleep at a time, for two or three weeks. Should we lose our ship and have to make our way over the ice southward from anywhere below Lady Franklin Bay, or possibly beyond there — it was good-by to my life's dream and probably to some of my companions.

CHAPTER IX

A WALRUS HUNT

THE walrus are among the most picturesque and powerful fauna of the far North. More than that, their pursuit and capture, a process by no means devoid of peril, is an important part of every serious arctic expedition, for on every expedition of mine these huge creatures, weighing as they do all the way from 1,200 to 3,000 pounds, are hunted for the purpose of obtaining the maximum of meat for dog food in a minimum of time.

Wolstenholm and Whale Sounds, which are passed before reaching Etah, are favorite haunts of the walrus. The hunting of these monsters is the most exciting and dangerous sport in the arctic regions. The polar bear has been called the tiger of the North; but a contest between one or two, or even three, of these animals and a man armed with a Winchester repeating rifle is an entirely one-sided affair. On the contrary, a contest with a herd of walrus, — the lions of the North, — in a small whale-boat, will give more thrills to the minute than anything else I know of within the Arctic Circle.

On the last expedition I did not go after walrus myself, leaving that exhilarating labor to the younger men. I have seen so much of it in the past that my first vivid impression is somewhat blunted. I have

therefore asked George Borup to write for me an
account of walrus-hunting, as it appears to a novice,
and his story is so vivid that I give it to the reader in
his own words, graphic with the keen impressions
of a young man and picturesque with college slang.
He says:

"Walrus-hunting is the best sport in the shooting
line that I know. There is something doing when you
tackle a herd of fifty-odd, weighing between one and
two tons each, that go for you whether wounded or not;
that can punch a hole through eight inches of young
ice; that try to climb into the boat to get at or upset
you,—we never could make out which, and didn't care,
as the result to us would have been the same, — or
else try to ram your boat and stave holes in it.

"Get in a mix-up with a herd, when every man in
the whale-boat is standing by to repel boarders, hitting them over the head with oars, boat-hooks, axes,
and yelling like a cheering section at a football game
to try to scare them off; with the rifles going like
young Gatling guns, and the walruses bellowing from
pain and anger, coming to the surface with mad rushes,
sending the water up in the air till you would think a
flock of geysers was turned loose in your immediate
vicinity — oh, it's great!

"When we were walrus-hunting, the *Roosevelt*
would steam along, with all hands on the watch.
Then suddenly a keen-eyed Eskimo would sing out,
'Awick soah!' or, possibly, 'Awick tedicksoah!' ('Walruses! A great many walruses!')

"We would look to see if there were enough of
the animals to make a raid worth while; then, if the

prospect was satisfactory, the *Roosevelt* would steam along to leeward, for if they smelled her smoke they would wake up and we would never see them again.

"Henson, MacMillan, and I used to take turns going after these brutes. Four or five Eskimos, one sailor, and a whale-boat were assigned to each of us. The boats were painted white to resemble pieces of ice, and the row-locks were muffled, that we might steal along as noiselessly as possible.

"As soon as we sighted a herd worthy of our lead, we would sing out to our men, 'Shake her up!' and they would all come on the jump. After a hurried though careful look to see if we had four or five oars, five harpoons, lines, floats, two rifles, and ammunition, we would cry, 'Stand by to lower away'; and as the *Roosevelt* slackened speed we would slide down the davit ropes, man the oars, and go out to look for trouble — which we usually found.

"We would get as near as possible to the walruses on the ice. If they were sound asleep, we could row to within five yards and harpoon a couple; but generally they would wake up, when we were about twenty yards away, and begin to slide off into the water. We would then shoot, and if they attacked us it was easy to harpoon them; while if they started to leave the country, it might be a Marathon race before we got close enough to make the harpoons fast in their hides.

"A walrus when killed will go to the bottom like a ton of lead, and our business was to get a harpoon into him before that event took place. The harpoon is fastened to the float by a long thong made of sealskin, and a float is made of the entire skin of a seal filled with air for buoyancy.

"A thing we soon learned to look out for was to let this thong, which was neatly coiled up like a lasso before it was thrown, have the right of way and all the space it needed; for if it happened to take a turn around one of our legs when the other end was fast to a walrus, we would be missing that useful member, and be pulled into the water — and possibly drowned.

"Now a crew that goes through a scrimmage with these monsters develops teamplay of a high order in a surprisingly short time. The sailor would steer, four Eskimos would row, and in the bow would be the best harpooner with one of us beside him. The two men forward would enable the men rowing to be spelled, if we had a long chase.

"I shall never forget my first mix-up with a herd. We had sighted about ten walruses two miles away, and MacMillan and I, Dennis Murphy, a sailor, and three Eskimos manned a whale-boat, and off we went. About two hundred yards from the walruses we quit rowing and let Murphy scull us, while Mac and I crouched side by side in the bow, the Eskimos with their harpoons being ready right behind us.

"When we were about twenty yards from the herd, one bull woke up, gave a grunt, poked another, woke him, and then — bang! bang! bang! we opened fire. Mac had a Winchester automatic rifle, and he got off five shots so fast that before the first one left the muzzle the other four were chasing it. He dropped a large bull, which gave a convulsive flop and rolled into the water with a splash. I hit a couple,

and with hoarse grunts of pain and fury they all
wriggled off the ice and dived out of sight. The boat
was hurried to within five yards of Mac's bull, and an
Eskimo hurled a harpoon, hit the large bull, and threw
overboard the sealskin float. At this stage of the game
about forty other walruses, that had been feeding
below, came up to the surface to see what the noise
was about, spitting the clam shells out of their mouths
and snorting. The water was alive with the brutes,
and many of them were so close to us that we could
hit them with the oars. A harpoon was driven into
another by a corking throw; and just then, when my
magazine was empty, things began to come our way.

"Suddenly a large bull, followed by two others,
all wounded, came to the surface twenty yards off,
gave tongue to their battle-cry and charged. The
Eskimos were not pleased at the look of things. They
grabbed the oars and began to bang them on the gunwale of the boat, yelling like so many steam sirens,
hoping to scare the invaders off; but they might as
well have been crooning lullabies.

"Mac, who had never before shot anything larger
than a bird, was cool, and his automatic was going
off like a pom-pom, when we cut loose on the charging
trio. Their numerous companions added to the general din; and the reports of the rifles, the shouts and
pounding of the Eskimos, with the bellowing of the
infuriated animals, sounded like Vesuvius blowing
its head off. We sank one walrus, then disabled another; but the biggest one dived and came up with a
snort right alongside of the boat, so that he blew water
in our faces. With our guns almost touching his head,

we let drive — and he began to sink. With a triumphant cheer, the Eskimos harpooned him.

"Then we signaled to the *Roosevelt* to come up, and as soon as the friends and neighbors of the deceased smelled the smoke, they made for parts unknown.

"In this hunt, as in all other walrus hunts I was in, I had a hard time in trying not to take a crack at the floats. They were black, and jumped around in the weirdest way, so that they appeared to be alive. I knew that if I shot one, I would never hear the last of it, so took good care.

"Another time we went for a herd of fifty-odd walruses that were sleeping on the ice. The wind was blowing fairly hard, and it is never easy to shoot accurately from a whale-boat which is doing a cake-walk in the arms of a choppy sea. When we got twenty yards from the ice cake, we began to fire. I hit a couple of walruses, but did not kill them, and with fierce grunts the huge brutes wriggled into the sea. They were coming our way, and all hands stood by to show the visitors how we loved to speed the parting guest — our way of showing this being the vocal and instrumental method already described.

"Wesharkoopsi, an Eskimo, who stood right behind me and who had been telling us what an expert he was with the harpoon, was making threatening gestures which boded ill for any walrus that came near us.

"Suddenly, with a loud 'Ook! Ook!' a bull rose like a giant jack-in-the-box right alongside of me, giving us a regular shower bath, and he got both tusks on the gunwale of the boat.

"Wesharkoopsi was not expecting a fight at such close quarters, and he got badly rattled. Instead of throwing his harpoon he dropped it, yelled madly, and began to spit in the monster's face. It is needless to state that we never again took Wesharkoopsi walrus-hunting in a whale-boat.

"The others were shouting, swearing in English and Eskimo at Wesharkoopsi, the walrus, and everything in general; some were trying to hit the brute, others to back water.

"I was not eager just then to test the soundness of one arctic explorer's dictum: 'If a walrus gets his tusks over the side of the boat, you must not hit him, as such a course would induce him to back water and upset you; but gently grasp the two-thousand-pound monster by the tusks and drop him overboard' — or words to that effect. If this one had got his tusks a quarter inch further my way, he would have had them clear over the gunwale; so I held my rifle at port arms, stuck its business end into the visitor's face, and let him have it — which settled his account.

"That walrus had tried to upset us, but almost immediately another one tried a new variation of the game, an almost successful effort to sink us — a regular dive-tackle.

"He was a large bull that an Eskimo had harpooned. He showed what he was made of by promptly attacking the float and putting it out of commission, then he proceeded to make off with the harpoon, float, and all. He happened to come near my end of the boat, and I shot at him; but whether I hit the mark or not I do not know. Anyhow, he dived, and while we were all looking over the side for him to appear, our craft was hit a tremendous whack by something under the stern — so hard that it upset the bosun, who was standing there peacefully sculling.

"Our friend was getting a little too strenuous; but he dived before I could shoot again, and came up fifty yards off. Then I hit him with a bullet, and he disappeared. Maybe we were not an anxious crowd in that boat for the next few minutes, as we knew that that submarine earthquake was due for another blow-up at any instant — but when and where! We stared at the surface of the water, to see if possible from what direction the next attack would come.

"One more such scrimmage as the last and we would be all in — both literally and metaphorically; for he had put a big hole through the bottom of the boat, and as she had a double bottom we could not check the leak, and one man had to bale rapidly. We always carried along a lot of old coats to stop holes in the boats, but in this case they might as well have been pocket handkerchiefs.

"Suddenly an Eskimo who was looking over the side yelled: 'Kingeemutt! Kingeemutt!' ('Back her! Back her!') But the words were hardly out of his mouth when — smash! rip! bang! — the stern of the boat rose under the shock, the bosun was nearly knocked overboard, an Eskimo catching him on the fly, and a hole I could have put both fists through suddenly appeared within an inch of his foot, just above the water line.

"I looked over the gunwale. There the brute lay on his back, tusks upright under the stern; then with

HOISTING A WALRUS TO THE DECK OF THE ROOSEVELT

A NARWHAL KILLED OFF CAPE UNION, JULY, 1909.
THE MOST NORTHERLY SPECIMEN EVER CAPTURED

a quick flop he dived. The men did their usual stunts to scare him off. Up he came fifteen yards away, gave his battle-cry, 'Ook! Ook! Ook!' to warn us to look out for trouble, and came tearing along the surface of Whale Sound like a torpedo boat destroyer, or an unmuffled automobile with a bicycle policeman on its trail.

"I got my rapid-fire gun into the game and sank him; then we made for the nearest cake of ice — and reached it none too soon."

To take up the story where Borup leaves it, when the first wounded walrus had been despatched with a bullet, and the floats were all taken in, an oar was erected in the boat for a signal, and the *Roosevelt* steamed up. The floats and the lines were taken over the rail of the ship, the walrus raised to the surface of the water, a hook inserted, and the winch on deck hoisted the monster on board, to be later skinned and cut up by the expert knives of the Eskimos. While this work was going on, the deck of the ship looked like a slaughterhouse, with the ravenous dogs— at this stage of the journey we had already about one hundred and fifty—waiting, ears erect and eyes sparkling, to catch the refuse thrown them by the Eskimos.

In the Whale Sound region we sometimes obtained narwhal and deer, but there was no narwhal hunting to speak of on the upward journey this last time. Walrus, narwhal, and seal meat are valuable food for dogs, but a white man does not usually enjoy it — unless he is nearly starved. Many times, however, during my twenty-three years of arctic exploration, I have thanked God for even a bite of raw dog.

CHAPTER X

FROM Etah to Cape Sheridan! Imagine about three hundred and fifty miles of almost solid ice — ice of all shapes and sizes, mountainous ice, flat ice, ragged and tortured ice, ice that, for every foot of height revealed above the surface of the water, hides seven feet below — a theater of action which for diabolic and Titanic struggle makes Dante's frozen circle of the Inferno seem like a skating pond.

Then imagine a little black ship, solid, sturdy, compact, strong and resistant as any vessel built by mortal hands can be, yet utterly insignificant in comparison with the white, cold adversary she must fight. And on this little ship are sixty-nine human beings, men, women, and children, whites and Eskimos, who have gone out into the crazy, ice-tortured channel between Baffin Bay and the Polar Sea — gone out to help prove the reality of a dream which has bewitched some of the most daring minds of the world for centuries, a will-o'-the-wisp in the pursuit of which men have frozen, and starved, and died. The music that ever sounded in our ears had for melody the howling of two hundred and forty-six wild dogs, for a bass accompaniment the deep, low grumbling of the ice, surging around us with the impulse of the tides, and for punctuation the shock and jar of our crashing assaults upon the floes.

We steamed northward into the fog beyond Etah, Greenland, on the afternoon of August 18, 1908. This was the beginning of the last stage of the *Roosevelt's* journey. All now on board would, if they lived, be with me until my return the following year. As an ungentle reminder of what was ahead of us, though going at half speed because of the fog, we struck a small berg a little way out from the harbor. Had the *Roosevelt* been an ordinary ship instead of the sturdy ice-fighter that she is, my story might have ended right here. As it was, the shock of the impact jarred things considerably. But the berg suffered more than the ship, which only shook herself like a dog coming out of the water, and with the main mass of the berg swaying heavily on one side from the blow we had given it, and a large fragment we had broken off churning the water on the other side, the *Roosevelt* scraped between them and went on.

This little incident made a strong impression on the new members of my party, and I did not think it necessary to tell them that it was only a mosquito bite to the crunching and grinding between the jaws of the heavier ice that was in store for us a little farther on. We were working in a northwesterly direction toward the Ellesmere Land side, and headed for Cape Sabine, of terrible memories. As we steamed on, the ice became thicker, and we had to turn south to get out of the way of it, worming our course among the loose floes. The *Roosevelt* avoided the heavier ice; but the lighter pack she shoved aside without much difficulty. South

of Brevoort Island we were fortunate in finding a strip
of open water, and steamed northward again, keeping
close to the shore.

It must be remembered that from Etah to Cape
Sheridan, for the greater part of the course, the shores
on either side are clearly visible, — on the east the
Greenland coast, on the west the coast of Ellesmere
Land and Grant Land. At Cape Beechey, the narrowest and most dangerous part, the channel is only eleven
miles wide, and when the air is clear it almost seems
as if a rifle bullet might be fired from one side to the
other. These waters, save in exceptional seasons, are
filled with the heaviest kind of ice, which is constantly
floating southward from the Polar Sea toward Baffin
Bay.

Whether this channel was carved in the solid land
by the force of pre-Adamite glaciers, or whether it is a
Titanic cleft formed by the breaking off of Greenland
from Grant Land, is a question still undetermined by
geologists; but for difficulty and danger there is no
place to compare with it in the whole arctic region.

It is hard for a layman to understand the character
of the ice through which the *Roosevelt* fought her way.
Most persons imagine that the ice of the arctic regions
has been formed by direct freezing of the sea water;
but in the summer time very little of the floating ice
is of that character. It is composed of huge sheets
broken off from the glacial fringe of North Grant Land
broken up by contact with other floes and with the
land, and driven south under the impetus of the violent
flood tides. It is not unusual to see there ice between
eighty and one hundred feet thick. As seven-eighths

of these heavy floes are under water, one does not realize how thick they are until one sees where a huge mass, by the pressure of the pack behind it, has been driven upon the shore, and stands there high and dry, eighty or a hundred feet above the water, like a silver castle guarding the shore of this exaggerated and ice-clogged Rhine.

The navigation of the narrow and ice-encumbered channels between Etah and Cape Sheridan was long considered an utter impossibility, and only four ships besides the *Roosevelt* have succeeded in accomplishing any considerable portion of it. Of these four ships, one, the *Polaris*, was lost. Three, the *Alert*, the *Discovery*, and the *Proteus*, made the voyage up and back in safety; but one of those, the *Proteus*, was lost in an attempt to repeat the dash. The *Roosevelt* had on the expedition of 1905–6 made the voyage up and back, though she was badly smashed on the return.

Going north, the *Roosevelt* of necessity followed the coast a portion of the way, as only close to the shore could any water be found which would enable the ship to advance. With the shore ice on one side, and the moving central pack on the other, the changing tides were almost certain to give us an occasional opportunity to steam ahead.

This channel is the meeting place between the tides coming from Baffin Bay on the south and from Lincoln Sea on the north, the actual point of meeting being about Cape Frazer. South of that point the flood tide runs north, and north of it the flood tide runs south. One may judge of the force of these tides from the fact that on the shores of the Polar Sea the mean rise is only a little over a foot, while in the narrowest part of the channel the tide rises and falls twelve or fourteen feet.

As a rule, looking across the channel, there seems to be no water — nothing but uneven and tortured ice. When the tide is at the ebb, the ship follows the narrow crack of water between the shore and the moving pack of the center, driving ahead with all her force; then, when the flood tide begins to rush violently southward, the ship must hurry to shelter in some niche of the shore ice, or behind some point of rock, to save herself from destruction or being driven south again.

This method of navigation, however, is one of constant hazard, as it keeps the vessel between the immovable rocks and the heavy and rapidly drifting ice, with the ever-present possibility of being crushed between the two. My knowledge of the ice conditions of these channels and their navigation was absolutely my own, gained in former years of traveling along the shores and studying them for this very purpose. On my various expeditions I had walked every foot of the coast line, from Payer Harbor on the south to Cape Joseph Henry on the north, from three to eight times. I knew every indentation of that coast, every possible shelter for a ship, every place where icebergs usually grounded, and the places where the tide ran strongest, as accurately as a tugboat captain in New York harbor knows the piers of the North River water front. When Bartlett was in doubt as to making a risky run, with the chance of not finding shelter for the ship, I could usually say to him:

"At such and such a place, so far from here, is a little niche behind the delta of a stream, where we can drive the *Roosevelt* in, if necessary"; or:

"Here icebergs are almost invariably grounded, and we can find shelter behind them"; or:

"Here is a place absolutely to be shunned, for the floes pile up here at the slightest provocation, in a way that would destroy any ship afloat."

It was this detailed knowledge of every foot of the Ellesmere Land and Grant Land coasts, combined with Bartlett's energy and ice experience, that enabled us to pass four times between this arctic Scylla and Charybdis.

The fog lifted about nine o'clock the first night out, the sun peeped through the clouds, and as we passed Payer Harbor, on the Ellesmere Land side, we saw, sharply outlined against the snow, the house where I wintered in 1901–2. A flood of memories rushed over me at sight of the place. It was in Payer Harbor that Mrs. Peary and my little daughter had waited for me, on the *Windward* from September, 1900, to May, 1901, the ice being so heavy that year that the ship could neither reach Fort Conger, three hundred miles beyond, where I was, nor regain the open water to the south and return home. That was the spring when I had been obliged to turn back at Lincoln Bay, because the exhaustion of my Eskimos and dogs made a dash for the Pole impossible. It was at Payer Harbor that I had rejoined my family; it was at Payer Harbor that I had parted from them, determined to make one fight more to reach the goal.

"One fight more," I said in 1902; but I had only reached 84° 17'.

"One fight more," I had said in 1905; but I had only reached 87° 6'.

And now, at Payer Harbor again, on August 18, 1908, it was still "One fight more!" Only this time I knew it was the last, in truth, whatever the result.

At ten o'clock that night we were steaming past the desolate, wind-swept and ice-ground rocks of Cape Sabine, the spot that marks one of the most somber chapters in arctic history, where Greely's ill-fated party slowly starved to death in 1884 — seven survivors only being rescued out of a party of twenty-four! The ruins of the rude stone hut built by these men for shelter during the last year of their lives can still be seen on the bleak northern shore of Cape Sabine, only two or three miles from the extreme point. It is doubtful if a more desolate and unsheltered location for a camp could be found anywhere in the arctic regions, fully exposed to the biting winds from the north, cut off by the rocks back of it from the rays of the southern sun, and besieged by the ice pack surging down from Kane Basin in the north.

I first saw the place in August, 1896, in a blinding snowstorm, so thick that it was impossible to see more than a few yards in any direction. The impressions of that day will never be forgotten — the pity and the sickening sense of horror. The saddest part of the whole story for me was the knowledge that the catastrophe was unnecessary, that it might have been avoided. My men and I have been cold and have been near to starvation in the Arctic, when cold and hunger were inevitable; but the horrors of Cape Sabine were not inevitable. They are a blot upon the record of American arctic exploration.

From Cape Sabine north there was so much open water that we thought of setting the lug sail before the southerly wind; but a little later the appearance of ice to the north caused us to change our minds. About sixty miles north of Etah, we came to a dead stop in the ice pack off Victoria Head. There we lay for hours; but the time was not altogether wasted, for we filled our tanks with ice from a floe.

In the afternoon of the second day out, the wind came on strong from the south, and we slowly drifted northward with the ice. After some hours, the wind began to form pools of open water through the pack, and we steamed westward toward the land, with the spray flying clear across the decks. An Eskimo declared that this was the devil spitting at us. After a few miles, we ran into denser ice and stopped again.

Dr. Goodsell, MacMillan and Borup were busy storing food and medical supplies in the boats, to be ready for an emergency. Had the *Roosevelt* been crushed by the ice or sunk, we could have lowered the boats at a moment's notice, fitted and equipped for a voyage, and retreated to the Eskimo country — thence back to civilization on some whaler, or in a ship which would have been sent up with coal the following year by the Peary Arctic Club, though that, of course, would have meant the failure of the expedition.

In each of the six whale-boats were placed a case containing twelve six-pound tins of pemmican, the compressed meat food used on arctic expeditions; two twenty-five pound tins of biscuit; two five-pound tins of sugar, a few pounds of coffee and several cans of condensed milk; an oil stove and five one-gallon tins of oil; a rifle with one hundred rounds of ammunition and a shotgun with fifty rounds; matches, a hatchet, knives, a can opener, salt, needles and thread; and the following medical supplies: catgut and needles, bandages and cotton, quinine, astringent (tannic acid), gauze, plaster-surgical liniment, boracic acid, and dusting powder.

The boats were swung at the davits, with a full complement of oars, mast, sails, etc., and the emergency outfit above described would have fitted them for a voyage of a week or ten days. On leaving Etah the essential items of supplies, such as tea, coffee, sugar, oil, pemmican, and biscuit, had been stowed on deck, close to the rail on both sides, ready instantly to be thrown over the rail onto the ice, in case the ship should be crushed.

Every person on board, both the men of the ship and the Eskimos, was ready with a little bundle packed to get right over the side at a moment's notice, after lowering the boats and throwing onto the ice the essential supplies stowed near the ship's rail. Nobody thought of undressing regularly; and the bathtub in my cabin might as well have been a trunk, for all the time I dared to spend in it between Etah and Cape Sheridan.

CHAPTER XI

THAT no time should be lost on the upward voyage, and also that my Eskimos might not have too much leisure in which to consider the dangers which constantly threatened their floating home, I kept them all busy. The men were put to work making sledges and dog-harness, so that when we reached Cape Sheridan—if we reached it,— we might be ready for the fall hunting. I had on board the raw materials, and each Eskimo built a sledge for himself, putting his best work into it. This pride of the Eskimo in personal achievement has been of great service to me, and has been encouraged by special prizes and special praise.

The Eskimo women were put to work on our winter garments as soon as possible after leaving Etah, so that, in the event of our losing the ship, every man would have a comfortable outfit. In the North we wear practically the same clothing as the Eskimos, including the fur stockings with the fur on the inside. Otherwise we should have frozen feet often instead of only occasionally. A man who could not live without silk stockings would not be likely to attempt the North Pole. As we had altogether, including the Eskimos, sixty-nine persons on board the ship — men, women, and children — it will be seen that there

was considerable sewing to be done. Old garments
had to be overhauled and mended, and new ones
made.

The worst of the ice fighting did not begin immediately, and the new members of the expedition, Mac-
Millan, Borup, and Dr. Goodsell, were at first much
interested in watching the Eskimo women at their
sewing. They sit on anything that is convenient, a
chair, a platform, or the floor. In their own quarters
they remove their footgear, put up one foot, and hold
one end of the fabric between their toes, sewing a
seam over and over from them, instead of toward
them, as our women do. The foot of an Eskimo
woman is a sort of third hand, and the work is gripped
between the great toe and the second toe.

The Eskimo women have great confidence in their
own skill at garment-making, and they take suggestions from the inexperienced white men with a good-
natured and superior tolerance. When one of the
northern belles was shaping a garment for Bartlett
to wear on the spring sledge journey, he anxiously
urged her to give him plenty of room. Her reply
was a mixed Eskimo and English equivalent for:

"You just trust me, Captain! When you get out
on the road to the Nor Pol, you'll need a draw-string
in your jacket, and not gussets." She had seen me
and my men come back from previous sledge journeys, and she knew the effect of long continued fatigue
and scanty rations in making a man's clothes fit him
loosely.

The Eskimos had the run of the ship, but the port
side of the forward deck house was given to them

entirely. A wide platform three or four feet high, made of packing boxes, was placed around the wall of the deck house for them to sleep on. Each family had its own quarters, partitioned off by planks, and screened in front by a curtain. They cooked their own meat and whatever else they desired, though Percy, the ship's steward, provided them with tea and coffee. If they had baked beans, or hash, or anything of that kind from the ship's store, it was cooked for them by Percy; and he also furnished them with his famous bread, which for lightness and crispness is unsurpassed in the round world.

The Eskimos seemed always to be eating. There was no table for the crowd of them, as they do not incline to regular meal hours; but each family ate by itself, as appetite dictated. I gave them pots, pans, plates, cups, saucers, knives, forks, and oil stoves. They had access to the ship's galley, day and night; but Percy was always amiable, and the Eskimos at length learned not to wash their hands in the water in which he purposed to boil meat.

The third day out the weather was villainous. It rained steadily, and there was a strong southerly wind. The group of dogs on the main deck stood about with low, dejected heads and dripping tails. Only at feeding time did they take courage even to fight or snap at one another. Most of the time the ship was stationary, or drifting slowly with the ice toward the mouth of Dobbin Bay. When at last the ice loosened, we made about ten miles in open water — then the wheel rope broke, and we had to stop for repairs, unable to take advantage of the stretch of water still before us. The captain's remarks when the strands of that cable parted I will leave to the imagination of the reader. Had the accident occurred at a time when the ship was between two big floes, the fortress of the North Pole might still remain uncaptured. It was after midnight before we got under way, and half an hour later we were stopped again by the impassable ice.

On the fourth day we lay quiet all day long, with a slight breeze from Princess Marie Bay setting us slowly eastward; but, as the sun was shining, we utilized the time in drying our clothing, wet and soggy from the almost continuous rain and snow of the previous two days. As it was still summertime in the Arctic, we did not suffer from cold. The pools between the ice floes were slowly enlarging, and at nine in the evening we were on our way again, but at eleven we ran into a thick fog. All night we bored and twisted through the ice, which, though thick, was not heavy for the *Roosevelt*, and only once or twice we had to back her. An ordinary ship could have made no headway whatever.

Wardwell, the chief engineer, stood his eight-hour or twelve-hour watch the same as his assistants, and during the passage of these dangerous channels he was nearly always in the engine-room, watching the machinery to see that no part of it got out of order at a crucial moment — which would have meant the loss of the ship. When we were between two big floes, forcing our way through, I would call down the tube leading from the bridge to the engine-room:

"Chief, you've got to keep her moving until I give you word, no matter what happens."

Sometimes the ship would get stuck between the corners of two floes which were slowly coming together. At such a time a minute is an eternity. I would call down the tube to Wardwell, "You've got to jump her now, the length of fifty yards," or whatever it might be. And I could feel the ship shaking under me as she seemed to take the flying leap, under the impulse of live steam poured directly from the boilers into the fifty-two-inch low-pressure cylinder.

The engines of the *Roosevelt* have what is called a by-pass, by which the live steam can be turned into the big cylinder, more than doubling the power of the engines for a few minutes. This simple bit of mechanism has saved us from being crushed flat by the ice on more than one occasion.

The destruction of a ship between two ice floes is not sudden, like her destruction by a submarine mine, for instance. It is a slow and gradually increasing pressure from both sides, sometimes till the ice meets in the vitals of the ship. A vessel might stay thus, suspended between two floes, for twenty-four hours — or until the movement of the tides relaxed the pressure, when she would sink. The ice might open at first just sufficiently to let the hull go down, and the ends of the yards might catch on the ice and break, with the weight of the water-filled hull, as was the case with the ill-fated *Jeannette*. One ship, in the Gulf of St. Lawrence, was caught in the ice and dragged over the rocks like a nutmeg over a nutmeg grater. The bottom was sliced off as one would slice a cucumber with a knife, so that the iron blubber tanks in the hold dropped out of her. The ship became nothing but the sides and ends of a box. She remained some twenty-four hours, gripped between the floes, and then went down.

On the 22d of August, the fifth day, our lucky stars must have been working overtime; for we made a phenomenal run — more than a hundred miles, right up the middle of Kennedy Channel, uninterrupted by ice or fog! At midnight the sun burst gloriously through the clouds, just over Cape Lieber. It seemed a happy omen.

Could such good fortune continue? Though my hopes were high, the experience of former journeys reminded me that the brightest coin has always a reverse side. In a day we had run the whole length of Kennedy Channel, and immediately before us there was only scattered ice. But beyond lay Robeson Channel, only some thirty miles away, and the navigator who knows Robeson Channel will never be sanguine that it has anything good in store for him.

Soon we encountered both ice and fog, and, while working slowly along in search of an opening, we were forced clear across to the Greenland coast at Thank God Harbor, the winter quarters of the *Polaris* in 1871–72. I have mentioned the lane of water which often lies at ebb tide between the land and the moving central pack; but the reader must not fancy that this is an unobstructed lane. On the contrary, its passage means constant butting of the smaller ice, and constant dodging of larger pieces.

Of course the steam is up at all times, ready, like ourselves, for anything at a moment's notice. When the ice is not so heavy as to be utterly impenetrable, the ship under full steam moves back and forth continually, butting and charging the floes. Sometimes a charge will send the ship forward half her length, sometimes her whole length — sometimes not an inch. When, with all the steam of the boilers, we can make no headway whatever, we wait for the ice to loosen up, and economize our coal. We do not mind using the ship as a battering ram — that is what she was made for; but beyond Etah coal is precious, and every ounce of it must yield its full return of northward steaming. The coal at present in our bunkers was all that we should have until our return the following year, when the Peary Arctic Club would send a ship to meet us at Etah.

It must be remembered that during all this time we were in the region of constant daylight, in the season of the midnight sun. Sometimes the weather was foggy, sometimes cloudy, sometimes sunny; but there was no darkness. The periods of day and night were measured only by our watches — not, during the passage of these channels, by sleeping and waking, for we slept only in those brief intervals when there was nothing else to do. Unresting vigilance was the price we paid for our passage.

Bartlett's judgment was reliable, but the cabin had no attraction for me when the ship and the fortunes of the expedition were swaying in the balance. Then, too, when the ship was butting the ice, the shock of the impact would have made

Morpheus himself sit up and rub his eyes every few minutes.

Owing to the stupendous and resistless character of the heavier ice, a ship would be utterly helpless if she were ever caught fairly and squarely between two giant floes. In such a case there would be no escape for any structure which man could design or build. More than once a brief nip between two big blue floes has set the whole one hundred and eighty-four-foot length of the *Roosevelt* vibrating like a violin string. At other times, under the pressure on the cylinders of the by-pass before described, the vessel would rear herself upon the ice like a steeplechaser taking a fence. It was a glorious battle — this charging of the ship against man's coldest enemy and possibly his oldest, for there is no calculating the age of this glacial ice. Sometimes, as the steel-shod stem of the *Roosevelt* split a floe squarely in two, the riven ice would emit a savage snarl that seemed to have behind it all the rage of the invaded immemorial Arctic struggling with the self-willed intruder, man. Sometimes, when the ship was in special peril, the Eskimos on board would set up their strange barbaric chant — calling on the souls of their ancestors to come from the invisible realm and help us.

Often on this last expedition of the *Roosevelt*, as on the former one, have I seen a fireman come up from the bowels of the ship, panting for a breath of air, take one look at the sheet of ice before us, and mutter savagely:

"By God, she's *got* to go through!"

Then he would drop again into the stoke hole, and

CAPTAIN BARTLETT IN THE CROW'S NEST

TABULAR ICEBERG AND FLOE ICE

a moment later an extra puff of black smoke would rise from the stack, and I knew the steam pressure was going up.

During the worst parts of the journey, Bartlett spent most of his time in the crow's nest, the barrel lookout at the top of the main mast. I would climb up into the rigging just below the crow's nest, where I could see ahead and talk to Bartlett, backing up his opinion with my own, when necessary, to relieve him, in the more dangerous places, of too great a weight of responsibility.

Clinging with Bartlett, high up in the vibrating rigging, peering far ahead for a streak of open water, studying the movement of the floes which pressed against us, I would hear him shouting to the ship below us as if coaxing her, encouraging her, commanding her to hammer a way for us through the adamantine floes:

"Rip 'em, Teddy! Bite 'em in two! Go it! That's fine, my beauty! Now — again! Once more!"

At such a time the long generations of ice and ocean fighters behind this brave, indomitable young New-foundland captain seemed to be re-living in him the strenuous days that carried the flag of England 'round the world.

CHAPTER XII

THE ICE FIGHT GOES ON

TO recount all the incidents of this upward journey of the *Roosevelt* would require a volume. When we were not fighting the ice, we were dodging it, or — worse still — waiting in some niche of the shore for an opportunity to do more fighting. On Sunday, the sixth day out from Etah, the water continued fairly open, and we made good progress until one o'clock in the afternoon, when we were held up by the ice pack as we were nearing Lincoln Bay. A cable was run out, and the ship secured to a great floe, which extended some two miles to the north and several to the east. The tide, which was running north at the time, had carried the smaller ice with it, leaving the *Roosevelt* in a sort of lake. While we were resting there, some of the men observed a black object far out on the great ice floe to which we were attached, and Dr. Goodsell and Borup, with two Eskimos, started out to investigate. This walking across the floes is dangerous, as the ice is full of cracks, some of them quite wide, and on the day in question the cracks were for the most part concealed by a recent snowfall. In jumping across a lead, the men had a narrow escape from drowning, and when they got within shooting distance of the black object they were seeking, it proved to be only a block of stone.

Before the return of Borup and the doctor the ice had already begun to close in around the ship and, as soon as the men were safe on board, the cable was hauled in and the *Roosevelt* drifted south with the pack. So close was the ice that night, that we had to swing the boats inward on the davits to protect them from the great floes, which at times crowded the rail. Finally, the captain worked the ship into another small lake to the southeast of our former position by the great floe, and there we remained several hours, steaming back and forth in order to keep the pool open.

About eleven o'clock that night, for all our efforts, the ice closed in again around the *Roosevelt;* but I observed a small lead to the southeast, which led into another body of open water, and gave orders to ram the vessel through, if possible. By working the nose of the ship into the small opening, and then by butting the ice on alternate sides, we succeeded in widening the lead sufficiently to allow of our passing through to the pool of open water beyond.

At four o'clock the next morning we were again under way, working northward through slack ice to a point a little beyond Shelter River, where we were again stopped by ice about nine o'clock in the forenoon. The *Roosevelt* moved in near the shore and her head was shoved against a big floe, to avoid her being jammed or carried southward by the now swiftly running tide and the ice pack.

After supper that night, MacMillan, Borup, and Dr. Goodsell, with two Eskimos, started for the shore over the jammed ice, with the intention of getting some game; but before they reached the shore there was so much movement in the adjacent floes that I considered their journey too hazardous for inexperienced men. A recall was sounded with the ship's whistle, and they started back over the now moving floes. Their movements were impeded by their guns, but fortunately they carried boat hooks, without which they could never have made their way back.

Using the boat hooks as vaulting poles, they leaped from one floe to another, when the leads were not too wide. When the open water was impassable in that way, they crossed it on small floating pieces of ice, using their hooks to push and pull themselves along. First the doctor slipped on the edge of a floe, and went into the icy water to the waist, but he was quickly hauled up by Borup. Then Borup slipped and went in to the waist, but he was out again as quickly.

Meanwhile the ice had separated about the *Roosevelt*, leaving a wide lane of water between her and the men; but by running the ship against one of the larger floes, we enabled them to clamber aboard. They lost no time in exchanging their wet garments for dry ones, and in a few minutes they were all laughing and recounting their exploits to an interested — and possibly amused — group of listeners.

A man who could not laugh at a wetting or take as a matter of course a dangerous passage over moving ice, would not be a man for a serious arctic expedition. It was with a feeling of intense satisfaction that I watched these three men, MacMillan, Borup, and Dr. Goodsell, my arctic "tenderfeet," as I called them, proving the mettle of which they were made.

I had selected these three men from among a host of applicants for membership in the expedition, because of the special fitness of each one. Dr. Goodsell was a solid, sturdy, self-made physician of Pennsylvania stock. His specialism in microscopy I trusted might give valuable results in a field not hitherto investigated in the North. He was to make microscopic studies of the germ diseases of the Eskimos.

MacMillan, a trained athlete and physical instructor, I had known, and known about, for years. I chose him because of his intense interest in the work, his intense desire to be of the party, and his evident mental and physical fitness for the rigorous demands of the Arctic.

Borup, the youngest member of the party, impressed me with his enthusiasm and physical abilities. He had a record as a Yale runner, and I took him on general principles, because I liked him, satisfied that he was of the right stuff for arctic work. It was a fortunate selection, as the photographs brought back by the expedition are due in a large measure to his expert knowledge of film developing.

I have been asked how the members of my party amused themselves during the long waits, when the ship was held up by the ice. The principal amusement of the new members was in trying to acquire from the Eskimos on board a smattering of their language. As interpreter, they had Matt Henson. Sometimes, looking down from the bridge of the ship onto the main deck, I would see one of these new men surrounded by a group of Eskimos, gesticulating and laughing, and I knew that a language lesson was in progress. The women were delighted at the opportunity to teach Borup the Eskimo words for jacket, hood, boots, sky, water, food, et cetera, as they seemed to be of the opinion that he was a fine boy.

The *Roosevelt* lay quietly in open water all night on the 24th of August, but in the forenoon of the 25th steamed northward nearly to Cape Union. Beyond there the ice was densely packed. I climbed up into the rigging to take a look but, finding no suitable shelter, decided to turn back to Lincoln Bay, where we made the ship fast between two grounded ice floes. The day before had been calm and sunny, but the 25th was snowy and disagreeable, with a raw northerly wind. The snow was driving in horizontal sheets across the decks, the water was black as ink, the ice a spectral white, and the coast near us looked like the shores of the land of ghosts. One of our berg pieces was carried away by the flood tide, and we were obliged to shift our position to the inner side of the other one; but there were other grounded bergs outside us to take the impact of the larger floes.

On general principles, I landed a cache of supplies at this point on the following day. The possibility of losing the ship was always present; but if everything went well the cache could be made use of in the hunting season. The supplies, in their wooden boxes, were simply piled upon the shore. Wandering arctic hares, reindeer, and musk-oxen never attempt to regale themselves on tin cans or wooden boxes.

I went ashore and walked over to Shelter River, living over again the experiences there in 1906, when, during my absence at Cape Thomas Hubbard, Captain

Bartlett — for he was then, as now, the master of the *Roosevelt* — had tried to drive the ship south from her exposed position at Cape Sheridan to a more sheltered place in Lincoln Bay, where I was to rejoin them.

At Shelter River, the *Roosevelt* had been caught between the moving pack and the vertical face of the ice-foot, receiving almost a fatal blow. She had been lifted bodily out of the water, the stern-post and rudder smashed into kindling wood, and a blade ripped off the propeller. Everything was landed from the vessel in the expectation that when the ice slacked off and she settled into the water, she would be leaking so badly it would be impossible to keep her afloat.

Bartlett and his men worked manfully in stopping the leaks, as far as possible; and when the pressure from the ice was partially released, the ship was floated. But she lay there nearly a month, and twice during that time even the rigging of the ship was landed, when it seemed impossible that she could survive.

Here at Shelter River I had found the *Roosevelt* on my return from "farthest west." A new rudder was improvised, and the crippled and almost helpless ship floated around into Lincoln Bay, whence she finally limped home to New York.

After an hour of retrospection at this place I walked back to the ship. Borup and MacMillan had also gone ashore, in the hope of obtaining game but had not found any. It was a dull, raw, overcast day and MacMillan, Borup, the doctor, and Gushue, the mate, amused themselves by target-shooting with their Winchesters.

The next day was seemingly endless, and still we lay there at Lincoln Bay, with a strong, raw, northeast wind blowing steadily and with increasing violence. The edge of the moving pack was only a few yards from the ship, but we were fairly well protected by large pieces which had grounded outside of us. Every little while a big floe came rushing past, crowding everything out of its way and giving our protectors a shove that set them and us nearer the shore. From the crow's nest we could see a little open water near the east coast of the channel, but there was none in our vicinity — only ice, ice, ice, of every imaginable shape and thickness.

Still another day, and the *Roosevelt* was in the same position, with the ice crowding against her; but at the crest of the high tide the grounded floe-berg to which we were attached by cable went adrift, and we all hurried on deck. The lines were hastily detached from the berg. As the ice went south, it left a stretch of open water before us about a mile long, and we steamed northward along the shore, pushing our way behind the grounded bergs, trying to find another niche where we might be secure from the now rapidly approaching pack.

It was well for us that the wind was blowing violently off shore, as it eased the pressure of the pack against us. One place seemed secure, and we were making ready to attach the cables, when an ice-floe, about an acre in extent with a sharp, projecting point like the ram of a battleship, came surging along toward the *Roosevelt*, and we were obliged to shift our position. Before the ship was secured, she was again threatened by the same floe, which seemed to be endowed with malign intelligence and to follow us like a bloodhound. We retired to still another position, and secured the vessel and finally the threatening floe passed onwards to the south.

There was no sleep for any one that sunlit night. About ten o'clock the berg fragment to which we were attached drifted loose under the pressure of the furious wind and the rising tide. In contracted space, with the ice whirling and eddying about us, we hastily got our lines in and shifted to another place, only to be driven out of it. We sought still another place of shelter, and in turn were also driven out of that. A third attempt to find safety was successful, but before it was accomplished the *Roosevelt* had twice been aground forward, her heel had been caught by a berg's spur, and her after rail smashed by the onslaught of another berg.

Saturday, the 29th, was another day of delay but I found some comfort in thinking of my little son in the far-away home. It was his fifth birthday, and Percy, Matt, and I, his three chums, drank a bottle of champagne in his honor. Robert E. Peary, Junior! What were they doing at home? I wondered.

I think that none of the members of the expedition will ever forget the following day, the 30th of August. The *Roosevelt* was kicked about by the floes as if she had been a football. The game began about four o'clock in the morning. I was in my cabin trying to get a little sleep — with my clothes on, for I had not dared to remove them for a week. My rest was cut short by a shock so violent that, before I realized

that anything *had* happened, I found myself on deck
— a deck that inclined to starboard some twelve or
fifteen degrees. I ran, or rather climbed the deck, to
the port side and saw what had happened. A big
floe, rushing past with the current, had picked up
the grounded berg to which we were attached by the
hawsers, as if that thousand-ton berg had been a toy,
and dashed it against the *Roosevelt* and clear along her
port side, smashing a big hole in the bulwarks at
Marvin's room. The berg brought up against another
one just aft of us, and the *Roosevelt* slipped from
between the two like a greased pig.

As soon as the pressure was relaxed and the ship
regained an even keel, we discovered that the cable
which had been attached to the floe-berg at the stern
had become entangled with the propeller. It was a
time for lightning thought and action; but by attach-
ing a heavier cable to the parted one and taking a hitch
round the steam capstan, we finally disentangled it.

This excitement was no sooner over than a great
berg that was passing near us split in two of its own accord, a cube some twenty-five or thirty feet in diameter
dropping toward the ship, and missing our quarter
by only a foot or two. "Bergs to the right of them,
bergs to the left of them, bergs on top of them," I
heard somebody say, as we caught our breath at this
miraculous escape.

The ship was now quite at the mercy of the drifting
ice, and with the pressure from the outer pack the *Roosevelt* again careened to starboard. I knew that if she
were driven any higher upon the shore, we should have
to discharge a large part of the coal in order to lighten

her sufficiently to get her off again. So I decided to dynamite the ice.

I told Bartlett to get out his batteries and dynamite, and to smash the ice between the *Roosevelt* and the heavy floes outside, making a soft cushion for the ship to rest on. The batteries were brought up from the lazaret, one of the dynamite boxes lifted out with caution, and Bartlett and I looked for the best places in the ice for the charges.

Several sticks of dynamite were wrapped in pieces of old bagging and fastened on the end of long spruce poles, which we had brought along specially for this purpose. A wire from the battery had, of course, been connected with one of the primers buried in the dynamite. Pole, wire, and dynamite were thrust down through cracks in the ice at several places in the adjacent floes. The other end of each wire was then connected with the battery, every one retreated to a respectful distance on the far side of the deck, and a quick, sharp push on the plunger of the battery sent the electric current along the wires

Rip! Bang! Boom! The ship quivered like a smitten violin string, and a column of water and pieces of ice went flying a hundred feet into the air, geyser fashion.

The pressure of the ice against the ship being thus removed, she righted herself and lay quietly on her cushion of crushed ice — waiting for whatever might happen next. As the tide lowered, the *Roosevelt* was bodily aground from amidships forward, heeling first to one side and then to the other with the varying pressure of the ice. It was a new variation of "Rocked in the Cradle of the Deep" — one that sent Eskimo babies, the dogs, the boxes, and even ourselves, tumbling about the decks.

When the tide rose, efforts were made to dislodge the ship from her stranded position. From the port side of the bow a line was made fast to a stationary floe-berg, and the captain called for full steam, first ahead, then astern. For some time there was no perceptible movement of the ship. Finally, the pull on the port bow from the cable, with full speed astern, had the desired effect and the vessel slid off and floated free; but the ice was so heavily packed behind us that we could not move her away. It was far from a pleasant spot.

CHAPTER XIII

CAPE SHERIDAN AT LAST

TO put it mildly, the position in which we now found ourselves was dangerous — even with the assistance of so experienced and steady an ice fighter as Bartlett. As day followed day and still we hung there at Lincoln Bay, we should doubtless have been extremely anxious had the *Roosevelt* not had a similar experience on the preceding voyage. But we believed that sooner or later the movement of the ice would enable us to steam the few remaining miles to Cape Sheridan, and possibly beyond there; for our objective point was some twenty-five miles to the northwest of our former winter quarters in 1905–06. We tried to possess our souls in patience, and if sometimes the delay got on our nerves, there was nothing to be gained by talking about it.

On the first of September the ice did not seem to be moving quite so rapidly. The evening before MacMillan had been sent ashore to the bluffs beyond Shelter River, and he had reported that there was considerable open water along the shore. Bartlett then went forward to reconnoiter. On his return he also reported open water, but with corners of big floes barring it in every direction.

That the fall hunting might get under way, Ootah, Aletah, Ooblooyah, and Ookeyah started off for the

117

Lake Hazen region, with a sledge and eight dogs, after musk-oxen and reindeer. It had been planned that they should hunt there until joined by other Eskimos from the ship, after she reached Cape Sheridan or Porter Bay. But in the absence of snow, the going was too rough for even a light sledge, and the Eskimos returned.

At last, a little before midnight on the 2d, we got out of the *impasse* at Lincoln Bay, where we had been held up for ten days. The cables were taken in, and the *Roosevelt*, steaming first forward and then astern, extricated herself from the shore pack. We felt as men must feel who are released from prison. There was a narrow lane of open water following the shore, and along that course we steamed, rounding Cape Union about half an hour before midnight.

But we were soon held up again by the ice, a little below Black Cape, a dark cone-shaped mountain standing alone, on the eastern side washed by the waters of the sea, on the west separated by deep valleys from the adjacent mountains. It was a scene of indescribable grandeur, for the coast was lined for miles with bergs, forced shoreward, broken and tilted at right angles. At Black Cape we had made half the distance between our former position at Lincoln Bay and the longed-for shelter at Cape Sheridan.

As we made fast against the land ice, a sixty-foot thick fragment of a floe was driven with frightful force up on the shore a little to the north of us. Had we been in the way of it — but a navigator of these channels must not dwell too much on such contingencies.

As an extra precaution, I had the Eskimos with axes bevel off the edge of the ice-foot abreast of the ship, to facilitate her rising if she should be squeezed by the heavy floes outside. It was snowing lightly all day long; but I went ashore, walking along the ice-foot to the next river, and up to the summit of Black Cape. An occasional walk on land was a relief from the stench and disorder of the ship, for the dogs kept the *Roosevelt* in a very unclean condition. Many persons have asked how we could endure the presence of nearly two hundred and fifty dogs on the deck of a small ship; but every achievement has its drawbacks, and it must not be forgotten that without the dogs we could not have reached the Pole.

At this point we landed another cache, similar to the one at Lincoln Bay, to be ready for anything that might happen.

On the 4th, the wind came strong from the south, and as there seemed to be a little open water ahead, at eight in the morning we started to get out of our berth. It took an hour to break up the "slob" ice which had cemented about the ship. We were happy to be under way again; but at the delta just ahead of us the ice refused to open, the drift ice from the south was coming up rapidly before the wind, and we were compelled to hurry back to our former berth below Black Cape. We did not get in again without some trouble as the strong wind made the *Roosevelt* hard to manage. The starboard quarter boat was badly smashed against the corner of a big berg piece, and the starboard corner of the forward deck house was almost ripped from the decking.

But all hands were stimulated by the thought that we were now only a few miles from Cape Sheridan — so near our goal that we were restless to be off again. That evening, with the ebb tide, the ice slackened, and the order was given to steam ahead. After one or two narrow escapes between the rapidly running floes, we reached the delta of Black Cape River, a few miles beyond our former place. But when the tide turned we were obliged to hurry back about a quarter of a mile to the shelter of a grounded berg.

When the hawsers were made fast I went ashore and up to the delta to look at the ice beyond. Not a crack or hole was visible to the north, and the path by which we had retreated to our present position was now a sea of solid ice. Should we *ever* be able to make the few remaining miles?

The wind continued to blow violently from the south, the ice began to slack off a little behind us, and at three o'clock in the morning of the 5th of September there was a gradually widening lead to the north. I felt that it was now or never, and the order went down for every pound of steam and full speed. Thus we rounded Cape Rawson, and Cape Sheridan was in view. At last! That sloping headland looked more beautiful than the gates of paradise to our vigil-wearied eyes.

We rounded the cape at a quarter past seven, fifteen minutes later than the time of our arrival in 1905. Since the 23d of August, thirteen days before, neither Bartlett nor I had had our clothes off.

Should we stop here? There was still open water beyond. I gave orders to steam ahead, hoping that we might reach Porter Bay. But after two miles we came to another impassable barrier of ice, and it was decided that it was Cape Sheridan again for this year's winter quarters. Back we went, and the work of getting the *Roosevelt* inside the tide crack was begun.

My heart was light. Those two miles beyond Cape Sheridan had given us the record of "farthest north" which any vessel had ever reached under her own steam, 82° 30'. One vessel only, Nansen's *Fram*, had been farther north, but she had drifted there stern foremost, a plaything of the ice. Again the little black, strenuous *Roosevelt* had proven herself the champion.

There are some feelings which a man cannot express in words. Such were mine as the mooring lines went out onto the ice foot at Cape Sheridan. We had kept the scheduled time of our program and had negotiated the first part of the difficult proposition— that of driving a ship from New York to a point within striking distance of the Pole. All the uncertainties of ice navigation — the possible loss of the *Roosevelt* and a large quantity of our supplies — were at an end. Another source of gratification was the realization that this last voyage had further accentuated the value of detailed experience in this arduous work. Notwithstanding the delays which had sometimes seemed endless, we had made the voyage with only a small percentage of the anxieties and injury to the ship which we had experienced on the former upward journey in 1905.

Lying there, with the northern bounds of all known lands — except those close to us — lying far to the south, we were in a position properly to attack the second part of our problem, the projection of a sledge party from the ship to the Pole itself. This rounding of Cape Sheridan was not the ultimate achievement probable.

So great was our relief at having driven the *Roosevelt* through the ice of Robeson Channel, that as soon as the mooring lines were out at Cape Sheridan we set to work unloading the ship with light-hearted eagerness. The *Roosevelt* was grounded inside the tide crack, and the first things we got ashore were the two hundred and forty-six dogs, which had made the ship a noisy and ill-smelling inferno for the last eighteen days. They were simply dropped over the rail onto the ice, and in a few minutes the shore in all directions was dotted with them, as they ran, leaped and barked in the snow. The decks were washed down with hose, and the work of unloading began. First the sledges came down from the bridge deck, where they had been built during the upward voyage, a fine fleet of twenty-three.

We wanted to get the ship well inside the ice barrier where she would be really safe, so we lightened her that she might float with the high tide. We made chutes from planks, and down these we slid the oil cases from the main deck and the hold. It was necessary to work carefully, as the ice was thin at that season. Later two or three sledge loads of supplies broke through, and the Eskimos with them; but as the water was only five or six feet deep, and the supplies were packed in tins, no serious damage was done.

THE ROOSEVELT DRYING OUT HER SAILS AT CAPE SHERIDAN, SEPTEMBER, 1908

(The Dark Spots on the Shore are the Supplies and Equipment of the Expedition)

THE ROOSEVELT ON SEPTEMBER 12, 1908
Marie Ahnighito Peary's Birthday

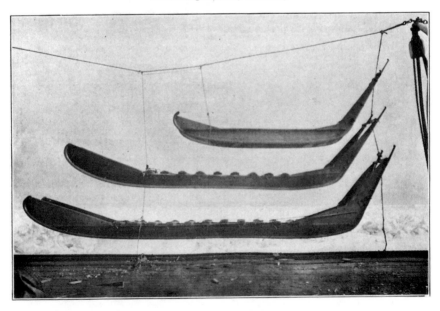

"PEARY" SLEDGES ON BOARD THE ROOSEVELT

While the oil was being unloaded, a party of men went out with ice chisels, poles, saws, and so forth, chopping away the ice so that we could warp the *Roosevelt* in, broadside to the shore. Bartlett and I were determined to get the ship beyond the floeberg barrier and into the shallow water of the ice-foot. We were not looking forward to another winter of such torment as we had lived through on the last previous expedition, with the ship just on the edge of the ice-foot and subject to every movement of the hostile pack outside.

After the oil cases came the tons of whale meat from the quarter-deck, some of it in chunks as large as a Saratoga trunk. It was thrown over the side onto the ice, sledged ashore by the Eskimos, some hundred yards over the ice-foot, and heaped in great piles, protected by the bags of coal which had also been taken from the quarter-deck. Then came the whale-boats, which were lowered from the davits and run ashore like sledges. They were later turned bottom side up for the winter and weighted down, so that the wind could not move them.

The work of landing the supplies and equipment consumed several days. This is the very first work of every well-managed arctic expedition on reaching winter quarters. With the supplies ashore, the loss of the ship by fire or by crushing in the ice, would mean simply that the party might have to walk home. It would not interfere with the sledge work, nor seriously cripple the expedition. Had we lost the *Roosevelt* at Cape Sheridan, we should have spent the winter in the box houses which we constructed and in the spring should have made the dash for the Pole just the same. We should then have walked the three hundred and fifty miles to Cape Sabine, crossed the Smith Sound ice to Etah, and waited for a ship.

The adjacent shore for a quarter of a mile was lined with boxes, each item of provisions having a pile to itself. This packing-box village was christened Hubbardville, in honor of General Thomas H. Hubbard, president of the Peary Arctic Club. When the boxes which had served as a bed platform in the Eskimo quarters of the *Roosevelt's* forward deck were removed, the place was swept and scrubbed; then a bed platform was built of boards, divided into sections for the various families and screened in front by curtains. Under the bed platform was an open space, where the Eskimos could keep their cooking utensils and other personal belongings. The fastidious reader who is shocked at the idea of keeping frying-pans under the bed should see an Eskimo family in one of their native houses of stone and earth, eight feet across, where meat and drink, men, women, and children are crowded indiscriminately for month upon month in winter.

We next landed about eighty tons of coal, so that, in case we should have to live in the box houses, there would be plenty of fuel. At that time of the year it was not very cold. On the 8th of September the thermometer stood at 12 above zero, the next day at 4.

The heavier cases, containing the tins of bacon, pemmican (the condensed meat food used in the Arctic), flour, et cetera, were utilized ashore like so many blocks of granite in constructing three houses, about fifteen feet by thirty. All the supplies were especially packed for this purpose, in boxes of specified dimensions — one of the innumerable details which made for the success of the expedition. In building the houses the tops of the boxes were placed inside, the covers removed, and the contents taken out as needed, as from a shelf, the whole house being one large grocery.

The roofs were made of sails thrown over boat booms or spars, and later the walls and roof were banked in solidly with snow. Stoves were set up, so that, if everything went well, the houses could be used as workshops during the winter.

So here we were, safely bestowed at Cape Sheridan, and the prize seemed already in our grasp. The contingencies which had blocked our way in 1906 were all provided for on this last expedition. We knew just what we had to do, and just how to do it. Only a few months of waiting, the fall hunting, and the long, dark winter were all that lay between me and the final start. I had the dogs, the men, the experience, a fixed determination (the same impulse which drove the ships of Columbus across the trackless western sea) — and the end lay with that Destiny which favors the man who follows his faith and his dream to the last breath.

CHAPTER XIV

WHEN the removal of supplies had lightened the *Roosevelt* so much that Bartlett got her considerably farther in shore, she lay with her nose pointing almost true north. It cheered us, for this was her constant habit. It seemed almost like the purpose of a living creature. Whenever on the upward voyage — either this time or on her first trip in 1905 — the ship was beset in the ice so that we lost control of her, she always swung around of her own accord and pointed north. When twisting through the ice, if we got caught when the ship was headed east or west, it was only a little while before the pressure would swing her round till once more she looked northward. Even on the return journey, in 1906, it was the same — as if the ship realized she had not accomplished her purpose and wanted to go back. The sailors noticed it, and used to talk about it. They said the *Roosevelt* was not satisfied, that she knew she had not done her work.

When we got the vessel as near the shore as possible, the ship's people began to make her ready for the winter. The engine-room force was busy blowing down the boilers, putting the machinery out of commission, removing every drop of water from the pipes and elbows so the cold of winter should not burst them;

and the crew was busy taking down the sails, slacking off the rigging, so the contraction from the intense cold of winter should not cause damage, with a thousand and one details of like character.

Before the sails were taken down, they were all set, that they might be thoroughly dried out by sun and wind. The ship was a beautiful sight, held fast in the embrace of the ice and with her cables out, but with every sail filled with wind like a yacht in a race.

While this work was going on small hunting parties of Eskimos were sent to the Lake Hazen region, but they met with little success. A few hares were secured, but musk-oxen seemed to have vanished. This troubled me, for it raised a fear that the hunting of the former expedition had killed off the game, or driven it away. The Eskimo women set their fox traps all along the shore for five miles or so each way, and they were more successful than the men, obtaining some thirty or forty foxes in the course of the fall and winter. The women also went on fishing trips to the ponds of the neighborhood, and brought in many mottled beauties.

The Eskimo method of fishing is interesting. The fish in that region will not rise to bait but are captured by cutting a hole in the ice and dropping in a piece of ivory carved in the shape of a small fish. When the fish rises to examine this visitor, it is secured with a spear. The Eskimo fish spear has a central shaft with a sharp piece of steel, usually an old nail, set in the end. On each side is a piece of deer antler pointing downward, lashed onto the shaft with a fine line, and sharp nails, pointing inward, are set in the two fragments of antler. When this spear is thrust down on the fish, the antlers spread as they strike the fish's back; he is impaled by the sharp point above him, and the sharp barbs on either side keep him from getting away.

The char (?) of North Grant Land is a beautiful mottled fish, weighing sometimes as much as eleven or twelve pounds. I believe that the pink fiber of these fish — taken from water never warmer than 35° or 40° above zero — is the firmest and sweetest fish fiber in the world. During my early expeditions in this region, I would spear one of these beauties and throw him on the ice to freeze, then pick him up and fling him down so as to shatter the flesh under the skin, lay him on the sledge, and as I walked away pick out morsels of the pink flesh and eat them as one would eat strawberries.

In September of 1900 with these fish a party of six men and twenty-three dogs were supported for some ten days, until we found musk-oxen. We speared the fish in the way the Eskimos taught us, using the regular native spear.

The new members of the expedition were naturally anxious to go sight-seeing. MacMillan had an attack of the grip, but Borup and Dr. Goodsell scoured the surrounding country. Hubbardville could not boast its Westminster Abbey nor its Arc de Triomphe, but there were Petersen's grave and the *Alert* and *Roosevelt* cairns, both in the neighborhood, and visible from the ship.

About a mile and a half southwest from our winter quarters was the memorial headboard of Petersen, the

Danish interpreter of the English expedition of 1875–76. He died as the result of exposure on a sledge trip, and was buried there abreast of the *Alert's* winter quarters. The grave is covered with a large flat slab, and at the head is a board covered with a copper sheet from the boiler room of the *Alert,* with the inscription punched in it. There may be a lonelier grave somewhere on earth, but if so I have no knowledge of it. No explorer, not even the youngest and most thoughtless, could stand before that "mute reminder of heroic bones" without a feeling of reverence and awe. There is something menacing in that dark silhouette against the white snow, as if the mysterious Arctic were reminding the intruder that he might be chosen next to remain with her forever.

Not far away is the *Alert's* cairn, from which I took the British record in 1905, a copy of it being replaced by Ross Marvin, according to the custom of explorers. In view of his tragic end, in the spring of 1909, the farthest north of all deaths known to man, this visit of Marvin's to the neighborhood of Petersen's grave has a peculiar pathos.

The *Roosevelt* cairn, erected by Marvin in 1906, is directly abreast of the ship's location at Cape Sheridan in 1905–06 and about one mile inland. It is on a high point of land, about four hundred feet above the water. The record is in a prune can, at the bottom of the pile of stones, and was written by Marvin himself in lead-pencil. The cairn is surmounted by a cross, made of the oak plank from our sledge runners. It faces north, and at the intersection of the upright and the crosspiece there is a large

"R" cut in the wood.   When I went up to see it, soon
after our arrival this last time, the cross was leaning
toward the north, as if from the intentness of its three
years' northward gazing.

On the 12th of September we had a holiday, it
being the fifteenth birthday of my daughter, Marie
Ahnighito, who was born at Anniversary Lodge,
Greenland — the most northerly born of all white
children.   Ten years before, we had celebrated her
fifth birthday on the Windward.   Many icebergs had
drifted down the channels since then, and I was still
following the same ideal which had given my daughter
so cold and strange a birthplace.

There was a driving snowstorm that day, but Bartlett dressed the ship in all the flags, the full inter-
national code, and the bright colors of the bunting
made a striking contrast to the gray-white sky.   Percy,
the steward, had baked a special birthday cake, and
we had it, surmounted with fifteen blazing candles,
on our supper table.   Just after breakfast the Eskimos
came in with a polar bear, a female yearling six feet
long, and I determined to have it mounted for Marie's
birthday bear.   It should be standing and advancing,
one paw extended as if to shake, the head on one side
and a bearish smile on the face.   The bear provided
us with juicy steaks, and we had a special tablecloth,
our best cups and saucers, new spoons, et cetera.

A day or two later we began to get the dogs made
fast, in preparation for the first sledge parties.   There
was now sufficient snow to begin the transportation of
supplies toward Cape Columbia, and Black Cliffs
Bay was frozen over.   The Eskimos tied the dogs, in

teams of five or six, to stakes driven into the shore or holes cut in the ice. They made a fine picture, looking shoreward from the ship — nearly two hundred and fifty of them — and their barking could be heard at all hours.

It must be remembered that day and night were still determined only by the clock, as the ever-circling sun had not yet set. By reason of the industry of all hands on the upward voyage, everything was now ready for the fall work. The Eskimos had built the sledges and made the dog harnesses, and Matt Henson had finished the "kitchen boxes," which enclosed our oil stoves in the field, while the busy needles of the Eskimo women had provided every man with a fur outfit.

In the North we wear the regular Eskimo garments, with certain modifications. First of all, there is the *kooletah*, a fur jacket with no buttons, which goes on over the head. For summer wear the Eskimos make it of sealskin, but for winter it is made of fox or deerskin.

For our own use, we had jackets made of Michigan sheepskin. We took the skins up with us, and the women made the garments, but when it was very cold we wore the deerskin or foxskin jacket of the Eskimos. Attached to this jacket is a hood, and around the face is a thick roll made of fox-tails.

The *ahteah* is a shirt, usually of fawn skin, with the hair inside, and the Eskimos wear it even in summer. In some of the photographs of natives, the skilful piecing together of the skins in the shirt can be traced. The Eskimo women are more adept at this work than are

any of the furriers of civilization. They sew the skins
with the sinew taken from the back of the deer — the
jumping muscle. It is absolutely unbreakable, and
moisture does not rot it. For the coarser work of sewing
boots, canoes, and tents, they use the sinew from the
tail of the narwhal. The sewing is now done with the
steel needles I have given them; but in former years
they used a punch made of bone, passing the sinew
through the hole, as a shoemaker uses a "waxed end."
They do not cut the skins with shears, as that would
injure the fur; but with a "woman's knife," similar
to an old-fashioned mincemeat chopper.

The shaggy fur trousers are invariably made from
the skins of the polar bear. Then there are stockings
of hareskin, and the *kamiks*, or boots, of sealskin, soled
with the heavier skin of the square-flipper seal. On
the ship, on sledge journeys, and in all the field work
of the winter, the regular footgear of the Eskimos
was worn. Add the warm fur mittens, and the winter
wardrobe is complete.

It may reasonably be inquired whether the close
housing for so long a time of such a considerable number of human beings did not result in personal friction,
due to the inevitable accumulation of a thousand and
one petty irritations. To some extent it did. But the
principal members of the expedition were men of
such character that they were able to exercise an
admirable self-restraint that prevented any unpleasant
results of consequence. Practically the only trouble
of a personal sort that was of any importance occurred
between one of the sailors and an Eskimo whom we
called Harrigan.

Harrigan acquired this sobriquet on account of his ear for music. The crew used to be fond of singing that energetic Irish air which was popular for some years along Broadway and which concludes ungrammatically with the words "Harrigan — that's me." The Eskimo in question seemed fascinated by this song and in time learned those three words and practised them with so much assiduity that he was ultimately able to sing them in a manner not wholly uncouth.

In addition to his musical leanings, Harrigan was a practical joker, and on one occasion he was exercising his humorous talents in the forecastle to the considerable discomfort of one of the crew. Ultimately the sailor, unable to rid himself of his persecutor in any other way, resorted to the use of his fists. The Eskimos, while good wrestlers, are far from adepts at the "manly art of self-defense," and the result was that Harrigan emerged from the forecastle with a well-blackened eye and a keen sense of having been ill used. He complained bitterly of his treatment, but I gave him a new shirt and told him to keep away from the forecastle where the sailors were, and in a few hours he had forgotten it like a school boy, so that the affair passed off without leaving any permanent ill feeling, and soon Harrigan was again cheerfully croaking his "Harrigan — that's me."

CHAPTER XV

THE main purpose of the autumn sledge parties was the transportation to Cape Columbia of supplies for the spring sledge journey toward the Pole. Cape Columbia, ninety miles northwest from the ship, had been chosen because it was the most northerly point of Grant Land, and because it was far enough west to be out of the ice current setting down Robeson Channel. From there we could strike straight north over the ice of the Polar Sea.

The moving of thousands of pounds of supplies for men and dogs for a distance of ninety miles, under the rigorous conditions of the Arctic, presented problems for calculation. The plan was to establish stations along the route, instead of sending each party through to Cape Columbia and back. The first party was to go to Cape Belknap, about twelve miles from the ship, deposit their supplies, and return the same day. The second party was to go to Cape Richardson, about twenty miles away, deposit their supplies, return part way and pick up the supplies at Cape Belknap, taking them forward to Cape Richardson. The next station was at Porter Bay, the next at Sail Harbor, the next at Cape Colan, and the final station at Cape Columbia itself. Parties would thus be going back and forth the whole time, the trail would constantly be kept open, and hunting could be done along the way. The tractive force was, of course, the Eskimo dogs, and sledges were the means of transportation. The sledges were of two types: the Peary sledge, which had never been used before this expedition, and the regular Eskimo sledge, increased somewhat in length for special work. The Peary type of sledge is from twelve to thirteen feet in length, two feet in width, and seven inches in height; the Eskimo type of sledge is nine feet in length, two feet in width, and seven inches in height. Another difference is that the Eskimo sledge is simply two oak runners an inch or an inch and a quarter thick and seven inches wide, shaped at the front to give the easiest curve for passage over the ice, and shod with steel, while the Peary sledge has oak sides rounded, both in front and behind, with two-inch wide bent ash runners attached, the runners being shod with two-inch wide steel shoes. The sides of both are solid, and they are lashed together with sealskin thongs.

The Peary sledge is the evolution of twenty-three years of experience in arctic work and is believed to be the strongest and easiest running sledge yet used for arctic traveling. On a level surface this sledge will support ten or twelve hundred pounds.

The Eskimos have used their own type of sledge from time immemorial. When they had no wood, before the advent of the white man, they made their sledges of bone — the shoulder-blades of the walrus, and the ribs of the whale, with deer antlers for up-standers.

For dog harnesses, I have adopted the Eskimo pattern, but have used different material. The Eskimo harness is made of sealskin — two loops joined by a cross strip at the back of the neck and under the throat. The dog's forelegs pass through the loops, and the ends are joined over the small of the back, where the trace is attached. This harness is very simple and flexible, and it allows the dog to exert his whole strength. The objection to sealskin as a harness material is a gastronomic one. When the dogs are on short rations they eat their harnesses at night in camp. To obviate this difficulty, I use for the harnesses a special webbing or belting, about two or two and a half inches in width, and replace the customary rawhide traces of the Eskimos by a braided linen sash cord.

The dogs are hitched to the sledge fanwise. The standard team is eight dogs; but for rapid traveling with a heavy load, ten or twelve are sometimes used. They are guided by the whip and the voice. The Eskimo whip has a lash sometimes twelve, sometimes eighteen, feet long, and so skilful are the Eskimos in its manipulation that they can send the lash flying through the air and reach any part of any particular dog they wish. A white man can learn to use an Eskimo whip, but it takes time. It takes time also to acquire the exact Eskimo accent to the words "*How-eh, how-eh, how-eh,*" meaning to the right; "*Ash-oo, ash-oo, ash-oo,*" to the left; as well as the standard, "*Huk, huk, huk,*" which is equivalent to "go on." Sometimes, when the dogs do not obey, the usual "*How-eh, how-eh, how-eh,*" will reverse its accent, and

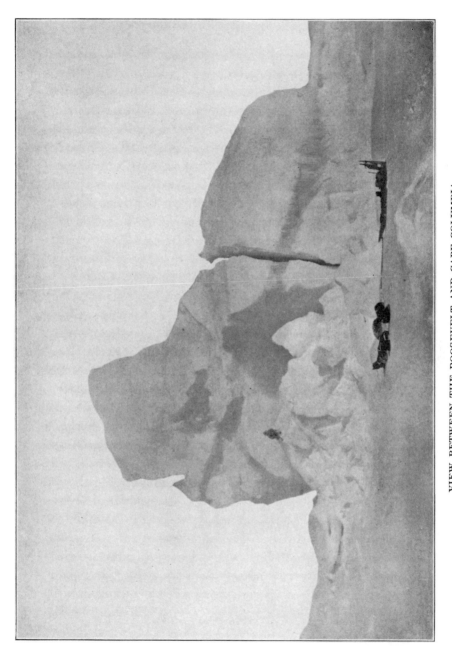

VIEW BETWEEN THE ROOSEVELT AND CAPE COLUMBIA

"PEARY" TYPE OF SLEDGE
12½ ft. Long, 2 ft. Wide, 7 in. High; With Steel Shoes 2 in. Wide

ESKIMO TYPE OF SLEDGE USED ON JOURNEY
9 ft. 6 in. Long, 2 ft. Wide, 8 in High; With Steel Shoes 1¼ in. Wide
Each has standard load of supplies for team and driver for fifty days—
pemmican, biscuit, milk, tea, oil, alcohol

the driver will yell, "*How-ooooooo*," with an accompaniment of other words in Eskimo and English which shall be left to the imagination of the reader. The temperature of a new man trying to drive a team of Eskimo dogs is apt to be pretty high. One is almost inclined to believe with the Eskimos that demons take possession of these animals. Sometimes they seem to be quite crazy. A favorite trick of theirs is to leap over and under and around each other, getting their traces in a snarl beside which the Gordian knot would be as nothing. Then, in a temperature anywhere between zero and 60° below, the driver has to remove his heavy mittens and disentangle the traces with his bare hands, while the dogs leap and snap and bark and seem to mock him. And this brings me to an incident which practically always happens when a new man starts out to drive Eskimo dogs.

A member of the expedition — I, who have also suffered, will not give his name away — started out with his dog team. Some hours later shouts and hilarious laughter were heard from the Eskimos. It was not necessary to inquire what had happened. The dog team had returned to the ship — without the sledge. The new dog driver, in attempting to unsnarl the traces of his dogs, had let them get away from him. Another hour or two went by, and the man himself returned, crestfallen and angry clear through. He was greeted by the derisive shouts of the Eskimos, whose respect for the white man is based primarily on the white man's skill in the Eskimo's own field. The man gathered up his dogs again and went back for the sledge.

The gradual breaking in of the new men is one of the purposes of the short trips of the fall. They have to become inured to such minor discomforts as frosted toes and ears and noses, as well as the loss of their dogs. They have to learn to keep the heavy sledges right side up when the going is rough and sometimes, before a man gets hardened, this seems almost to rip the muscles from the shoulder blades. Moreover, they have to learn how to wear their fur clothing.

On the 16th of September the first train of supplies was sent to Cape Belknap: Marvin, Dr. Goodsell, and Borup, with thirteen Eskimos, sixteen sledges, and about two hundred dogs. They were an imposing procession as they started northwest along the ice-foot, the sledges going one behind the other. It was a beautiful day — clear, calm, and sunny, — and we could hear, when they were a long distance away, the shouts of the Eskimo drivers, "*Huk, huk, huk,*" "*Ash-oo,*" "*How-eh,*" the cracking of the whips, and the crisp rustle and creaking of the sledges over the snow.

It is often asked how we keep warm when riding on the sledges. We do not ride, save in rare instances. We walk, and when the going is hard we have to help the dogs by lifting the sledges over rough places.

The first party returned the same day with the empty sledges, and the next day two Eskimo hunting parties came in with three deer, six hares, and two eider ducks. Neither party had seen any tracks of musk-oxen. On the 18th, the second sledge party was sent out to carry fifty-six cases of crew pemmican to Cape Richardson, where they were to camp, bring up the biscuit from Cape Belknap to Cape Richardson the following day, and then return to the ship.   That gave them one night in the field.

A man's first night in a canvas tent in the Arctic is likely to be rather wakeful.   The ice makes mysterious noises; the dogs bark and fight outside the tent where they are tethered; and as three Eskimos and one white man usually occupy a small tent, and the oil-stove is left burning all night, the air, notwithstanding the cold, is not over-pure; and sometimes the Eskimos begin chanting to the spirits of their ancestors in the middle of the night, which is, to say the least, trying.   Sometimes, too, the new man's nerves are tried by hearing wolves howl in the distance.

The tents are specially made.   They are of light-weight canvas, and the floor of the tent is sewed directly into it.   The fly is sewed up, a circular opening cut in it, just large enough to admit a man, and that opening fitted with a circular flap which is closed by a draw-string, making the tent absolutely snow-proof.   An ordinary tent, when the snow is flying, would be filled in no time.

The tent is pyramidal, with one pole in the center, and the edges are usually held down by the sledge runners or by snowshoes used as tent pegs.   The men sleep on the floor in their clothes, with a musk-ox skin under, and a light deerskin over them.   I have not used sleeping bags since my arctic trip of 1891–92.

The "kitchen box" for our sledge journeys is simply a wooden box containing two double-burner oil-stoves, with four-inch wicks.   The two cooking pots are the bottoms of five-gallon coal-oil tins, fitted with covers.   When packed they are turned bottom

side up over each stove, and the hinged cover of the
wooden box is closed.   On reaching camp, whether tent
or snow igloo, the kitchen box is set down inside, the
top of the box is turned up and keeps the heat of
the stove from melting the wall of the igloo or burning
the tent; the hinged front of the box is turned down
and forms a table. The two cooking pots are filled
with pounded ice and put on the stoves; when the ice
melts one pot is used for tea, and the other may be
used to warm beans, or to boil meat if there is any.

Each man has a quart cup for tea, and a hunting
knife which serves many purposes. He does not
carry anything so polite as a fork, and one teaspoon
is considered quite enough for a party of four.   Each
man helps himself from the pot — sticks in his knife
and fishes out a piece of meat.

The theory of field work is that there shall be two
meals a day, one in the morning and one at night.   As
the days grow short, the meals are taken before light
and after dark, leaving the period of light entirely
for work. Sometimes it is necessary to travel for
twenty-four hours without stopping for food.

The Cape Richardson party returned on the evening of the 19th, and was sent out again on the 21st,
nineteen Eskimos and twenty-two sledges, to take 6,600
pounds of dog pemmican to Porter Bay. MacMillan,
being still under the weather with the grip, missed this
preliminary training; but I felt certain that he would
overtake the experience of the others as soon as he
was able to travel. When the third party returned,
on the 24th, they brought back the meat and skins
of fourteen deer.

CAPTAIN BARTLETT AND HIS PARTY

Panikpah, "Harrigan," Ooqueah, Bartlett. (A Typical Unit Division of the Expedition)

(Tents Were Used for Shelter in Earlier Autumn Hunting and Transportation of Supplies. In Winter Traveling and in the Sledge Journey Igloos Were Used)

On the 28th there was a general exodus from the ship: Henson, Ootah, Alletah, and Inighito were to hunt on the north side of Lake Hazen; Marvin, Poodloonah, Seegloo, and Arco on the east end and the south side of Lake Hazen; and Bartlett, with Panikpah, Inighito, Ookeyah, Dr. Goodsell, with Inighito, Keshungwah, Kyootah, and Borup, with Karko, Tawchingwah, and Ahwatingwah, were to go straight through to Cape Columbia.

I had planned from the beginning to leave most of the hunting and other field work to the younger members of the expedition. Twenty odd years of arctic experience had dulled for me the excitement of everything but a polar-bear chase; the young men were eager for the work; there was much to do on board ship in planning for the spring, and I wished to conserve my energies for the supreme effort.

There was no systematic training, because I do not believe in it. My body has always been able thus far to follow my will no matter what the demands might be, and my winter's work was largely a matter of refinement of equipment, and of mathematical calculations of pounds of supplies and miles of distance. It was the lack of food which had forced us to turn back at 87° 6'. Hunger, not cold, is the dragon which guards the Rhinegold of the Arctic.

I did allow myself one break in the monotony of ship life — a trip to Clements Markham Inlet, in October. Ever since April, 1902, when I had looked around the angle of Cape Hecla into the unexplored depths of this great fiord, I had had a longing to penetrate it. On the previous expedition I had started twice with that purpose, but had been prevented from carrying it out, partly on account of bad weather, partly by reason of my anxiety for the *Roosevelt*, which I had left in a precarious position. But now the *Roosevelt* was safe; and though the sun was circling near the horizon and the winter night would soon be upon us, I decided to make the trip.

On the 1st of October I left the ship with three Eskimos, Egingwah, Ooblooyah, and Koolatoonah, three sledges with teams of ten dogs each, and supplies for two weeks only. With the sledges thus lightly loaded, and the trail broken for us by the parties which had preceded us, we made rapid progress, reaching Porter Bay, thirty-five miles from the ship, for our first camp in a few hours.

Here we found two Eskimos, Onwagipsoo and Wesharkoopsee, who had been sent out a day or two before. Onwagipsoo went back to the ship, but Wesharkoopsee we took along with us to carry a load of supplies to Sail Harbor, which we expected to reach on the next march; from there he also would return to the ship.

Our camp at Porter Bay was in the permanent tent which had been erected there by the first of the autumn parties, the canvas tent with the sewed-in floor which has already been described. It was not very cold that night, and we slept comfortably after a hearty supper of beans and tea. Beans and tea! Perhaps it does not sound like a Lucullan feast, but after a day in the field in Grant Land it tastes like one.

CHAPTER XVI

THE BIGGEST GAME IN THE ARCTIC

WE slept splendidly on that banquet, and, breaking out early the next morning, we passed up the ice of Porter Bay to its head, then, taking to the land, crossed the five-mile-wide isthmus which separates Porter Bay from the head of James Ross Bay. Every foot of this route was familiar to me and rich with memories. Reaching the other side, we descended to the ice again and made rapid progress along the western shore. The dogs were lively and well-fed, trotting along with tails and ears erect; the weather was good, and the sun, now low on the horizon, cast long, fantastic shadows on the ice from every man and dog.

Suddenly the quick eyes of Egingwah spied a moving speck on the slope of the mountain to our left. "*Tooktoo*," he cried, and the party came to an instant standstill. Knowing that the successful pursuit of a single buck reindeer might mean a long run, I made no attempt to go after him myself; but I told Egingwah and Ooblooyah, my two stalwart, long-legged youngsters, to take the 40–82 Winchesters and be off. At the word they were flying across country, eager as dogs loosed from the traces, crouching low and running quickly. They took a course which would intercept the deer a little farther along the slope of the mountain.

I watched them through my glasses. The deer, when he caught sight of them, started off leisurely in another direction, looking back every now and then, suspiciously alert. When the deer halted suddenly and swung round facing them, it was clear that they had given the magic call taught by Eskimo father to Eskimo son through generation after generation, the imitation call at which every buck reindeer stops instantly — a peculiar hissing call like the spitting of a cat, only more lingering.

The two men leveled their rifles, and the magnificent buck went down in his tracks. The dogs had been watching, with heads and ears erect; but at the report of the rifles they swung sharply to the shore, and the next instant we were hurrying across the rocks and over the snow, the dogs dragging the sledges as if they had been empty.

When we reached the two hunters they were standing patiently beside the deer. I had told them not to disturb him, as some good photographs were desired. He was a beautiful creature, almost snow-white, with magnificent branching antlers. When the photographs were taken, all four of the men set to work, skinning and cutting him up.

The scene is vivid in memory: the towering mountains on both sides of James Ross Bay, with the snow-covered foreshore stretching down to the white surface of the bay; in the south the low-lying sun, a great glare of vivid yellow just showing through the gap of the divide, the air full of slowly dropping frost crystals; and the four fur-clad figures grouped around the deer, with the dogs and the sledges at a little distance

POLAR BEAR, ARRANGED BY "FROZEN TAXIDERMY" AND PHOTO-
GRAPHED BY FLASHLIGHT

FAMILY GROUP OF PEARY CARIBOU (RANGIFER PEARYI), ARRANGED BY "FROZEN TAXIDERMY", AND PHOTOGRAPHED BY FLASHLIGHT

— the only signs of life in that great white wilderness.

When the deer was skinned and dressed, the pelt was carefully rolled and put on one of the sledges, the meat was made into a pile for Wesharkoopsee to take back to the ship when he returned from Sail Harbor with empty sledge, and we pushed along the western shore of the bay; then, taking to the land again, still westward across this second peninsula and low divide, till we came to the little bight, called Sail Harbor by the English, on the western side of Parry Peninsula.

Here, out at the mouth of the harbor, under the lee of the protecting northern point, we made our second camp.

Wesharkoopsee deposited his load of supplies, and I wrote a note for Bartlett, who was west of us on his way to Cape Columbia. That night we had deer steak for supper — a feast for a king.

After a few hours' sleep we started, straight as the crow flies, across the eastern end of the great glacial fringe, heading for the mouth of Clements Markham Inlet. Reaching the mouth of the inlet, we kept on down its eastern shore, finding very good going; for the tides rising in the crack next the shore had saturated the overlying snow, then freezing had formed a narrow but smooth surface for the sledges.

A part of this shore was musk-ox country, and we scanned it carefully, but saw none of the animals. Some miles down the bay we came upon the tracks of a couple of deer. A little farther on we were electrified by a tense whisper from the ever sharp-sighted Egingwah:

"*Nanooksoah!*"

He was pointing excitedly toward the center of the fiord, and following the direction of his finger we saw a cream-colored spot leisurely moving toward the mouth of the fiord — a polar bear!

If there is anything that starts the blood lust in an Eskimo's heart more wildly than the sight of a polar bear, I have yet to discover it. Hardened as I am to arctic hunting, I was thrilled myself.

While I stood in front of the dogs with a whip in each hand, to keep them from dashing away — for the Eskimo dog knows the meaning of *"nanooksoah"* as well as his master — the three men were throwing things off the sledges as if they were crazy.

When the sledges were empty, Ooblooyah's team shot by me, with Ooblooyah at the up-standers. Egingwah came next, and I threw myself on his sledge as it flew past. Behind us came Koolatoonah with the third team. The man who coined the phrase "greased lightning" must have ridden on an empty sledge behind a team of Eskimo dogs on the scent of a polar bear.

The bear had heard us, and was making for the opposite shore of the fiord with prodigious bounds. I jumped to the up-standers of the flying sledge, leaving Egingwah to throw himself on it and get his breath, and away we went, wild with excitement, across the snow-covered surface of the fiord.

When we got to the middle the snow was deeper, and the dogs could not go so fast, though they strained

ahead with all their might. Suddenly they scented
the trail — and then neither deep snow nor anything
else could have held them. Ooblooyah, with a crazy
team and only himself at the up-standers, distanced
the rest of us, arriving at the farther shore almost as
soon as the leaping bear. He loosed his dogs immediately, and we could see the bear in the distance,
followed by minute dots that looked hardly larger
than mosquitoes swarming up the steep slope. Before
our slower teams got to the shore, Ooblooyah had
reached the top of the slope, and he signaled us to
go around, as the land was an island.

When we reached the other side, we found where
the bear had descended to the ice again and kept on
across the remaining width of the fiord to the western
shore, followed by Ooblooyah and his dogs.

A most peculiar circumstance, commented on by
Egingwah as we flew along, was that this bear, contrary to the custom of bears in Eskimo land, did not
stop when the dogs reached him, but kept right on
traveling. This to Egingwah was almost certain proof
that the great devil himself — terrible Tornarsuk —
was in that bear. At the thought of chasing the devil,
my sledge companion grew even more excited.

On the other side of the island the snow was deeper
and our progress slower, and when we reached the
western shore of the fiord, up which, as on the island,
we had seen from a distance the bear and Ooblooyah's
dogs slowly climbing, both we and our dogs were
pretty well winded. But we were encouraged by hearing the barking of the free dogs up somewhere among
the cliffs. This meant that the bear had at last been

brought to bay. When we reached the shore our dogs were loosed from the sledges. They swarmed up the hot trail, and we followed as best we could.

A little farther on we came to a deep cañon, and as we could tell by the sounds, the dogs and the bear were at the bottom. But where we stood the walls were too precipitous for even an Eskimo to descend, and we could not see our quarry. He was evidently under some projecting ledge on our side.

Moving up the cañon to find a place of descent, I heard Egingwah shout that the bear had started down the cañon and was climbing up the other side. Hurrying back through the deep snow and over the rough rocks, I suddenly saw the beast, perhaps a hundred yards away, and raised my rifle. But I must have been too much winded to take good aim, for though I fired two shots at him the bear kept right on up the cañon side. Surely Tornarsuk was in him!

I found that I had given the stumps of both my feet — my toes were frozen off at Fort Conger in 1899 — some severe blows against the rocks; and as they were complaining with vehemence, I decided not to follow the bear any farther along the steep boulder-strewn bluffs.

Handing my rifle to Egingwah, I told him and Koolatoonah to go after the bear while I went back down the bluffs to the sledges and followed along the bay ice. But before I had gone far along the bay ice shouting was heard in the distance, and soon an Eskimo appeared on a summit and waved his hand — a signal that they had bagged the bear.

Just ahead, and abreast of where the Eskimo had

appeared, was the mouth of a ravine, and I stopped the sledge there and waited. In a little while my men appeared slowly working their way down the ravine. The dogs which had been in at the death were attached to the bear, as if he had been a sledge, and they were dragging him after them. It was an interesting scene: the steep and rocky ravine in its torn mantle of snow, the excited dogs straining ahead with their unusual burden, the inert cream-colored, blood-streaked form of the great bear, and the shouting and gesticulating Eskimos.

When they finally got the bear down to the shore, and while I was taking photographs of him, the Eskimos walked up and down excitedly discussing the now certain fact that the devil had been in this animal, or he never would have traveled as he did after the dogs overtook him. The subtleties of arctic demonology being beyond the grasp of any mere white man, I did not join in the argument as to whither the devil had betaken himself when the rifle of Ooblooyah laid low his fleshly tenement.

Our prize was soon skinned and cut up by the skilful knives of the Eskimos, the meat was piled on the shore for future parties to bring back to the ship, the bearskin was carefully folded on one of the sledges, and we returned to the place where we had first seen the bear, on the other side of the bay.

There we found the supplies which had been thrown from the sledges to lighten them for the bear chase; and as the men and dogs were tired out, and we were satisfied with the day's work, we camped on the spot.

Our tent was unfolded and set up, the oil-stoves were lighted, and we had a plentiful supply of bear steak — all the juicier, perhaps, for the recent presence of Tornarsuk.

CHAPTER XVII

MUSK-OXEN AT LAST

ON the next march we had gone only some six or seven miles when, rounding a point on the eastern shore of the Inlet, we saw black dots on a distant hillside.

"*Oomingmuksue!*" said Ooblooyah, excitedly, and I nodded to him, well pleased.

To the experienced hunter, with one or two dogs, seeing musk-oxen should be equivalent to securing them. There may be traveling over the roughest kind of rough country, with wind in the face and cold in the blood; but the end should always be the trophies of hides, horns, and juicy meat.

For myself, I never associate the idea of sport with musk-oxen — too often in the years gone by the sighting of those black forms has meant the difference between life and death. In 1896, in Independence Bay, the finding of a herd of musk-oxen saved the lives of my entire party. On my way back from 87° 6', in 1906, if we had not found musk-oxen on Nares Land, the bones of my party might now be bleaching up there in the great white waste.

When we saw the significant black dots in the distance, we headed for them. There were five close together, and another a little way off. When we got within less than a mile, two of the dogs were loosed.

They were wild with excitement, for they also had seen the black dots and knew what they meant; and as soon as the traces were unfastened they were off — straight as the flight of a homing bee.

We followed, at our leisure, knowing that when we arrived the herd would be rounded up, ready for our rifles. A single musk-ox, when he sees the dogs, will make for the nearest cliff and get his back against it; but a herd of them will round up in the middle of a plain with tails together and heads toward the enemy. Then the bull leader of the herd will take his place outside the round-up, and charge the dogs. When the leader is shot, another takes his place, and so on.

A few minutes later I stood again, as I had stood on previous expeditions, with that bunch of shaggy black forms, gleaming eyes and pointed horns before me — only this time it did not mean life or death.

Yet, as I raised my rifle, again I felt clutching at my heart that terrible sensation of life hanging on the accuracy of my aim; again in my bones I felt that gnawing hunger of the past; that aching lust for red, warm, dripping meat — the feeling that the wolf has when he pulls down his quarry. He who has ever been really hungry, either in the Arctic or elsewhere, will understand this feeling. Sometimes the memory of it rushes over me in unexpected places. I have felt it after a hearty dinner, in the streets of a great city, when a lean-faced beggar has held out his hand for alms.

I pulled the trigger, and the bull leader of the herd fell on his haunches. The bullet had found the vulnerable spot under the fore shoulder, where one

HEAD OF BULL MUSK-OX KILLED ON PARRY PENINSULA

HERD OF MUSK-OXEN ROUNDED UP

should always shoot a musk-ox. To aim at the head is a waste of ammunition.

As the bull went down, out from the herd came a cow, and a second shot accounted for her. The others, a second cow and two yearlings, were the work of a few moments; then I left Ooblooyah and Koolatoonah to skin and cut them up, while Egingwah and I started for the single animal, a couple of miles away.

As the dogs approached this fellow, he launched up the hill and disappeared over a nearby crest. The light surface snow along the path he had taken was brushed away by the long, matted hair of his sides and belly, which hung down to the ground.

The dogs had disappeared after the musk-ox, but Egingwah and myself were guided by their wild barking. Our quarry had taken refuge among the huge rocks in the bottom of a stream-bed, where his rear and both sides were protected, and there he stood at bay with the yelping dogs before him.

One shot was enough; and leaving Egingwah to skin and cut up the animal, I started to walk back to the other two men, as it had been decided to camp at the place where they were cutting up the five musk-oxen. But as I emerged from the mouth of the cañon, I saw up the valley still another of the big, black shaggy forms. Quickly I retraced my steps, and gathering in two of the dogs, secured this fellow as easily as the others.

This last specimen was, however, of peculiar interest, as the white hair of the legs, just above the hoofs, was dashed with a bright red—a marking which I had never before seen in any of these arctic animals.

Taking the dogs with me and leaving the musk-ox, I went on to the place selected for a camp. Oob-loyah and Koolatoonah were just finishing cutting up the fifth musk-ox, and were immediately sent off with a sledge and team of dogs, to help Egingwah with the two big bulls.

When they were gone, I set up the tent myself and began to prepare the tea for our supper. As soon as the voices of the Eskimos were audible in the distance, I put on the musk-ox steaks to broil and in a few minutes we were enjoying the reward of our labor. Surely this was living on the fat of the land indeed, deer steak the second night, bear steak last night, to-night the luscious meat of the musk-ox!

In the morning we continued our course, and during the day three more musk-oxen were gathered in, the meat being cached as before. That night we camped at the head of the hitherto unexplored inlet, and I had the satisfaction of knowing that one more stretch of previously unknown territory had been added to the world's map.

Next day we started north along the west side of the inlet. We had been traveling for hours and were just looking for a suitable place to camp, being then at the foot of a steep bluff some fifty feet in height, when suddenly the dogs made a break for the shore and attempted to climb the bluff. Of course they could not do this on account of the sledges; but we knew what their wild action meant — more musk-oxen.

In a moment Egingwah and I, with rifles in our hands, were climbing the bluff. Peering over the top we saw a herd of five. It was nearly dark now, the arctic twilight being so dense that we could simply make out five dark spots. We waited for a moment to catch our breath, then I motioned to Ooblooyah to bring two of the dogs, leaving Koolatoonah with the others at the sledges. Notwithstanding the uncertain light, we made short work of this herd.

Again I pitched the tent and prepared supper, while my brown friends paid their final respects to the musk-oxen on the bluff. It is necessary to eviscerate these animals as soon as they are killed, otherwise the excessive heat of the great shaggy bodies will cause the meat to become tainted. When the three Eskimos came down to the tent the darkness was already upon us — a promise of the long black night to come.

The next day we completed the circuit of the western shore of the Inlet, then started on a bee line for Sail Harbor, making this a forced march. At Sail Harbor we found a note from Bartlett, showing that he had passed there the previous day on his way back from Cape Columbia to the ship.

There we camped again; and in the morning, while the men were breaking camp and lashing up the sledges, I started with the very first rays of the morning light across the peninsula towards James Ross Bay. As I crested the divide, I saw — down on the shore of the Bay — a group of dark spots which were clearly recognized as a camp; and a little later I sang out to the party, which comprised the divisions of Bartlett, Goodsell, and Borup.

By the time the sleepy-eyed, stiff figures of the

three men — who, as I soon learned, had been asleep only an hour or so — emerged from the tents, my sledges and Eskimos were close at my heels. I can see now the bulging eyes of the men, and particularly of young Borup, when they saw the sledge loads of shaggy skins. On the top of the leading sledge was the magnificent snowy pelt of the polar bear, with the head forward; behind this was the deerskin with its wide-antlered head, and more musk-ox heads than they had had time to count.

"Oh, gee!" exclaimed Borup, when his open-mouthed astonishment would permit of articulation.

I had no time for visiting, as I wanted to reach the ship on that march; and after a few words left the men to finish their interrupted sleep. It was long after dark when we reached the *Roosevelt*. We had been absent seven sleeps, had traveled over two hundred miles, had accomplished the exploration of Clements Markham Inlet, had made a rough map of it, and incidentally had obtained magnificent specimens of the three great animals of the arctic regions, thus adding a few thousand pounds of fresh meat to our winter supply. So, with a feeling of entire satisfaction, I had a hot bath in my cabin bathroom on the *Roosevelt*, and then turned in to my bunk for a long and refreshing sleep.

Throughout the month of October the work of transporting supplies and of hunting went on. The captain made two round trips from the ship to Cape Columbia; but he was working backward and forward all the time along the route. In the course of this work he obtained four musk-oxen.

WEE-SHAK-UP-SI AND MUSK-OX CALF

BEAR KILLED IN CLEMENTS MARKHAM INLET

CARIBOU HEADS IN THE RIGGING OF THE
ROOSEVELT

(From Photographs taken on the Return Voyage)

MUSK-OX HEADS IN THE RIGGING OF THE
ROOSEVELT

MacMillan recovered from his attack of grip, and on the 14th of October was sent with two sledges, two Eskimos, and twenty dogs to make a survey of Clements Markham Inlet and obtain musk-oxen and deer. He bagged five of the former. The last of the month the doctor also had an attack of grip, which kept him in bed for a week or two. Many small parties were sent out on short hunting trips and there was hardly a day during the fall when the men were all on the ship at one time.

While, from the time of our arrival at Cape Sheridan early in September to the date of our departure from land for the Pole on March 1, every member of the expedition was almost constantly engaged in work that had for its object the completing of preparations for the final sledge journey in the spring, no small part of this work was educational in purpose and result. That is to say, it was intended to inure the "tender-feet" of the party to the hardships of long journeys over rough going and through low temperatures, snow and wind. It taught them how to take care of themselves under difficult conditions, how to defend themselves against the ever-present peril of frost-bite, how to get the greatest comfort and protection from their fur clothing, how to handle their valuable dogs and how to manage their Eskimo helpers so as to get the best results from their efforts.

An entry in Dr. Goodsell's journal is so typical of the chief troubles of any arctic sledging journey that it is worth repeating here.

"Have been utilizing the time," wrote Dr. Goodsell, "in trying to dry out stockings and boots. It is extremely difficult to dry out stockings because of the cold and the necessity of economizing fuel.   The general procedure is to discard footgear when it is nearly saturated with moisture.   As long as the footgear is dry there is little danger of frosting the feet, if ordinary precautions are taken.   With wet footgear one is in constant danger of freezing the feet.   The oil-stove with the three-inch burner is barely sufficient to dry the gloves, of which two pairs are worn, an outer pair of bearskin, and an inner pair of deerskin."   Another journal entry deals with a different kind of peril:

"Toxingwa and Weesockasee were overcome by the lack of oxygen and the fumes of alcohol while MacMillan was preparing tea.   Weesockasee fell back as though asleep.   Toxingwa was twisting around, as though to get his arm free from one sleeve of his jacket. He too, finally fell back.   MacMillan surmised the cause and kicked the door to one side.   In about fifteen or twenty minutes they came around all right. The Commander on another of his expeditions nearly had a similar experience when he saw his Eskimos acting strangely, and quickly kicked out the side of the igloo."

Still another peril that is omnipresent in sledge journeys over a polar sea is that of falling through thin ice and getting thoroughly wet.   Perhaps it is not necessary to enlarge upon the gravity of this danger, since it was precisely such an accident that cost Professor Marvin his life.   Even if the victim of such an accident should be able to drag himself out of the water, he would in all probability speedily freeze to death.   Death by freezing comes speedily to a water-soaked man when temperatures are ranging anywhere from 20 to 60 degrees below zero.

"Just finished changing my boots for a dry pair," writes the doctor. "Crossing a lead covered with thin ice and fissured in the center, my left leg went in to the knee. Fortunately my .right foot was forward on firm ice and I threw myself ahead, going down on my left knee on the edge of firm ice and drawing my leg out of the water. At another lead the ice gave way as I sprang from its surface. My right foot dipped into the water to the ankle. I do not understand why I did not go down bodily into the water. Had I gone in to my waist there would have been a serious result, for the sledges were some distance away and the temperature was 47° below zero. In the absence of an igloo and a change of clothes near at hand, a ducking in this temperature would certainly have a serious termination."

Trying conditions these — yet the thing had its irresistible fascination, and now and then came reflective moments like the one on February 25, when the doctor, encamped on the way from the *Roosevelt* to Cape Columbia, wrote as follows:

"When I was nearing Point Good, insensibly I paused time and again to view the scene. I could see Cape Hecla to the rear and the Parry Peninsula. In advance the twin peaks of Cape Columbia beckoned us on to the second point of departure in the Commander's northward march. To the north as we progressed, beyond the comparatively smooth glacial fringe loomed the floes and pinnacles of rough ice which will try us all to the utmost for weeks to come.

To the south the circumference of the horizon was bounded by the sharp, jagged, serrated mountain ranges, mostly parallel to the coast. Every day we have a glorious dawn lasting for hours. A golden gleam is radiated from parallel ranges of serrated mountains. Individual peaks reflect the light of the sun, which will illuminate them with its direct rays in a few days. There is a cornea of golden glow, crimson and yellow, with strata of darker clouds floating parallel to the coast ranges — Turner effects for hours each day and for days in succession, the effect increasing from day to day. I am writing under difficulties, Innighito (an Eskimo) holding the candle. My hands are so cold that I can scarcely guide my pencil, as I recline on the bed platform of the igloo."

But all this anticipates. On the 12th of October the sun had bidden us good-by for the year, and the rapidly darkening twilight increased the difficulties of the field work. Our photographs grew daily less satisfactory. We had not been able to take snapshots since about the middle of September; for, when the sun is near the horizon, though the light is apparently as brilliant as in summer, it seems to have no actinic power. Our first time-exposures were five seconds; our last, on the 28th of October, were ninety minutes. The temperature also was gradually getting lower, and on the 29th of October it was 26° below zero.

The fall work ended with the return of Bartlett and his party from Cape Columbia, on November 5th, the other men having all returned before. By that time the light had disappeared, and it would be neces-

sary to wait for the recurring moons of the long winter
night before we could do any more work.

We had gone up there in the arctic noon, had
worked and hunted through the arctic twilight, and
now the night was upon us — the long arctic night
which seems like the valley of the shadow of death.
With nearly all the supplies for the spring sledge
journey already at Cape Columbia, with a good store
of fresh meat for the winter, and our party all in good
health, we entered the Great Dark with fairly contented
hearts. Our ship was apparently safe; we were well
housed and well fed; and if sometimes the terrible
melancholy of the dark clutched for a moment at
the hearts of the men, they bravely kept the secret
from each other and from me.

CHAPTER XVIII

THE LONG NIGHT

IT may well be doubted if it is possible for a person who has never experienced four months of constant darkness to imagine what it is. Every school boy learns that at the two ends of the earth the year is composed of one day and one night of equal length, and the intervening periods of twilight; but the mere recital of that fact makes no real impression on his consciousness. Only he who has risen and gone to bed by lamplight, and risen and gone to bed again by lamplight, day after day, week after week, month after month, can know how beautiful is the sunlight.

During the long arctic night we count the days till the light shall return to us, sometimes, toward the end of the dark period, checking off the days on the calendar — thirty-one days, thirty days, twenty-nine days, and so on, till we shall see the sun again. He who would understand the old sun worshipers should spend a winter in the Arctic.

Imagine us in our winter home on the *Roosevelt*, four hundred and fifty miles from the North Pole: the ship held tight in her icy berth, a hundred and fifty yards from the shore, the ship and the surrounding world covered with snow, the wind creaking in the rigging, whistling and shrieking around the corners of the deck houses, the temperature ranging from zero

ILLUMINATION OF THE ROOSEVELT IN WINTER QUARTERS ON A MOONLIGHT NIGHT
Showing the Ice Pressure Close to the Ship

to sixty below and the ice-pack in the channel outside groaning and complaining with the movement of the tides.

During the moonlit period of each month, some eight or ten days, when the moon seems to circle round and round the heavens, the younger members of the expedition were nearly always away on hunting trips; but during the longer periods of utter blackness most of us were on the ship together, as the winter hunting is done only by moonlight.

It must be understood that the arctic moon has its regular phases, its only peculiarity being the course it appears to travel in the sky. When the weather is clear there is starlight, even in the dark period; but it is a peculiar, cold, and spectral starlight, which, to borrow the words of Milton, seems but to make the "darkness visible."

When the stars are hidden, which may be much of the time, the darkness is so thick that it seems as if it could almost be grasped with the hand, and in a driving wind and snowstorm, if a man ventures to put his head outside the cabin door, he seems to be hurled back by invisible hands of demoniacal strength.

During the early part of the winter the Eskimos lived in the forward deck house of the ship. There was always a fire in the galley stove, a fire in the Eskimo quarters, and one in the crew's quarters; but though I had a small cylindrical coal stove in my cabin, it was not lighted throughout the winter. Leaving the forward door of my cabin open into the galley a part of the time, kept my cabin comfortably warm. Bartlett occasionally had a fire in his cabin, and the other members of the expedition sometimes lighted their oil-stoves.

On the first of November we adopted the winter schedule of two meals a day, breakfast at nine, dinner at four. This is the weekly bill of fare which Percy, the steward, and I made out and which was followed throughout the winter

Monday. *Breakfast:* Cereal. Beans and brown bread. Butter. Coffee. *Dinner:* Liver and bacon. Macaroni and cheese. Bread and butter. Tea.

Tuesday. *Breakfast:* Oatmeal. Ham and eggs. Bread and butter. Coffee. *Dinner:* Corned beef and creamed peas. Duff. Tea.

Wednesday. *Breakfast:* Choice of two kinds of cereal. Fish, forward (that is, for the sailors); sausage, aft (for the members of the expedition). Bread and butter. Coffee. *Dinner:* Steak and tomatoes. Bread and butter. Tea.

Thursday. *Breakfast:* Cereal. Ham and eggs. Bread and butter. Coffee. *Dinner:* Corned beef and peas. Duff. Tea.

Friday. *Breakfast:* Choice of cereal. Fish. Hamburger on starboard (our own) table. Bread and butter. Coffee. *Dinner:* Pea soup. Fish. Cranberry pie. Bread and butter. Tea.

Saturday. *Breakfast:* Cereal. Meat stew. Bread and butter. Coffee. *Dinner:* Steak and tomatoes. Bread and butter. Tea.

Sunday. *Breakfast:* Cereal. "Brooze" (Newfoundland hard biscuit, softened and boiled with salt codfish). Bread and butter. Coffee. *Dinner:* Salmon trout. Fruit. Chocolate.

Our table conversation was mainly with regard to our work. We would discuss the details of the last sledge trip, or talk over the plans for the next one. There was always something going on, and the minds of the men were so occupied that they did not have time to yield themselves to the traditional, maddening winter melancholy of the Arctic. Moreover, men of sanguine temperament had been selected, and much material in the rough had been carried along in order to keep everybody busy working it into shape for use.

On Sunday mornings I breakfasted in my cabin, thus leaving the men to themselves. On these occasions conversation was less technical and ranged from books to table manners, and sometimes Bartlett seized the opportunity to give his companions half-serious, half-humorous advice on the matter of table conduct, telling them that the time would come when they must return to civilization, and that they must not allow themselves to get into careless habits. Thus the academic and the practical elements of the party met on even ground.

I have never adopted rigorous rules for the members of my expeditions, because it is not necessary. There were regular hours for meals in the mess rooms. It was understood that lights should be out at midnight, but if any man wanted a light later, he could have it. These were our rules.

The Eskimos were allowed to eat when they pleased. They might sit up late at night, if they chose, but their work of making sledges and fur clothing had to proceed just the same the next day. There was only one rigid rule for them: that no loud noises, such as chopping dog meat or shouting, were to be made from ten o'clock at night until eight in the morning.

While living on the *Roosevelt*, in winter quarters, we abandoned much of the routine of ship life afloat. The only regular bells were those at ten and twelve at night, the first a signal for all loud noises to cease, the latter a signal for lights to be turned out. The only watches were those of the regular day and night watchmen.

With the exception of a few cases of grip, the health of the party was good during the whole period of our life at winter quarters. Grip in the Arctic, coincident with epidemics in Europe and America, is rather an interesting phenomenon. My first experience with it was in 1892, following one of the peculiar Greenland storms, similar to those in the Alps — a storm which evidently swept over the entire width of Greenland from the southeast, raising the temperature from the minus thirties to plus forty-one in twenty-four hours. Following that atmospheric disturbance every member of my party, and even some of the Eskimos, had a pronounced attack of grip. It was our opinion that the germs were brought to us by this storm, which was more than a local disturbance.

Aside from rheumatism and bronchial troubles, the Eskimos are fairly healthy; but the adults are subject to a peculiar nervous affection which they call *piblokto* — a form of hysteria. I have never known a child to have *piblokto;* but some one among the adult Eskimos would have an attack every day or two, and one day there were five cases. The immediate cause of this affection is hard to trace, though sometimes it seems to be the result of a brooding over absent or dead relatives, or a fear of the future. The manifestations of this disorder are somewhat startling.

The patient, usually a woman, begins to scream and tear off and destroy her clothing. If on the ship, she will walk up and down the deck, screaming and gesticulating, and generally in a state of nudity, though the thermometer may be in the minus forties. As the intensity of the attack increases, she will sometimes leap over the rail upon the ice, running perhaps half a mile. The attack may last a few minutes, an hour, or even more, and some sufferers become so wild that they would continue running about on the ice perfectly naked until they froze to death, if they were not forcibly brought back.

When an Eskimo is attacked with *piblokto* indoors, nobody pays much attention, unless the sufferer should reach for a knife or attempt to injure some one. The attack usually ends in a fit of weeping, and when the patient quiets down, the eyes are bloodshot, the pulse high, and the whole body trembles for an hour or so afterward.

The well-known madness among the Eskimo dogs is also called *piblokto*. Though it does not seem to be infectious, its manifestations are similar to those of hydrophobia. Dogs suffering from *piblokto* are usually shot, but they are often eaten by the Eskimos.

The first winter moon came early in November, and on the 7th MacMillan started for Cape Columbia for a month of tidal observations, taking with him Jack Barnes, a sailor, Egingwah, and Inighito and their wives. Poodloonah, Ooblooah and Seegloo went as MacMillan's supporting party, to carry supplies, and

Wesharkoopsee and Keshungwah started for Cape
Richardson to bring back the musk-ox skins which had
been left there during the fall hunting trips.

The tidal observations by MacMillan at Cape
Columbia were made in connection with the tidal
observations which were constantly going on at Cape
Sheridan during the fall and winter, and with those
taken later at Cape Bryant on the other side of Robeson
Channel. These tidal observations of the expedition
of 1908–09 were the farthest north of all continuous
series ever recorded anywhere, though similar observations had been taken by the Lady Franklin Bay
Expedition at Fort Conger, about sixty miles southwest.

Marvin and Borup, during the November moon,
continued the tidal observations at Cape Sheridan.
The tidal igloo, which was built on the ice just inside
the tide crack, about one hundred and eighty yards
from the ship, was an ordinary Eskimo snow igloo and
was used as a protection to the men in taking the observations at the tide staff. This staff, about twelve feet
long, was driven into the bottom, and its length was
marked off in feet and inches. As the tide rose and
fell, the ice and the igloo moved with the water, but the
staff remained stationary, and by the position of
the ice upon the staff we measured the tides, varying
with the day, the moon and the season.

The tides along the north coast of Grant Land are
remarkable for the slightness of the rise and fall, which
varies from an average of 1.8 feet at Cape Sheridan to
.8 at Cape Columbia. As is well known to navigators,
the tides at Sandy Hook, New York, sometimes rise
twelve feet, while the tides in the Bay of Fundy are

often over fifty feet; in Hudson Strait they are about forty, and there are places on the coast of China where the extreme rise is even greater.

The two Eskimo women were sent to Cape Columbia with MacMillan's party because the Eskimo men like to have their families with them when they go on long trips. The women are useful in drying and mending the fur garments which are constantly going to pieces in the rough usage of the sledge trips. Some of them can drive a dog team as well as the men, and many of them are good shots. I have known them to shoot musk-oxen and even bears. They do not attempt the walrus, yet they can paddle a kayak as well as the men — to the limit of their strength.

The accomplishments of the Eskimo women are of the useful rather than the ornamental kind. The handling of the native lamp, for instance, requires great skill. If the lamp is well trimmed, it is as clear and smokeless as our own lamps; if it is neglected, it smokes and smells vilely. As the Eskimos are not highly romantic, a woman's skill in dressing skins and in making clothes largely determines the quality of husband she is likely to get. The Eskimo men have not a very critical eye for feminine beauty, but they are strong in appreciation of domestic accomplishments.

Even so early as November we began to be worried about the dogs. Many of them had died; they were nearly all in poor condition, and the food was none too abundant. It is always necessary to take up twice as many dogs as will be needed, in order to provide for probable accidents. On the 8th of November there were only one hundred and ninety-three out of the two hundred and forty-six with which we had left Etah in August. The whale meat brought for them seemed to be lacking in nutrition.

Four more that were in the worst condition were killed, to save the dog food, and on the 10th we had to kill five more. Then we tried the experiment of feeding them on pork, with the result that seven more died. I began to wonder whether we should have enough dogs left for the spring journey toward the Pole.

It is absolutely impossible to figure on the Eskimo dog's uncertain tenure of life. The creatures will endure the severest hardships; they will travel and draw heavy loads on practically nothing to eat; they will live for days exposed to the wildest arctic blizzard; and then, sometimes in good weather, after an ordinary meal of apparently the best food, they will lie down and die.

On the 25th of November we again overhauled and counted the dogs. There were now only one hundred and sixty left, and ten of these were in bad condition. But I discovered that day, on having the frozen walrus meat ripped up on the forecastle, that we had a greater supply than we had believed, and the discovery drove away the nightmare which had been haunting us. From now on the dogs could be fed a little more generous allowance of the best kind of food. For, after we had tried practically everything, including our bacon, it was found that walrus meat agreed with them better than anything else.

The importance of this matter must not be lost sight of for an instant. Dogs, and plenty of them, were vitally necessary to the success of the expedition. Had an epidemic deprived us of these animals, we might just as well have remained comfortably at home in the United States. All the money, brains and labor would have been utterly thrown away, so far as concerned the quest of the North Pole.

CHAPTER XIX

THE ROOSEVELT'S NARROW ESCAPE

IT is perfectly true that the building business is not
extensive in the arctic regions, but it is also a fact
that if you expect to travel extensively there you
must know how to build your own dwellings. If you
neglect to instruct yourself in this direction the chances
are that some time or other you will regret it.

Toward the end of the autumn field work, the use of
the canvas tents had been discontinued, and snow igloos
had been constructed along the line of march. These
were permanent, and were used by the various parties,
one after the other. The new members of the expedition were instructed in the art of igloo building by Marvin, Henson, and the Eskimos. No man should go into
the field in the North in winter unless he knows how to
build a shelter for himself against the cold and the
storm.

The size of the igloo depends usually upon the number of men in the party. If built for three men, it will
be about five by eight feet on the inside; if for five men,
it will be about eight by ten, in order to give greater
width to the sleeping platform.

Four good men can build one of these snow houses
in an hour. Each takes a saw knife from the up-standers of the sledge and sets to work cutting snow blocks.
The saw knives are about eighteen inches long and are

strong and stiff, with a cutting edge on one side and saw-teeth on the other. The blocks of snow are of different sizes, those for the bottom row being larger and heavier than those for the upper rows, and all are curved on the inner side, so that when set together they will form a circle. The thickness of the walls depends upon the hardness of the snow. If it is closely packed, the walls may be only a few inches thick; if the snow is soft, the blocks are thicker, that they may hold their shape. The blocks for the bottom layer are sometimes two or three feet long and two feet high; but sometimes they are much smaller, as there is no ironclad rule about it.

When sufficient blocks have been cut to make an igloo, an Eskimo takes his position on the spot (usually a sloping bank of snow) which is to be the center of the structure. Then the others bring the snow blocks and place them end to end, on edge, to form an egg-shaped ring about the man in the center, who deftly joints and fits them with his snow knife. The second row is placed on top of the first, but sloping slightly inward; and the following rows are carried up in a gradually ascending spiral, each successive layer leaning inward a little more, and each block held in place by the blocks on either side, until finally an aperture is left in the top to be filled with one block.

This block is then properly shaped by the man inside the igloo; he pushes it up endwise through the aperture, turns it over by reaching through the top, lowers it into place, and chips off with his knife until it fits the hole like the keystone of an arch, firmly keying the structure, whose general proportions are not unlike those of a beehive.

A hole just large enough for a man to crawl through is cut close to the bottom on one side, and any superfluous snow inside the igloo is thrown out through this hole. In the rear or larger end, the sloping floor is leveled off to form a bed platform, and in front of this the floor is dug down a foot or more for a standing space and a place for the cookers.

Then the sleeping gear and cooking outfit are passed into the igloo, and, after the dogs have been fed and tethered for the night, the members of the party enter, the opening at the bottom is closed by a large block of snow, the edges of which have been shaped and chipped by a saw knife to make a tight joint, and everything is ready for the night.

After the cookers are lighted, the igloo is soon comparatively warm, and in the arctic regions, when men are tired out from a long march, they generally fall asleep easily. Insomnia is not one of the arctic annoyances.

We never carry alarm clocks in the field to arouse us in the morning. The first man who has had his sleep out looks at his watch, and if it is time to be on the march again, he wakes the others. After breakfast we break camp and are out again.

I did not join the field parties during the winter moons this time, but remained on the ship, going over and perfecting the plans for the spring campaign — the sledge journey toward the Pole — and giving considerable study to the new type of Peary sledge, to the improvement of details of clothing, and to experimenting with the new alcohol stove which I had designed for the spring work — determining the most effective charge of alcohol, the most effective size of broken ice for melting, and so on. The question of weights is a most important factor in all sledge equipment, and it was necessary constantly to study to obtain the maximum effectiveness with the minimum weight and bulk. For relaxation, I devoted many hours to a new form of taxidermy.

About the middle of November I had a large snow igloo built on the top of the hatch on the main deck of the *Roosevelt*, which we called "the studio," and Borup and I began to experiment with flashlight pictures of the Eskimos. They had become accustomed to seeing counterfeit presentments of themselves on paper, and were very patient models. We also got some good moonlight pictures — time exposures varying from ten minutes to two or three hours.

On this last expedition I did not permit myself to dream about the future, to hope, or to fear. On the 1905–06 expedition I had done too much dreaming; this time I knew better. Too often in the past had I found myself face to face with impassable barriers. Whenever I caught myself building air castles, I would either attack some work requiring intense application of the mind, or would go to sleep — it was hard sometimes to fight back the dreams, especially in my solitary walks on the ice-foot under the arctic moon.

On the evening of November 11, there was a brilliant paraselene, two distinct halos and eight false moons being visible in the southern sky. This phenomenon is not unusual in the Arctic, and is caused by the frost crystals in the air. On this particular occasion the inner halo had a false moon at its zenith, another at

its nadir, and one each at the right and left.   Outside
was another halo, with four other moons.

Sometimes during the summer we see the parhelion,
a similar phenomenon of the sun. I have seen the
appearance of the false suns — or sun-dogs as the sailors
call them — so near that the lowest one would seem to
fall between me and a snow-bank twenty feet away, so
near that by moving my head backward and forward I
could shut it out or bring it into view. This was the
nearest I ever came to finding the pot of gold at the
foot of the rainbow.

On the night of November 12, the ice of the channel
pack, which for more than two months had seemed
unmindful of our intrusive presence, arose in wrath and
tried to hurl us upon the equally inhospitable shore.

All that evening the wind had been gradually
increasing in violence, and about half-past eleven the
ship began to complain, creaking, groaning and mutter-
ing to herself. I lay in my bunk and listened to the
wind in the humming rigging, while the moonlight,
shining through the porthole, filled the cabin with dim
shadows. Toward midnight, mingled with the noises
of the ship, another and more ominous sound became
audible — the grinding of the ice in the channel outside.

I threw on my clothes and went on deck. The tide
was running flood, and the ice was moving resistlessly
past the point of the cape. The nearer ice, between us
and the outer pack, was humming and groaning with
the steadily increasing pressure. By the light of the
moon we could see the pack as it began to break and
pile up just beyond the edge of the ice-foot outside us.
A few minutes later the whole mass broke with a rabid

roar into a tumbling chaos of ice blocks, some upheaving, some going under, and a big rafter, thirty feet high, formed at the edge of the ice-foot within twenty feet of the ship. The invading mass grew larger and larger and steadily advanced toward us. The grounded piece off our starboard beam was forced in and driven against the big ice block under our starboard quarter. The ship shook a little, but the ice block did not move.

With every pulse of the tide the pressure and the motion continued, and in less than an hour from the time I had come on deck, a great floe berg was jammed against the side of the *Roosevelt* from amidships to the stern. It looked for a minute as if the ship were going to be pushed bodily aground.

All hands were called, and every fire on board was extinguished. I had no fear of the ship being crushed by the ice, but she might be thrown on her side, when the coals, spilled from a stove, might start that horror of an arctic winter night, the "ship on fire." The Eskimos were thoroughly frightened and set up their weird howling. Several families began to gather their belongings, and in a few minutes women and children were going over the port rail onto the ice, and making for the box houses on the shore.

The list of the *Roosevelt* toward the port or shore side grew steadily greater with the increasing pressure from outside. With the turn of the tide about half-past one in the morning, the motion ceased, but the *Roosevelt* never regained an even keel until the following spring. The temperature that night was 25° below zero, but it did not seem so very cold.

Marvin's tidal igloo was split in two, but he continued his observations, which were of peculiar interest that night; and as soon as the ice had quieted down Eskimos were sent out to repair the igloo.

Strange to say, none of the Eskimos was attacked with *piblokto* because of their fright, and I learned that one of the women, Ahtetah, had remained quietly sewing in the Eskimo quarters during the whole disturbance. After this experience, however, some of the Eskimo families took up their winter residence in the box houses and in snow igloos ashore.

The winter winds of the Far North are almost unimaginable by any one who has never experienced them. Our winter at Cape Sheridan this last time was less severe than the winter of 1905–06, but we had several storms that reminded us of old times. The north and northwest winds sweeping down along the coast are the coldest; but for absolutely insane fury the winds from the south and the southwest, falling off the highland of the coast with almost the impact of a wall of water, are unsurpassed anywhere else in the arctic regions.

Sometimes these storms come on gradually, the wind from the northwest steadily increasing in force and swinging through the west to the southwest, gathering fury with every hour, until the snow is picked up bodily from the land and the ice-foot and carried in blinding, horizontal sheets across the ship. On deck it is impossible to stand or move, except in the shelter of the rail, and so blinding is the cataract of snow that the lamps, powerful as are their reflectors, are absolutely indistinguishable ten feet away.

When a party in the field is overtaken by a storm,

they have to stay in the snow igloo until the fury is over. If there is no igloo near them, they build one just as quickly as they can when they see the storm approaching, or, if there is not time for that, they have to make a dugout in a snow bank.

Thursday, the 26th of November, was proclaimed to be Thanksgiving Day in Grant Land. For dinner we had soup, macaroni and cheese, and mince pie made of musk-ox meat. During the December moon Captain Bartlett, with two Eskimos, two sledges, and twelve dogs, went out to scour the region between the ship and Lake Hazen for game. Henson, with similar equipment, went to Clements Markham Inlet. Borup, with seven Eskimos, seven sledges, and forty-two dogs, set out for Cape Colan and Cape Columbia. Dr. Goodsell started at the same time with three Eskimos, two sledges, and twelve dogs, to hunt in the region from Black Cliffs Bay to James Ross Bay. The parties were to use the regular arctic ration of tea, pemmican, and biscuit, unless they found game, in which case they were to use fresh meat for both men and dogs. In addition to the hunting, supplies for the spring sledge work were to be moved from one cache to another along the coast.

To give variety to the work, the men who remained with the ship during one moon went into the field the next. The ship's men, engineers and sailors, seldom went on hunting trips but remained with the ship, attending to their regular duties and sometimes helping with the work of equipment.

I had in my cabin a good arctic library — absolutely complete as regards the work of later years. This included Abruzzi's "On the *Polar Star* in the Arctic Sea," Nansen's "Farthest North," Nares' "Voyage to the Polar Sea," Markham's two volumes on arctic explorations, the narratives of Greely, Hall, Hayes, Kane, Inglefield — in fact, all the stories of the navigators of the Smith Sound region, as well as those who have attempted the Pole from other directions, such as the Austrian expedition under Payer and Weyprecht, Koldewey's East Greenland expedition, and so forth.

Then, in antarctic literature I had Captain Scott's two magnificent volumes, "The Voyage of the *Discovery*," Borchgrevink's "The *Southern Cross* Expedition to the Antarctic," Nordenskjöld's "Antarctica," the "Antarctica" of Balch, and Carl Fricker's "The Antarctic Regions," as well as Hugh Robert Mills' "Siege of the South Pole."

The members of the expedition used to borrow these books, one at a time, and I think that before the winter was over they all knew pretty well what had been done by other men in this field.

Every week or ten days throughout the winter we had to remove from our cabins the ice caused by the condensation of the moist air where it came in contact with the cold outer walls. Behind every article of furniture near the outer wall the ice would form, and we used to chop it out from under our bunks by the pailful.

The books were always placed far forward on the shelves, because if a book were pushed back it would freeze solid to the wall. Then, if a warmer day came, or a fire was built in the cabin, the ice would melt, the water would run down and the leaves of the book would mold.

The sailors amused themselves after the manner of sailors everywhere, playing dominoes, cards and checkers, boxing and telling stories. They used to play at feats of strength, such as finger-pulling, with the Eskimos. One of the men had an accordion, another a banjo, and as I sat working in my cabin I used often to hear them singing "Annie Rooney," "McGinty," "The Spanish Cavalier," and sometimes "Home, Sweet Home." Nobody seemed to be bored. Percy, who had special charge of the phonograph, often treated the men to a concert, and all through the winter I heard nobody complain of monotony or homesickness.

CHAPTER XX

CHRISTMAS ON THE ROOSEVELT

THE four December field parties returned to the ship one after the other. Captain Bartlett was the only one who had found any game, and he got only five hares. During this trip the captain had an experience which might have been decidedly uncomfortable for him, had it turned out a bit less fortunately. He was up in the Lake Hazen region with his Eskimos, and he had left them at the igloo while he looked around for game. He had just found some deer tracks when the moon went behind a bank of clouds and the night became suddenly black.

He waited an hour or two for the moon to come out that he might see where he was, and meanwhile the two Eskimos, thinking he was lost, broke camp and set out for the ship. As soon as there was light enough, he started off to the south of the igloo, and after a time overtook his companions. Had he gone even a little way to the north he would not have met them, and would have had to walk back alone to the ship, without supplies, a distance of seventy or eighty miles, with a storm brewing.

This party had bad weather nearly all the way home. The temperature was comparatively mild, only ten or fifteen degrees below zero, and the sky was overcast. The captain made the last march a long one, notwithstanding the darkness. Of course he could not always keep the trail. Sometimes he would be walking along over snow as level as a floor, then suddenly the level would drop ten or fifteen feet, and, walking right on in the dark, he would land on the back of his head with such force that he saw stars which do not appear in any scientific celestial map.

At one point in the journey they struck going so rough that it was impossible to push ahead and drive the dogs without light. They had no lantern, but Bartlett took a sugar tin, cut holes in the sides, and put a candle in it. With this makeshift beacon he was able to keep somewhere near the trail. But there was considerable wind, and he declared that he used enough matches in relighting the candle on that march to keep an Eskimo family cheerful throughout a whole winter.

The failure of these parties to obtain game was a serious matter. In order to save food I had still further to reduce the number of dogs. We overhauled them, and fourteen of the poorest — they would not have survived the winter — were killed and used as food for the others.

I am often asked how the wild herbivorous animals, like the musk-ox and the reindeer, survive the winter in that snow-covered land. By a strange paradox, the wild winds that rage in that country help them in their struggle for existence, for the wind sweeps the dried grasses and scattered creeping willows bare of snow over great stretches of land, and there the animals can graze.

December 22 marked the midnight of the "Great Night," the sun from that day starting on the return journey north. In the afternoon all the Eskimos were assembled on deck, and I went to them with my watch in my hand, telling them that the sun was now coming back. Marvin rang the ship's bell, Matt Henson fired three shots, and Borup set off some flashlight powder. Then the men, women, and children formed in line and marched into the after deck house by the port gangway, passing the galley, where each one received, in addition to the day's rations, a quart of coffee, with sugar and milk, ship's biscuit, and musk-ox meat; the women were also given candy and the men tobacco.

After the celebration, Pingahshoo, a boy of twelve or thirteen, who helped Percy in the galley, started confidently south over the hills to meet the sun. After a few hours he returned to the ship, quite crestfallen, and Percy had to explain to him that while the sun was really on its way back, it would not get to us for nearly three months more.

The next day after the winter solstice, our supply of water from the Cape Sheridan River having failed, Eskimos were sent out to reconnoiter the ponds of the neighborhood. The English expedition on the *Alert* had melted ice during their entire winter, and on the expedition of 1905–06 we had been obliged to melt ice for a month or two; but this year the Eskimos sounded the ponds, and about fifteen feet of water was found in one a mile inland from the *Roosevelt*. Over the hole in the ice they built a snow igloo with a light wooden trap-door, so as to keep the water in the hole from freezing too quickly. The water was brought to the ships in barrels on sledges drawn by the Eskimo dogs.

As Christmas fell in the dark of the moon, all the members of the expedition were on the ship, and we celebrated with a special dinner, field sports, raffles, prizes, and so on. It was not very cold that day, only minus 23°.

In the morning we greeted each other with the "Merry Christmas" of civilization. At breakfast we all had letters from home and Christmas presents, which had been kept to be opened on that morning. MacMillan was master of ceremonies and arranged the program of sports. At two o'clock there were races on the ice-foot. A seventy-five-yard course was laid out, and the ship's lanterns, about fifty of them, were arranged in two parallel rows, twenty feet apart. These lanterns are similar to a railway brakeman's lantern, only larger. It was a strange sight — that illuminated race-course within seven and a half degrees of the earth's end.

The first race was for Eskimo children, the second for Eskimo men, the third for Eskimo matrons with babies in their hoods, the fourth for unencumbered women. There were four entries for the matrons' race, and no one could have guessed from watching them that it was a running race. They came along four abreast, dressed in furs, their eyes rolling, puffing like four excited walruses, the babies in their hoods gazing with wide and half-bewildered eyes at the glittering lanterns. There was no question of cruelty to children, as the mothers were not moving fast enough to spill their babies. Then there were races for the ship's men and the members of the expedition, and a tug of war between the men aft and forward.

Nature herself participated in our Christmas celebrations by providing an aurora of considerable brilliancy. While the races on the ice-foot were in progress, the northern sky was filled with streamers and lances of pale white light. These phenomena of the northern sky are not, contrary to the common belief, especially frequent in these most northerly latitudes. It is always a pity to destroy a pleasant popular illusion; but I have seen auroras of a greater beauty in Maine than I have ever seen beyond the Arctic Circle.

Between the races and the dinner hour, which was at four o'clock, I gave a concert on the æolian in my cabin, choosing the merriest music in the rack. Then we separated to "dress for dinner." This ceremony consisted in putting on clean flannel shirts and neckties. The doctor was even so ambitious as to don a linen collar.

Percy, the steward, wore a chef's cap and a large white apron in honor of the occasion, and he laid the table with a fine linen cloth and our best silver. The wall of the mess room was decorated with the American flag. We had musk-ox meat, an English plum pudding, sponge cake covered with chocolate, and at each plate was a package containing nuts, cakes, and candies, with a card attached: "A Merry Christmas, from Mrs. Peary."

After dinner came the dice-throwing contests, and the wrestling and pulling contests in the forecastle. The celebration ended with a graphophone concert, given by Percy.

But perhaps the most interesting part of our day was the distribution of prizes to the winners in the various contests. In order to afford a study in Eskimo psychology, there was in each case a choice between prizes. Tookoomah, for instance, who won in the women's race, had a choice among three prizes: a box of three cakes of scented soap; a sewing outfit, containing a paper of needles, two or three thimbles, and several spools of different-sized thread; and a round cake covered with sugar and candy. The young woman did not hesitate. She had one eye, perhaps, on the sewing outfit, but both hands and the other eye were directed toward the soap. She knew what it was meant for. The meaning of cleanliness had dawned upon her — a sudden ambition to be attractive.

The last time that all the members of the expedition ate together was at the four o'clock dinner on December 29, for that evening Marvin, the captain, and their parties started for the Greenland coast; and when we met together at the ship after my return from the Pole there was one who was not with us — one who would never again be with us.

Ross Marvin was, next to Captain Bartlett, the most valuable man in the party. Whenever the captain was not in the field, Marvin took command of the work, and on him devolved the sometimes onerous, sometimes amusing labor of breaking in the new members. During the latter part of the former expedition in the *Roosevelt*, Marvin had grasped more fully than any other man the underlying, fundamental principles of the work.

He and I together had planned the details of the new method of advance and relay parties. This method, given a fixed surface over which to travel, could be mathematically demonstrated, and it has proved to be the most effective way to carry on an arctic sledge journey.

The party that started for the Greenland coast, across the ice of Robeson Channel, on the evening of December 29, consisted of Marvin, the captain, nine Eskimos, and fifty-four dogs. They were all to go south along the coast to Cape Union, then cross the channel to Cape Brevoort, Marvin, with his men and supporting parties, going north to Cape Bryant for a month of tidal observations, the captain and his men going south along the ice of Newman Bay and on to the Polaris Promontory to hunt.

The following day, Dr. Goodsell and Borup, each with his party of Eskimos and dogs, started by way of Cape Belknap, the doctor to hunt in Clements Markham Inlet, Borup to hunt in the region of the first glacier north of Lake Hazen. No such extensive field work had ever before been attempted by any arctic expedition, the radius of territory covered being about ninety miles in all directions from our winter quarters.

While distributing material for the spring sewing among the Eskimo women in the forward deck house and in the box houses and snow igloos on shore, I learned that some of the Eskimo men felt somewhat shaky about going north again on the ice of the polar sea. They had not forgotten the narrow escape we had had in recrossing the "big lead" on the return journey from the "farthest north" of 1906. Though I felt confident of my ability to handle them when the time came, still, I realized that we might have trouble with them yet. But I would not permit myself to worry about the outcome.

The first of the January hunting parties, Dr. Goodsell's, came in on the 11th. They had had no luck, though they had seen fresh tracks of musk-oxen. Borup came in the next morning with eighty-three hares, and an interesting story. They were right up against the glacier when they came across a whole colony of the little white arctic animals. He said there must have been nearly a hundred of them. The arctic hares are not wild; they will come so near to the hunter that he can almost grasp them with his hand. They have not learned the fear of man, because in their wilds man is practically unknown. Borup and the Eskimos surrounded the hares, until finally they got so near to them that instead of using any more ammunition they knocked the creatures over the heads with the butts of their rifles.

One day, during this hunting trip, Borup and his Eskimos became confused and were unable to find their igloo for twenty-four hours. The saw-knives, essential in constructing a snow igloo, had been left behind, and none of the men had even an ordinary knife which might have been used as a substitute. There was a gale of wind, the moon was obscured, the air was full of whirling snow, and it was very cold. They spent most of the time walking to and fro to keep warm. At last, when they were exhausted, they turned the sledges on their sides, the Eskimos worked out with their feet snow blocks which reinforced the shelter, and they were able to snatch a little sleep. When the weather cleared, they found themselves half a mile from their igloo.

The day following Borup's return, the captain came

in with his men and Marvin's supporting party of four. We were just beginning to be worried about them, as the ice of Robeson Channel in the dark of winter is not the safest road for a sledge party. The captain reported that they had been only six hours in crossing the channel; but, though he had reconnoitered the whole plain of the Polaris Promontory, he had seen no musk-oxen.

By the end of January we could see a faint redness in the south at noon, and the twilight was increasing. The last moon of the winter was now circling in the sky, and I wrote in my diary: "Thank Heaven, no more moons!" No matter how many dark winters a man may have gone through in the Arctic, the longing for the sun does not grow less intense.

In the February moon Bartlett went to Cape Hecla, Goodsell moved more supplies from Hecla to Cape Colan, and Borup went to Markham Inlet on another hunting trip. Before leaving, the doctor completed a record of the approximate mean temperatures for the season, which showed that every month except October had been colder than three years before. For December the mean was eight degrees lower.

Marvin was still at Cape Bryant, but the last of the February parties came in on the 9th, and from that time on we were all busy preparing for the great and last journey. On Sunday night, February 14, I had a brief talk with the Eskimo men, telling them what we proposed to do, what was expected of them, and what each man who went to the farthest point with me would get when he returned: boat, tent, Winchester repeater, shotgun, ammunition, box of tobacco, pipes, cartridges, numerous knives, hatchets, et cetera.

Their fears of the "big lead" took flight at the prospect of what to them was untold riches; and when it came to the point of making up my sledge parties, only one Eskimo, Panikpah, would admit any fears. They had seen me return so many times that they were ready to take their chances with me this one time more.

Bartlett left the ship on Monday, February 15, with instructions to go straight through to Cape Columbia, then put in two or three days hunting for musk-oxen in the neighborhood. The three divisions following Bartlett had instructions to go to Cape Columbia with their loads; then return to Cape Colan, where there was a cache, and take full loads from there to Cape Columbia. Goodsell's division started on Tuesday, on Wednesday it was stormy, and MacMillan and Henson got away on Thursday. They were all to meet me at Cape Columbia on the last day of February.

Marvin and his party had come in from Cape Bryant about six o'clock on Wednesday night. They were all well. Borup's division left the ship on Friday, Marvin's division got away on Sunday, the 21st, and I was left alone on the ship for one day.

That last day was one of perfect quiet and rest, free from interruption. The morning I devoted to going over carefully the details of the work already done, to see that no slenderest necessary thread had been overlooked, and to considering again, point by point, the details of the coming journey.

When I had satisfied myself (as I had not been able to do during the bustle and constant interruptions of the last two weeks) that everything was in its place and every possible contingency provided for, I had a few hours in which to look the situation squarely in the face, and to think of those other times, when, as now, I was on the eve of departure into the void and unknown North.

When at last I turned in for a few hours' sleep before the morning start, it was with the consciousness that so far as my knowledge and ability went, everything had been done, and that every member of the party, as well as myself, would put into his efforts all there was in him of will and sinew and vitality. This being settled, the outcome rested with the elements — the vagaries of the arctic pack, and the quality and amount of our own physical and mental stamina.

This was my final chance to realize the one dream of my life. The morning start would be the drawing of the string to launch the last arrow in my quiver.

CRANE CITY, CAPE COLUMBIA, AT THE TIME OF DEPARTURE
March 1st. 1909

FACE OF THE LAND ICE, "GLACIAL FRINGE," OFF CAPE COLUMBIA

PINNACLE NEAR THE SHORE

CHAPTER XXI

ARCTIC ICE SLEDGING AS IT REALLY IS

PERHAPS it will assist the reader to form a more vivid picture of the sort of work that now lay before the expedition and which the expedition eventually performed, if an effort is made to make him understand exactly what it means to travel nearly a thousand miles with dog sledges over the ice of the polar pack. In that belief, I shall at this point endeavor to describe as briefly as is consistent with clearness the conditions that confronted us and the means and methods by which those conditions were met.

Between the winter quarters of the *Roosevelt* at Cape Sheridan, and Cape Columbia, the most northerly point on the north coast of Grant Land, which I had chosen as the point of departure for the ice journey, lay ninety miles in a northwesterly direction along the ice-foot and across the land, which we must traverse before plunging onto the trackless ice fields of the Arctic Ocean.

From Cape Columbia we were to go straight north over the ice of the Polar Sea, — four hundred and thirteen geographical miles. Many persons whose memories go back to the smooth skating ponds of their childhood, picture the Arctic Ocean as a gigantic skating pond with a level floor over which the dogs drag us merrily — we sitting comfortably upon the sledges with hot bricks to keep our toes and fingers warm. Such ideas are distinctly different from the truth, as will appear.

There is no land between Cape Columbia and the North Pole and no smooth and very little level ice.

For a few miles only after leaving the land we had level going, as for those few miles we were on the "glacial fringe." This fringe, which fills all the bays and extends across the whole width of North Grant Land, is really an exaggerated ice-foot; in some places it is miles in width. While the outer edge in places is afloat and rises and falls with the movement of the tides, it never moves as a body, except where great fields of ice break off from it and float away upon the waters of the Arctic Ocean.

Beyond the glacial fringe is the indescribable surface of the shore lead, or tidal crack — that zone of unceasing conflict between the heavy floating ice and the stationary glacial fringe. This shore lead is constantly opening and shutting; opening when there are offshore winds, or spring ebb-tides, crushing shut when there are northerly winds or spring flood-tides. Here the ice is smashed into fragments of all sizes and piled up into great pressure ridges parallel with the shore.

The ice is smashed into these pressure ridges by the sheer and unimaginable force with which the floes are driven against the edge of the glacial fringe, just as farther out the pressure ridges are caused by the force with which the great floes themselves are crushed and smashed together by the force of the wind and the tides.

These pressure ridges may be anywhere from a few feet to a few rods in height; they may be anywhere from a few rods to a quarter of a mile in width; the individual masses of ice of which they are composed may vary, respectively, from the size of a billiard ball to the size of a small house.

Going over these pressure ridges one must pick his trail as best he can, often hacking his way with pick-axes, encouraging the dogs by whip and voice to follow the leader, lifting the five-hundred-pound loaded sledges over hummocks and up acclivities whose difficulties sometimes seem likely to tear the muscles from one's shoulder-blades.

Between the pressure ridges are the old floes, more or less level.   These floes, contrary to wide-spread and erroneous ideas, are not formed by direct freezing of the water of the Arctic Ocean.   They are made up of great sheets of ice broken off from the glacial fringe of Grant Land and Greenland, and regions to the westward, which have drifted out into the polar sea.   These fields of ice are anywhere from less than twenty to more than one hundred feet in thickness, and they are of all shapes and sizes.   As a result of the constant movement of the ice during the brief summer, when great fields are detached from the glaciers and are driven hither and thither under the impulse of the wind and the tides — impinging against one another, splitting in two from the violence of contact with other large fields, crushing up the thinner ice between them, having their edges shattered and piled up into pressure ridges — the surface of the polar sea during the winter may be one of almost unimaginable unevenness and roughness.

At least nine-tenths of the surface of the polar sea between Cape Columbia and the Pole is made up of these floes. The other one-tenth, the ice between the floes, is formed by the direct freezing of the sea water each autumn and winter. This ice never exceeds eight or ten feet in thickness.

The weather conditions of the fall determine to a great extent the character of the ice surface of the polar sea during the following winter. If there have been continuous shoreward winds at the time when the increasing cold was gradually cementing the ice masses together, then the heavier ice will have been forced toward the shore; and the edges of the ice-fields farther out, where they come in contact, will have piled up into a series of pressure ridges, one beyond the other, which any one traveling northward from the land must go over, as one would go over a series of hills.

If, on the other hand, there has been little wind in the fall, when the surface of the polar sea was becoming cemented and frozen over, many of these great floes will have been separated from other floes of a like size and character, and there may be stretches of comparatively smooth, young, or new, ice between them. If, after the winter has set in, there should still be violent winds, much of this thinner ice may be crushed up by the movement of the heavier floes; but if the winter remains calm, this smoother ice may continue until the general breaking up in the following summer.

But the pressure ridges above described are not the worst feature of the arctic ice. Far more troublesome and dangerous are the "leads" (the whalers' term for lanes of open water), which are caused by the movement of the ice under the pressure of the wind and tides. These are the ever-present nightmare of the traveler over the frozen surface of the polar ocean — on the upward journey for fear that they may prevent further advance; on the return journey for fear they may cut him off from the land and life, leaving him to wander about and starve to death on the northern side. Their occurrence or non-occurrence is a thing impossible to prophesy or calculate. They open without warning immediately ahead of the traveler, following no apparent rule or law of action. They are the unknown quantity of the polar equation.

Sometimes these leads are mere cracks running through old floes in nearly a straight line. Sometimes they are zigzag lanes of water just wide enough to be impossible to cross. Sometimes they are rivers of open water from half a mile to two miles in width, stretching east and west farther than the eye can see.

There are various ways of crossing the leads. One can go to the right or the left, with the idea of finding some place where the opposite edges of the ice are near enough together so that our long sledges can be bridged across. Or, if there are indications that the lead is closing, the traveler can wait until the ice comes quite together. If it is very cold, one may wait until the ice has formed thick enough to bear the loaded sledges going at full speed. Or, one may search for a cake of ice, or hack out a cake with pickaxes, which can be used as a ferry-boat on which to transport the sledges and teams across.

But all these means go for naught when the "big lead," which marks the edge of the continental shelf where it dips down into the Arctic Ocean, is in one of its tantrums, opening just wide enough to keep a continual zone of open water or impracticable young ice in the center, as occurred on our upward journey of 1906 and the never-to-be-forgotten return journey of that expedition, when this lead nearly cut us off forever from life itself.

A lead might have opened right through our camp, or through one of the snow igloos, when we were sleeping on the surface of the polar sea. Only — it didn't.

Should the ice open across the bed platform of an igloo, and precipitate its inhabitants into the icy water below, they would not readily drown, because of the buoyancy of the air inside their fur clothing. A man dropping into the water in this way might be able to scramble onto the ice and save himself; but with the thermometer at 50° below zero it would not be a pleasant contingency.

This is the reason why I have never used a sleeping-bag when out on the polar ice. I prefer to have my legs and arms free, and to be ready for any emergency at a moment's notice. I never go to sleep when out on the sea ice without my mittens on, and if I pull my arms inside my sleeves I pull my mittens in too, so as to be ready for instant action. What chance would a man in a sleeping-bag have, should he suddenly wake to find himself in the water?

The difficulties and hardships of a journey to the North Pole are too complex to be summed up in a paragraph. But, briefly stated, the worst of them are: the ragged and mountainous ice over which the traveler must journey with his heavily loaded sledges; the often terrific wind, having the impact of a wall of water, which he must march against at times; the open leads already described, which he must cross and recross, somehow; the intense cold, sometimes as low as 60° below zero, through which he must — by fur clothing and constant activity — keep his flesh from freezing; the difficulty of dragging out and back over the ragged and "lead" interrupted trail enough pemmican, biscuit, tea, condensed milk, and liquid fuel to keep sufficient strength in his body for traveling. It was so cold much of the time on this last journey that the brandy was frozen solid, the petroleum was white and viscid, and the dogs could hardly be seen for the steam of their breath. The minor discomfort of building every night our narrow and uncomfortable snow houses, and the cold bed platform of that igloo on which we must snatch such hours of rest as the exigencies of our desperate enterprise permitted us, seem hardly worth mentioning in comparison with the difficulties of the main proposition itself.

At times one may be obliged to march all day long facing a blinding snowstorm with the bitter wind searching every opening in the clothing. Those among my readers who have ever been obliged to walk for even an hour against a blizzard, with the temperature ten or twenty degrees *above* zero, probably have keen memories of the experience. Probably they also remember how welcome was the warm fireside of home at the end of their journey. But let them imagine tramping through such a storm all day long, over jagged and uneven ice, with the temperature between fifteen and thirty degrees *below* zero, and no shelter to look forward to at the end of the day's march excepting a narrow and cold snow house which they would themselves be obliged to build in that very storm before they could eat or rest.

I am often asked if we were hungry on that journey. I hardly know whether we were hungry or not. Morning and night we had pemmican, biscuit and tea, and the pioneer or leading party had tea and lunch in the middle of the day's march. Had we eaten more, our food supply would have fallen short. I myself dropped twenty-five pounds of flesh between my departure from the ship and my return to it.

But fortitude and endurance alone are not enough in themselves to carry a man to the North Pole. Only with years of experience in traveling in those regions, only with the aid of a large party, also experienced in that character of work, only with the knowledge of arctic detail and the equipment necessary to prepare himself and his party for any and every emergency, is it possible for a man to reach that long sought goal and return.

CHAPTER XXII

ESSENTIALS THAT BROUGHT SUCCESS

SOMETHING has already been said regarding the fact that our journey to the North Pole was no haphazard, hit or miss "dash." It was not really a "dash" at all. Perhaps it may properly be described as a "drive" — in the sense that when the sledge journey got under way we pressed forward with a speed at times almost breathless. But nothing was done impulsively. Everything was done in accordance with a scheme long contemplated and plotted out in advance with every possible care.

The source of our success was a carefully planned system, mathematically demonstrated. Everything that could be controlled was controlled, and the indeterminate factors of storms, open leads and accidents to men, dogs and sledges, were taken into consideration in the percentage of probabilities and provided for as far as possible. Sledges would break and dogs would fall by the way, of course; but we could generally make one sledge out of two broken ones, and the gradual depletion of the dogs was involved in my calculations.

The so-called "Peary system" is too complex to be covered in a paragraph, and involves too many technical details to be outlined fully in any popular narrative. But the main points of it are about as follows:

To drive a ship through the ice to the farthest possible northern land base from which she can be driven back again the following year.

To do enough hunting during the fall and winter to keep the party healthily supplied with fresh meat.

To have dogs enough to allow for the loss of sixty per cent. of them by death or otherwise.

To have the confidence of a large number of Eskimos, earned by square dealing and generous gifts in the past, so that they will follow the leader to any point he may specify.

To have an intelligent and willing body of civilized assistants to lead the various divisions of Eskimos — men whose authority the Eskimos will accept when delegated by the leader.

To transport beforehand to the point where the expedition leaves the land for the sledge journey, sufficient food, fuel, clothing, stoves (oil or alcohol) and other mechanical equipment to get the main party to the Pole and back and the various divisions to their farthest north and back.

To have an ample supply of the best kind of sledges.

To have a sufficient number of divisions, or relay parties, each under the leadership of a competent assistant, to send back at appropriate and carefully calculated stages along the upward journey.

To have every item of equipment of the quality best suited to the purpose, thoroughly tested, and of the lightest possible weight.

To know, by long experience, the best way to cross wide leads of open water.

To return by the same route followed on the upward march, using the beaten trail and the already con-structed igloos to save the time and strength that would have been expended in constructing new igloos and in trail-breaking.

To know exactly to what extent each man and dog may be worked without injury.

To know the physical and mental capabilities of every assistant and Eskimo.

Last, but not least, to have the absolute confidence of every member of the party, white, black, or brown, so that every order of the leader will be implicitly obeyed.

Bartlett's division was to pioneer the road, and keep one day ahead of the main party. It was my plan at this time to keep the pioneer party close to the main party, and thus prevent the possibility of its being cut off from the main party by a rapidly forming lead, with insufficient supplies either for a further advance or for regaining the main division. Bartlett's pioneer division comprised himself and three Eskimos, Pooadloonah, "Harrigan," and Ooqueah, with one sledge and team of dogs, carrying their own gear and five days' supplies for the division.

Borup's division comprised himself and three Eski-mos, Keshungwah, Seegloo, and Karko, with four sledges and dog teams carrying nearly the standard loads. His division was to act as an advance supporting party, and was to accompany Bartlett for three marches and then return to Cape Columbia in one march with empty sledges. He was to deposit his loads and one sledge at the place where he left Bartlett, making a cache on the line of march; then hurry back to Columbia, re-load, and overtake the main party, which would leave the land one day after himself and Bartlett.

By this arrangement, if there were no delays, the main party would begin its third march at the same time when Borup started back; the evening of the third day would find the main party at Borup's cache, and Borup at Cape Columbia; the next morning, when the main party began its fourth march, Borup would be leaving Cape Columbia three marches behind, which difference, with a well-traveled trail to follow, he could probably eliminate in three marches.

It chanced that this sending back of Borup for additional loads to overtake the main party, with the later complications which grew out of it, through the opening of leads between him and the main party, was a link in the chain of delays which might have caused serious trouble, as will be hereafter explained.

In order that the reader may understand this journey over the ice of the polar sea, it is necessary that the theory and practise of both pioneer and supporting parties should be fully understood. Without this system, as has been amply demonstrated by the experience of previous expeditions, it would be a physical impossibility for any man to reach the North Pole, and return. The use of relay parties in arctic work is, of course, not new, though the idea was carried further in the last expedition of the Peary Arctic Club than ever before; but the pioneer party is original with my expeditions and for that reason it is perhaps worth while to describe it in detail.

The pioneer party was one unit division, made up of four of the most active and experienced men of the expedition, with sledges lightly loaded with five or six days' provisions, drawn by the best dog teams of the entire pack. When we started from Cape Columbia, this pioneer party, headed by Bartlett, went out twenty-four hours in advance of the main party. Later on, when we reached the time of continuous daylight and sunlight through the twenty-four hours, the pioneer party was but twelve hours in advance of the main party.

The duty of this pioneer party was to make a march in every twenty-four hours in spite of every obstacle — excepting, of course, some impassable lead. Whether there was a snowstorm or violent winds to be faced, or mountainous pressure ridges were to be climbed over, the march of the pioneer party must be made; for past experience had proved that whatever distance was covered by the advance party with its light sledges could be covered in less time by the main party even with heavily loaded sledges, because the main party, having the trail to follow, was not obliged to waste time in reconnoitering. In other words, the pioneer party, was the pace-maker of the expedition, and whatever distance it made was the measure of accomplishment for the main party. The leader of the pioneer party, in the first instance Bartlett, would start out ahead of his division, usually on snowshoes; then the light sledges of the party would follow him. Thus the leader of the pioneer division was pioneering ahead of his own party, and that whole division was pioneering ahead of the main party.

It is necessary that the arduous work of trail-breaking for the first two-thirds of the distance over the rougher ice nearer the land should be done by one division after another, in succession, in order to save the strength of the main party for their final drive. One great advantage which I had on this expedition was that, owing to the size of my party, whenever the men in this pioneer division became exhausted with their arduous labor and lack of sleep, I could withdraw them into the main party, and send out another division to take their place.

Supporting parties are essential to success because, a single party, comprising either a small or a large number of men and dogs, could not possibly drag (in gradually lessening quantities) all the way to the Pole and back (some nine hundred odd miles) as much food and liquid fuel as the men and dogs of that party would consume during the journey. It will be readily understood that when a large party of men and dogs starts out over the trackless ice to the polar sea, where there is no possibility of obtaining a single ounce of food on the way, after several days' marching, the provisions of one or more sledges will have been consumed by the men and dogs. When this occurs, the drivers and dogs with those sledges should be sent back to the land at once. *They are superfluous mouths which cannot be fed from the precious supply of provisions which are being dragged forward on the sledges.*

Still further on, the food on one or two more sledges will have been consumed. These sledges also, with their dogs and drivers, must be sent back, in order to ensure the furthest possible advance by the main party. Later on, still other divisions must be sent back for the same reason.

But my supporting parties had another duty to perform, only a little less important than the one already noted; that was to keep the trail open for the rapid return of the main party.

The magnitude of this duty is clear. The ice of the polar sea is not an immovable surface. Twenty-four hours — or even twelve hours — of strong wind, even in the depth of the coldest winter, will set the big floes grinding and twisting among themselves, crushing up into pressure ridges in one place, breaking into leads in another place.

Under normal conditions, however, this movement of the ice is not very great in a period of eight or ten days, so that a party starting back over an outward trail at the end of several days is able to knit together all faults and breaks in the trail that have occurred during that period by reason of the movement of the ice.

The second supporting party, starting back several days later from a point still farther on, knits together the broken ends of the trail of its own division; and when it comes upon the trail of the first supporting party, reunites such other breaks as have occurred since the first supporting party went over it on its way back to land. So with the third and fourth supporting parties.

When I speak of knitting together breaks in the trail, I mean simply that the passage of the supporting party from that point where the trail was broken by the movement of the ice to the point where the trail went on again, some distance either to the east or west, would itself renew the broken trail, the passage of the men and dog teams packing down the ice and snow.

So that when the main party came back it would simply follow the track of the supporting party, and not have to scout for the trail.

As a result of this method of keeping the return trail continuously open, when the main party starts to return it has a continuous trail back to the land, which it can follow with from fifty to one hundred per cent. greater speed than it was possible to make on the outward journey. The reasons for this are obvious: no time is wasted in selecting and breaking a trail; the dogs are more energetic when following a beaten track and when on the road home; no time is wasted in making camp, the snow igloos built on the outward journey being reoccupied on the return journey.

It must be understood that when each supporting party reached the land again, its work in regard to the polar dash was over. It did not come back onto the ice with any further supplies for the main party.

At the very end, when the supporting parties have performed their important work of trail-breaking and transportation of supplies, the main party for the final journey *must* be small and carefully selected, as the small party resulting from the successive selection of the fittest, can travel much faster than a large one.

Each division of four men was absolutely independent and had its complete traveling outfit; in fact, except for the alcohol stove and cooking utensils, each sledge was complete in itself. On each sledge were the provisions for men and dogs, and clothing for the driver. The standard sledge load would support the driver and the dog team for about fifty days, and by sacrificing a few dogs and using them as food for the other dogs and

TYPICAL TRAIL IN SOFT SNOW (LOOKING BACKWARD)

TYPICAL VIEW OF THE ICE OF THE ARCTIC OCEAN, NORTH OF GRANT
LAND

TYPICAL CAMP ON THE ICE

the men, this time could have been extended to sixty days. Had any sledge and its provisions been cut off from the rest of the division, the man with it would have had everything he needed, except the cooking outfit. Had the sledge which carried the alcohol stove been lost, either in a lead or otherwise, the party to which it belonged would have had to double up with one of the other divisions.

The new alcohol stove, the design of which I had perfected during the winter, was used altogether on this northern sledge trip. We did not carry oil-stoves at all, except some very small ones with two-inch wicks, which we used for drying mittens.

The standard method for loading each sledge was as follows: On the bottom was a layer of dog pemmican in red tins, covering the entire length and width of the sledge; on this were two tins of biscuit, and crew pemmican in blue tins; then the tins of alcohol and condensed milk, a small skin rug for the man to sleep on at night in the igloo, snowshoes and spare footgear, a pickax and a saw knife for cutting snow blocks. Practically the only extra items of wearing apparel which were carried were a few pairs of Eskimo sealskin *kamiks* (boots), for it can readily be imagined that several hundred miles of such walking and stumbling over snow and ice would be rather hard on any kind of footgear which could be made.

Compactness was the main idea in packing one of these sledges, the center of gravity of the load being brought as low as possible in order that the sledges might not easily overturn.

The standard daily ration for work on the final

sledge journey toward the Pole on all expeditions has been as follows:

1 lb. pemmican, 1 lb. ship's biscuit, 4 oz. condensed milk, ½ oz. compressed tea, 6 oz. liquid fuel, alcohol or petroleum. A total of 2 lbs. 4½ oz. of solids per man, per day.

On this ration a man can work hard and keep in good condition in the lowest temperatures for a very long time. I believe that no other item of food, either for heat or muscle building, is needed.

The daily ration for the dogs is one pound of pemmican per day; but so hardy are these descendants of the arctic wolves that when there is a scarcity of food they can work for a long time on very little to eat. I have, however, always endeavored so to proportion provisions to the length of time in the field, that the dogs should be at least as well fed as myself.

A part of the scientific work of the expedition was a series of deep-sea soundings from Cape Columbia to the Pole. The sounding apparatus of the expedition on leaving Cape Columbia comprised two wooden reels of a length equal to the width of the sledge, a detachable wooden crank to go on each end of the reel, to each reel a thousand fathoms (six thousand feet) of specially made steel piano wire of a diameter .028 inches, and one fourteen-pound lead having at its lower end a small bronze clam-shell device, self-tripping when it reached the bottom, for the purpose of bringing up samples of the ocean bed. The weights of this outfit were as follows: each thousand fathoms of wire 12.42 pounds, each wooden reel 18 pounds, each lead 14 pounds. A complete thousand-fathom outfit weighed 44.42 pounds.

The two outfits, therefore, weighed 89 pounds, and a third extra lead brought this total up to 103 pounds.

Both the sounding leads and the wire were made especially for the expedition, and so far as I know they were the lightest, for their capacity, that have ever been used.

One sounding apparatus was carried by the main division and the other by the pioneer party, in the early stages of our progress. When there was a lead we sounded from the edge of it; when there was no open water we made a hole in the ice if we could find any that was thin enough for the purpose.

Two men could readily make these deep-sea soundings by reason of the lightness of the equipment.

The distance which we traveled day by day was at first determined by dead reckoning, to be verified later by observations for latitude. Dead reckoning was simply the compass course for direction, and for distance the mean estimate of Bartlett, Marvin, and myself as to the length of the day's march. On board ship dead reckoning is the compass course for direction and the reading of the log for distance. On the inland ice of Greenland my dead reckoning was the compass course, and the reading of my odometer, a wheel with a cyclometer registering apparatus. This could not possibly be used on the ice of the polar sea, as it would be smashed to pieces in the rough going. One might say in general that dead reckoning on the polar ice is the personal estimate of approximate distance, always checked and corrected from time to time by astronomical observations.

Three members of the expedition had had sufficient

experience in traveling over arctic ice to enable them to estimate a day's journey very closely. These three were Bartlett, Marvin, and myself. When we checked up our dead reckoning by astronomical observations, the mean of our three estimates was found to be a satisfactory approximation to the results of the observations.

It goes without saying that mere dead reckoning, entirely unchecked by astronomical observations, would be insufficient for scientific purposes. During the earlier stages of our journey there was no sun by which to take observations. Later, when we had sunlight, we took what observations were necessary to check our dead reckonings — but no more, since I did not wish to waste the energies or strain the eyes of Marvin, Bartlett, or myself.

As a matter of fact observations were taken every five marches, as soon as it was possible to take them at all.

CHAPTER XXIII

OFF ACROSS THE FROZEN SEA AT LAST

THE work of the expedition, to which all the former months of detail were merely preliminary, began with Bartlett's departure from the *Roosevelt* on the 15th of February for the final sledge journey toward the Pole. The preceding summer we had driven the ship through the almost solid ice of the channels lying between Etah and Cape Sheridan; we had hunted through the long twilight of the autumn to supply ourselves with meat; we had lived through the black and melancholy months-long arctic night, sustaining our spirits with the hope of final success when the returning light should enable us to attack the problem of our passage across the ice of the polar sea. Now these things were all behind us, and the final work was to begin.

It was ten o'clock on the morning of February 22d— Washington's Birthday — when I finally got away from the ship and started on the journey toward the Pole. This was one day earlier than I had left the ship three years before on the same errand. I had with me two of the younger Eskimos, Arco and Kudlooktoo, two sledges and sixteen dogs. The weather was thick, the air was filled with a light snow, and the temperature was 31° below zero.

There was now light enough to travel by at ten

o'clock in the morning. When Bartlett had left the ship a week before, it was still so dark that he had been obliged to use a lantern in order to follow the trail northward along the ice-foot.

When I finally got away from the ship, there were in the field, for the northern work, seven members of the expedition, nineteen Eskimos, one hundred and forty dogs, and twenty-eight sledges. As already stated, the six advance divisions were to meet me at Cape Columbia on the last day of February. These parties, as well as my own, had all followed the regular trail to Cape Columbia, which had been kept open during the fall and winter by the hunting parties and supply-trains. This trail followed the ice-foot along the coast the greater part of the way, only taking to the land occasionally to cut across a peninsula and thus shorten the road.

On the last day of February Bartlett and Borup got away to the North with their divisions, as soon as it was light enough to travel. The weather still remained clear, calm, and cold. After the pioneer division had started north, all the remaining sledges were lined up, and I examined them to see that each had the standard load and full equipment. On leaving the *Roosevelt* I had in the field exactly enough dogs to put twenty teams of seven dogs each on the ice, and had counted on doing this; but while we were at Cape Columbia the throat distemper broke out in one team, and six dogs died. This left me only enough for nineteen teams.

My plans were further disarranged by the disabling of two Eskimos. I had counted on having a pickax brigade, composed of Marvin, MacMillan, and Dr.

Goodsell, ahead of the main party, improving the road, but found that two Eskimos would be unfit to go on the ice — one having a frosted heel, and the other a swollen knee. This depletion in the ranks of sledge drivers meant that Marvin and MacMillan would each have to drive a dog team, and that the pickax squad would be reduced to one man — Dr. Goodsell. As it turned out, this did not make much difference. The going was not so rough in the beginning as I had anticipated, and most of the pickax work that was required could be done by the drivers of the sledges as they reached the difficult places.

When I awoke before light on the morning of March 1st, the wind was whistling about the igloo. This phenomenon, appearing on the very day of our start, after so many days of calm, seemed the perversity of hard luck. I looked through the peep-hole of the igloo and saw that the weather was still clear, and that the stars were scintillating like diamonds. The wind was from the east — a direction from which I had never known it to blow in all my years of experience in that region. This unusual circumstance, a really remarkable thing, was of course attributed by my Eskimos to the interference of their arch enemy, Tornarsuk — in plain English, the devil — with my plans.

After breakfast, with the first glimmer of daylight, we got outside the igloo and looked about. The wind was whistling wildly around the eastern end of Independence Bluff; and the ice-fields to the north, as well as all the lower part of the land, were invisible in that gray haze which, every experienced arctic traveler knows, means vicious wind. A party less perfectly clothed than we were would have found conditions very trying that morning. Some parties would have considered the weather impossible for traveling, and would have gone back to their igloos.

But, taught by the experience of three years before, I had given the members of my party instructions to wear their old winter clothing from the ship to Cape Columbia and while there, and to put on the new outfit made for the sledge journey when leaving Columbia. Therefore we were all in our new and perfectly dry fur clothes and could bid defiance to the wind.

One by one the divisions drew out from the main army of sledges and dog teams, took up Bartlett's trail over the ice and disappeared to the northward in the wind haze. This departure of the procession was a noiseless one, for the freezing east wind carried all sounds away. It was also invisible after the first few moments — men and dogs being swallowed up almost immediately in the wind haze and the drifting snow.

I finally brought up the rear with my own division, after getting things into some semblance of order, and giving the two disabled men left at Cape Columbia their final instructions to remain quietly in the igloo there, using certain supplies which were left with them until the first supporting party returned to Cape Columbia, when they were to go back with it to the ship.

An hour after I left camp my division had crossed the glacial fringe, and the last man, sledge, and dog of the Northern party — comprising altogether twenty-four men, nineteen sledges, and one hundred and thirty-three dogs — was at last on the ice of the Arctic Ocean, about latitude 83°.

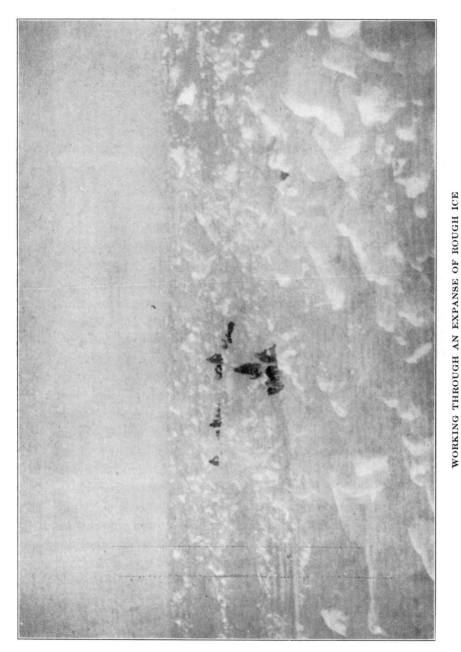

WORKING THROUGH AN EXPANSE OF ROUGH ICE

PASSING THROUGH A DEFILE IN ROUGH ICE

Our start from the land this last time was eight days earlier than the start three years before, six days of calendar time and two days of distance, our present latitude being about two marches farther north than Cape Hecla, our former point of departure.

When we were far enough out on the ice to be away from the shelter of the land, we got the full force of the violent wind. But it was not in our faces, and as we had a trail which could be followed, even if with heads down and eyes half closed, the wind did not impede us or cause us serious discomfort. Nevertheless, I did not like to dwell upon the inevitable effect which it would have upon the ice farther out — the opening of leads across our route.

When we dropped off the edge of the glacial fringe onto the pressure ridges of the tidal crack already described, in spite of the free use of our pickaxes and the pickaxes of the pioneer division, which had gone before, the trail was a most trying one for men, dogs, and sledges, especially the old Eskimo type of sledge. The new "Peary" sledges, by reason of their length and shape, rode much more easily and with less strain than the others. Every one was glad to reach the surface of the old floes beyond this crazy zone of ice which was several miles in width. As soon as we struck the old floes the going was much better. There appeared to be no great depth of snow, only a few inches, and this had been hammered fairly hard by the winter winds. Still the surface over which we traveled was very uneven, and in many places was distinctly trying to the sledges, the wood of which was made brittle by the low temperature, now in the minus fifties. On the whole, however,

I felt that if we encountered nothing worse than this in the first hundred miles from the land we should have no serious cause for complaint.

A little farther on, while walking alone behind my division, I met Kyutah of Marvin's division, hurrying back with empty sledge. He had smashed his sledge so badly that it seemed better to go back to Cape Columbia for one of the reserve sledges there than to attempt to repair the broken one. He was cautioned not to waste a minute and to be sure to overtake us at our camp that night, and he was soon disappearing into the wind haze in our rear.

Still farther on I met Kudlooktoo, returning on the same errand, and a little later came upon some of the other divisions that had been obliged to stop to repair their sledges which had suffered severely in their encounters with the rough ice.

Finally I reached the captain's first camp, ten miles out. Here I took one of the two igloos, and Marvin took the other. The divisions of Goodsell, MacMillan, and Henson were to build their own igloos this first night. Bartlett and Borup being in advance, would each build an igloo at every one of their camps. I, being the oldest man in the party, was to take one of these, and the order of precedence in which the divisions of Marvin, MacMillan, Goodsell, and Henson were to occupy the second of the already constructed igloos had been determined by lot at Columbia, the first lot falling to Marvin. Later, when Bartlett's division alone was in the lead, there was only one igloo already built at each camp on the line of march.

The day twilight, which now lasted about twelve

hours, had disappeared entirely by the time the last sledge reached this first camp. It had been a trying day for the sledges. The new "Peary" type, by reason of its shape and greater length, had come off best. Though two of these had suffered minor damages, none of them had been put out of commission. Two of the old Eskimo type had been smashed completely, and another nearly so.

The dogs were soon fed, and each division went for supper and rest to its own igloo, leaving the rugged surface of the ice to the darkness, and the howling wind and drift. The march had been a somewhat hard one for me, because, for the first time in sixteen years, the leg which I had broken in Greenland, in 1891, had been causing me considerable trouble.

The door of my igloo had scarcely been closed by a block of snow, when one of Henson's Eskimos came running over, blue with fright, to tell me that Tornar-suk was in camp, and that they could not light the alcohol in their new stove. I did not understand this, as the stoves had all been tested on board ship and had worked to perfection; but I got out and went over to Henson's igloo, where it appeared that he had used up a whole box of matches in unsuccessful efforts to light his stove. Our stoves were of an entirely new design, using no wicks, and a moment's examination disclosed the trouble. It was so cold that there was no vaporization from the alcohol, and it would not light directly as at higher temperatures. A bit of paper dropped into it and lighted was the solution, and there was no further trouble.

The failure of even one of our alcohol stoves would

have seriously impaired our chances, as the men of that division could not have boiled the tea which is absolutely necessary for work in those low temperatures. Kyutah, the Eskimo who had gone back to land with his broken sledge, came in during the night, but Kudlooktoo failed to put in an appearance. Thus the end of our first day over the polar ice found the expedition one man short.

CHAPTER XXIV

THE FIRST OPEN WATER

THE first serious obstacle of the sledge journey was encountered the second day out from land. The day was cloudy, the wind continuing to blow from the east with unabated violence. Again I intentionally brought up the rear of my division, in order to see that everything was going right and that every one was accounted for. The going was much the same as on the previous day, rough and trying to the endurance of men, dogs and sledges.

When we had made about three-quarters of a march we saw ahead of us a dark ominous cloud upon the northern horizon, which always means open water. There is always fog in the neighborhood of the leads. The open water supplies the evaporation, the cold air acts as a condenser, and when the wind is blowing just right this forms a fog so dense that at times it looks as black as the smoke of a prairie fire.

Sure enough, just ahead of us were black spots against the snow which I knew to be my various divisions held up by a lead. When we came up with them I saw a lane of open water, about a quarter of a mile wide, which had formed since the captain had passed the day before. The wind had been getting in its work!

I gave the word to camp (there was nothing else to

do), and while the igloos were being built, Marvin and MacMillan made a sounding from the edge of the lead, getting ninety-six fathoms.

This march to the edge of the lead put us beyond the British record of 83° 20′ made by Captain Markham, R. N., north of Cape Joseph Henry, May 12, 1876.

Before daylight the next morning we heard the grinding of the ice, which told us that the lead was at last crushing together, and I gave the signal to the other three igloos, by pounding with a hatchet on the ice floor of my igloo, to fire up and get breakfast in a hurry. The morning was clear again, excepting for the wind haze, but the wind still continued to blow with unabated violence.

With the first of the daylight we were hurrying across the lead on the raftering young ice, which was moving, crushing, and piling up with the closing of the sides of the lead. If the reader will imagine crossing a river on a succession of gigantic shingles, one, two, or three deep and all afloat and moving, he will perhaps form an idea of the uncertain surface over which we crossed this lead. Such a passage is distinctly trying, as any moment may lose a sledge and its team, or plunge a member of the party into the icy water. On the other side there was no sign of Bartlett's trail. This meant that the lateral movement (that is east and west) of the ice shores of the lead had carried the trail along with it.

After an hour or two of marching, we found ourselves in the fork of two other leads, and unable to move in any direction. The young ice (that is, the recently frozen ice) on the more westerly of these leads, though

too thin to sustain the weight of the sledges, was yet
strong enough to bear an Eskimo, and I sent Kyutah to
the west to scout for the captain's trail, while the other
Eskimos built out of snow blocks a shelter from the
wind, and repaired some minor damages to our sledges.

In half an hour or so Kyutah returned from the
west, signaling that he had found Bartlett's trail. Soon
after he reached us a movement of the shores of the lead
to the west crushed up the narrow ribbon of unsafe
young ice over which he had passed, and we were able
to hurry across with sledges and push west for the trail,
which was about a mile and a half distant.

When we reached the trail we saw, by the tracks of
men and dogs pointing south, that Borup had already
passed that way on his return to Columbia, in accordance with my program. He had probably crossed the
lead and was now scouting for our trail somewhere on
the southerly side.

As soon as Marvin, who was following me, came up,
I had Kyutah throw off his sledge load, and sent Marvin and the Eskimo on the back trail to "Crane City,"
Cape Columbia. I did this partly because of the possibility that there might be complications there in
which Borup, who was new to the work, would feel the
need of a man of Marvin's wider experience, and partly
because many of our alcohol and petroleum tins had
sprung leaks in the rough going of the last few days, and
an additional supply was needed to make up for present
and possible future loss. The change of the loads was
effected in a few minutes, without delay to the main
party, which kept right on, and Marvin and his dusky
companion were soon out of sight.

The captain's third camp was reached before dark that night. All day long the wind kept us company, and we could see by the water clouds all about us that the leads were open here and there in every direction. Fortunately none of them immediately crossed our trail, and the going was much as on the previous day.

During this march we saw, above the summits of the great land mountains which were still visible to the south of us, a flaming blade of yellow light which reached half way to the zenith — in other words, after nearly five months, we could almost see the sun again as he skimmed along just under the southern horizon. Only a day or two more, and his light would shine directly upon us. The feeling of the arctic traveler for the returning sun after the long darkness is a feeling hard to interpret to those who are accustomed to seeing the sun every morning.

On the following day, March 4, the weather changed. The sky was overcast with clouds, the wind had swung completely around to the west during the night, there were occasional squalls of light snow, and the thermometer had risen to only 9° below zero. This temperature, after that of the minus fifties, in which we had been traveling, seemed almost oppressively warm. The leads were even more numerous than the day before, and their presence was clearly outlined by the heavy black clouds. A mile or two east of us there was a lead stretching far to the north and directly parallel with our course, which did not cause us any apprehension. But a broad and ominous band of black extending far to the east and west across our course and apparently ten or fifteen miles to the north of us, gave me serious concern.

APPROACHING A LEAD THROUGH ROUGH ICE

STOPPED BY OPEN WATER

Evidently the ice was all abroad in every direction, and the high temperature and snow accompanying the west wind proved that there was a large amount of open water in that direction.

The outlook was not pleasant, but as some compensation the going was not quite so rough. As we advanced, I was surprised to find that as yet none of the leads cut Bartlett's trail. Consequently we made good progress, and though the march was distinctly longer than the previous one, we reached Bartlett's igloo in good time.

Here I found a note from Bartlett which had evidently been despatched by an Eskimo, informing me that he was in camp about a mile farther north — held up by open water. This explained the black, ominous band which I had been watching for hours on the northern horizon, and which had gradually risen as we approached until it was now almost overhead.

Pushing on, we soon reached the captain's camp. There I found the familiar unwelcome sight which I had so often before me on the expedition of 1905–06 — the white expanse of ice cut by a river of inky black water, throwing off dense clouds of vapor which gathered in a sullen canopy overhead, at times swinging lower with the wind and obscuring the opposite shore of this malevolent Styx.

The lead had opened directly through the heavy floes, and, considering that these floes are sometimes one hundred feet in thickness, and of almost unimaginable weight, the force that could open such a river through them is comparable with the forces that threw up the mountains on the continents and opened the channels between the lands.

Bartlett told me that during the previous night in the camp a mile farther south where I had found his note, the noise caused by the opening of this great lead had awakened him from sleep. The open water was now about a quarter of a mile in width, and extended east and west as far as we could see when we climbed to the highest pinnacle of ice in the neighborhood of our camp.

Two or three miles to the east of us, as we could see by the vapor hanging over it, the north and south lead which had paralleled our last two marches intersected the course of the lead beside which we were encamped.

Though farther south than where we had encountered the "Big Lead" in 1906, north of Cape Hecla, this one had every resemblance to that great river of open water which on the way up we had called "the Hudson," and on our way back — when it seemed that those black waters had cut us off forever from the land—we had renamed "the Styx." The resemblance was so strong that even the Eskimos who had been with me on the expedition three years before spoke about it.

I was glad to see that there was no lateral movement in the ice; that is, that the two shores of the lead were not moving east or west, or in opposite directions. The lead was simply an opening in the ice under the pressure of the wind and the spring tides, which were now swelling to the full moon on the 6th.

Captain Bartlett, with his usual thoughtfulness, had an igloo already built for me near his own when I arrived. While the other three divisions were building their igloos the captain took a sounding, and obtained a depth of one hundred and ten fathoms. We were now about forty-five miles north of Cape Columbia.

The next day, March 5, was a fine, clear day, with a light westerly breeze, and a temperature of 20° below zero. For a little while about noon the sun lay, a great yellow ball, along the southern horizon. Our satisfaction at seeing it again was almost compensation for our impatience at being delayed there — beside the gradually widening lead. Had it not been cloudy on the 4th, we should have seen the sun one day earlier.

During the night the lead had narrowed somewhat, raftering the young ice. Then, under the impulse of the tidal wave, it had opened wider than ever, leaving, in spite of the constantly forming ice, a broad band of black water before us. I sent MacMillan back with three dog teams and three Eskimos to bring up the load which Kyutah had thrown off before he went back to the land with Marvin, and also to bring up a portion of Borup's cache which we had not been able to load on our sledges. MacMillan also took a note to leave at Kyutah's cache, telling Marvin where we were held up, and urging him to hurry forward with all possible speed. The remainder of the party occupied themselves repairing damaged sledges and in drying their clothing over the little oil hand lamps.

All the next day we were still there beside the lead. Another day, and we were still there. Three, four, five days passed in intolerable inaction, and still the broad line of black water spread before us. Those were days of good traveling weather, with temperatures ranging from minus 5° to minus 32°, a period of time which might have carried us beyond the 85th parallel but for those three days of wind at the start which had been the cause of this obstruction in our course.

During those five days I paced back and forth, deploring the luck which, when everything else was favorable — weather, ice, dogs, men, and equipment — should thus impede our way with open water. Bartlett and I did not talk much to each other during those days. It was a time when silence seemed more expressive than any words. We looked at each other occasionally, and I could see from the tightening of Bartlett's jaw all that I needed to know of what was going on in his mind.

Each day the lead continued to widen before us, and each day we looked anxiously southward along the trail for Marvin and Borup to come up. But they did not come.

Only one who had been in a similar position could understand the gnawing torment of those days of forced inaction, as I paced the floe in front of the igloos most of the time, climbing every little while to the top of the ice pinnacle back of the igloos to strain my eyes through the dim light to the south, sleeping through a few hours out of each twenty-four, with one ear open for the slightest noise, rising repeatedly to listen more intently for the eagerly desired sound of incoming dogs — all this punctuated, in spite of my utmost efforts at self-control, with memories of the effect of the delay at the "Big Lead" on my prospects in the previous expedition. Altogether, I think that more of mental wear and tear was crowded into those days than into all the rest of the fifteen months we were absent from civilization.

The additional supply of oil and alcohol, which Marvin and Borup were to bring to me, was, I felt, vital to our success; but even if they did not come in with it, I could not turn back here. While pacing the floe, I figured out how we should use our sledges piecemeal as fuel in our cookers, to make tea after the oil and alcohol were gone. By the time the wood of the sledges was exhausted, it would be warm enough so that we could suck ice or snow to assuage our thirst, and get along with our pemmican and raw dog without tea. But, though I planned, it was a plan of desperation. It was a harrowing time, that period of waiting.

CHAPTER XXV

SOME OF MY ESKIMOS LOSE THEIR NERVE

THE protracted delay, hard as it was upon all the members of the expedition, had a demoralizing psychological effect upon some of my Eskimos. Toward the end of the period of waiting I began to notice that some of them were getting nervous. I would see them talking together in twos and threes, just out of earshot. Finally two of the older men, who had been with me for years and whom I had trusted, came to me pretending to be sick. I have had sufficient experience to know a sick Eskimo when I see one, and the excuses of Pooadloonah and Panikpah did not convince me. I told them by all means to go back to the land just as quickly as they could, and to take with them a note to Marvin, urging him to hurry. I also sent by them a note to the mate of the ship, giving instructions in regard to these two men and their families.

As the days went by, other Eskimos began to complain of this and that imaginary ailment. Two of them were rendered temporarily unconscious by the fumes of the alcohol cooker in their igloo, frightening all the rest of the Eskimos half out of their wits, and I was seriously puzzled as to what I should do with them. This was an illustration of the fact, which may not have occurred to every one, that the leader of a polar expedition has sometimes other things to contend with than the natural conditions of ice and weather.

On the 9th or 10th we might possibly have crossed the lead on the young ice, by taking desperate chances; but, considering our experience of 1906, when we had nearly lost our lives while recrossing the "Big Lead" on the undulating ice, and also considering that Marvin *must* be somewhere near by this time, I waited these two more days to give him a chance to catch up.

MacMillan was invaluable to me during this period. Seeing the restlessness of the Eskimos, and without waiting for any suggestion from me, he gave himself absolutely to the problem of keeping them occupied and interested in games and athletic "stunts" of one kind and another. This was one of those opportunities which circumstances give a man silently to prove the mettle of which he is made.

On the evening of March 10, the lead being nearly closed, I gave orders to get under way the next morning. The delay had become unendurable, and I decided to take the chance of Marvin's overtaking us with the oil and alcohol.

Of course there was the alternative of my going back to see what was the trouble. But that idea was dismissed. There was little attraction in ninety miles of extra travel, to say nothing of the psychological effect on the members of the expedition.

I had no anxiety about the men themselves. Borup, I felt sure, had reached the land without delay. Marvin, if he had been held up temporarily by the opening of the shore lead, had the load which had been thrown off by Kudlooktoo when his sledge was smashed, and this load contained all essential items of supplies. But I could not believe that the shore lead had remained open so long.

The morning of the 11th was clear and calm, with a temperature of minus 40°, which meant that all the open water was frozen over. We got under way early, leaving in my igloo at this camp the following note for Marvin:

4th CAMP, *March* 11, 1909.

Have waited here (6) days. Can wait no longer. We are short of fuel. Push on with all possible speed to overtake us. Shall leave note at each camp. When near us rush light sledge and note of information ahead to overhaul us.

Expect send back Dr. & Eskimos 3 to 5 marches from here. He should meet you & give you information.

We go straight across this lead (E. S. E.)

There has been no lateral motion of the ice during 7 days. Only open and shut. *Do not camp here.* CROSS THE LEAD. Feed full rations & speed your dogs.

It is *vital* you overtake us and give us fuel.

Leaving at 9 A.M., Thursday, Mar. 11.

PEARY.

P.S. On possibility you arrive too late to follow us, have asked captain take general material from your bags.

We crossed the lead without trouble, and made a fair march of not less than twelve miles. This day we crossed seven leads, each being from half a mile to one mile in width, all covered with barely negotiable young ice. At this time the various divisions, including Bartlett's, were all traveling together.

On this march we crossed the 84th parallel. That night the ice was raftering about our camp with the

ATHLETIC SPORTS AT THE LEAD CAMP

PICKAXING A ROAD THROUGH ZONE OF ROUGH ICE

A CHARACTERISTIC VIEW OF THE EXPEDITION ON THE MARCH IN FINE WEATHER

(Indian File Used to Economize the Strength of Men and Dogs and to Accentuate the Trail. The Passage of Each Sledge Makes the Trail Easier for the Ones Behind It)

movement of the tide. The continual grinding, groaning, and creaking, as the pieces of ice crunched together, kept up all night long. The noise, however, did not keep me from sleeping, as our igloos were on a heavy ice-floe, which was not likely itself to be broken up, most of the ice around it being young and thin.

In the morning it was still clear, and the temperature was down to minus 45°. Again we made a fair march of not less than twelve nautical miles, crossing in the first half many cracks and narrow leads, and in the latter half traversing an unbroken series of old floes. I felt confident that this zone of numerous leads which we had crossed in the last two marches was the "Big Lead," and was of the opinion that we were now safely across it.

We hoped that Marvin and Borup, with their men and vital supply of fuel, would get across the "Big Lead" before we had any more wind; for six hours of a good fresh breeze would utterly obliterate our trail, by reason of the movement of the ice, and their search for us in the broad waste of that white world would have been like the proverbial search for a needle in a haystack.

The following march, on the 13th, was distinctly crisp. When we started the thermometer was minus 53°, the minimum during the night having been minus 55°; and when the twilight of evening came on it was down to minus 59°. With the bright sunshine at midday, and with no wind, in our fur clothing we did not suffer from the cold. The brandy, of course, was solid, the petroleum was white and viscid, and the dogs as they traveled were enveloped in the white cloud of their own breath.

I traveled ahead of my division this march, and whenever I looked back could see neither men nor dogs — only a low-lying bank of fog glistening like silver in the horizontal rays of the sun behind it to the south — this fog being the steam of the dog teams and the men.

The going during this march was fairly good, except at the beginning, where for about five miles we zigzagged through a zone of very rough ice. The distance covered was at least twelve miles. Our camp that night was on a large old floe in the lee of a large hummock of ice and snow.

Just as we had finished building our igloos, one of the Eskimos who was standing on the top of the hummock shouted excitedly:

"Kling-mik-sue!" (Dogs are coming.)

In a moment I was on the hummock beside him. Looking south I could see, a long distance away, a little bank of silvery white mist lying on our trail. Yes, it was surely the dogs. A little later Seegloo, of Borup's party, dashed up on a light sledge drawn by eight dogs, with a note from Marvin containing the welcome news that he, Borup, and their men had slept the previous night at our second camp back; that they would sleep the next night at our first camp back, and catch up with us on the following day. The rear party, with its precious loads of oil and alcohol, was over the "Big Lead!"

Henson at once received instructions to get away early the next morning with his division of Eskimos and sledges, to pioneer the road for the next five marches.

The doctor was informed definitely that he was to return to the land the next morning with two men. The rest of the party would remain here repairing sledges and drying clothes until Marvin and Borup came in, when I could reapportion my loads, and send back all superfluous men, dogs, and sledges.

That night, my mind again at rest, I slept like a child. In the morning Henson got away early to the north with his pioneer division of three Eskimos, Ootah, Ahwatingwah, Koolootingwah, and sledges and teams. A little later Dr. Goodsell with two Eskimos, Wesharkoopsi and Arco, one sledge, and twelve dogs took the back trail.

The doctor had assisted me in every possible way; but his services in the field were gratuitous and were understood so to be. His place was naturally at the ship, where the greater number still remained, for the moral effect of his presence even if his medical services should not be much needed, and I did not feel justified in subjecting him further to the dangers of the leads with their treacherous young ice. The latitude where the doctor turned back was about 84° 29′.

In the latter part of the afternoon, March 14, another cloud of silvery smoke was seen advancing along our trail, and a little later Marvin came swinging in at the head of the rear division, men and dogs steaming like a squadron of battle-ships, and bringing in an ample supply of fuel. Otherwise his loads were light, to permit rapid traveling. Many times in the past had I been glad to see the true eyes of Ross Marvin, but never more glad than this time.

The sledges which were now repaired were laden with

the standard loads already described, and I found that I had just twelve. This left some men and dogs over, so that it was not serious news when MacMillan called my attention to a frosted heel with which he had been worrying along for several days without saying anything to any one about it. I saw at once that the only thing for him to do was to turn back.

It was a disappointment to me to lose MacMillan so early, as I had hoped that he would be able to go to a comparatively high latitude; but his disability did not affect the main proposition. I had ample personnel, as well as provisions, sledges, and dogs; and the men, like the equipment, were interchangeable.

Here it may be well to note that, beyond my saying to Bartlett at Cape Columbia that I hoped conditions might be such as to give me the benefit of his energy and sturdy shoulders to some point beyond Abruzzi's farthest, no member of the party knew how far he was to go, or when he was to turn back. Yet this made no difference in the eagerness of their work. Naturally I had my definite program; but conditions or accidents might necessitate such instant and radical modifications of it that it seemed hardly worth while to make it known. Few, if any, other explorers have had so efficient and congenial a party as mine this last time. Every man was glad to subordinate his own personal feelings and ambitions to the ultimate success of the expedition.

Marvin made a sounding about a half mile north of the camp and got eight hundred and twenty-five fathoms, which substantiated my belief that we had crossed the "Big Lead." This lead probably follows

the continental shelf which this sounding showed to
be between there and Camp No. 4 (with the probability of its being between Camp Nos. 4 and 5),
probably at about the 84th parallel.   The continental
shelf is simply a submerged plateau surrounding all the
continent, the "Big Lead" marking the northern edge
of that shelf where it dips into the polar sea.

Monday, March 15, was also clear and cold, with a
temperature between 45° and 50° below zero.   The
wind had shifted again to the east and was very pene-
trating.   Bartlett and Marvin started off with the
pickaxes as soon as they had finished their morning
tea and pemmican, and their divisions, with Borup and
his division, followed as soon as their sledges were
stowed.

MacMillan got away for Columbia with two
Eskimos, two sledges, and fourteen dogs.   The main
expedition now comprised sixteen men, twelve sledges,
and one hundred dogs.   One sledge had been broken
up to repair the others, three had been taken back with
the returning parties, and two were left at this camp
to be utilized on the return.   Of the sledges that now
went on, seven were the new type of Peary sledge and
five were the old Eskimo pattern.

After saying good by to MacMillan I followed the
other three divisions to the north, bringing up the rear
as previously.   The going in this march was similar to
that of the previous one, fairly good, as it was over the
old floes.   The soreness in my fractured leg which had
troubled me more or less all the way from Cape
Columbia was now almost entirely gone.

Late in the afternoon we began to hear loud reports

and rumblings among the floes, as well as the more sibilant sound of the raftering young ice in various directions. This meant more open water ahead of us. Soon an active lead cut right across our path, and on the farther or northern side of it we could see that the ice was moving. The lead seemed to narrow toward the west, and we followed it a little way until we came to a place where there were large pieces of floating ice, some of them fifty or a hundred feet across. We got the dogs and sledges from one piece of ice to another — the whole forming a sort of pontoon bridge.

As Borup was getting his team across the open crack between two pieces of floating ice, the dogs slipped and went into the water. Leaping forward, the vigorous young athlete stopped the sledge from following the dogs, and, catching hold of the traces that fastened the dogs to the sledge, he pulled them bodily out of the water. A man less quick and muscular than Borup might have lost the whole team as well as the sledge laden with five hundred pounds of supplies, which, considering our position far out in that icy wilderness, were worth more to us than their weight in diamonds. Of course, had the sledge gone in, the weight of it would have carried the dogs to the bottom of the sea. We drew a long breath, and, reaching the solid ice on the other side of this pontoon bridge, plunged on to the north. But we had gone only a short distance when right in front of us the ice separated with loud reports, forming another open lead, and we were obliged to camp.

The temperature that night was 50° below zero; there was a fresh breeze from the southeast and enough moisture in the open water close by us to give the wind a keen edge, which made the time occupied in building igloos decidedly unpleasant. But we were all so thankful over our escape from losing that imperiled sledge with its precious load that personal discomforts seemed indeed of small account.

CHAPTER XXVI

BORUP'S FARTHEST NORTH

THAT night was one of the noisiest that I have ever spent in an igloo, and none of us slept very soundly. Hour after hour the rumbling and complaining of the ice continued, and it would not have surprised us much if at any moment the ice had split directly across our camp, or even through the middle of one of our igloos. It was not a pleasant situation, and every member of the party was glad when the time came to get under way again.

In the morning we found a passage across the lead a short distance to the east of our camp over some fragments which had become cemented together during the cold night. We had only gone forward a few hundred yards when we came upon the igloo which Henson had occupied. This did not indicate rapid progress.

At the end of six hours we came upon another of Henson's igloos — not greatly to my surprise. I knew, from experience, that yesterday's movement of the ice and the formation of leads about us would take all the spirit out of Henson's party until the main party should overtake them again. Sure enough, the next march was even shorter. At the end of a little over four hours we found Henson and his division in camp, making one sledge out of the remains of two. The

A TYPICAL EXAMPLE OF THE DIFFICULTIES OF WORKING SLEDGES OVER
A PRESSURE RIDGE

damage to the sledges was the reason given for the delay.

This march having been largely over a broad zone of rough rubble ice, some of my own sledges had suffered slight damage, and the entire party was now halted and the sledges were overhauled.

After a short sleep I put Marvin ahead to pick the trail, with instructions to try to make two long marches to bring up the average.

Marvin got away very early, followed a little later by Bartlett, Borup, and Henson, with pickaxes to improve further the trail made by Marvin. After that came the sledges of their divisions, I, as usual, bringing up the rear with my division, that I might have everything ahead of me and know just how things were going. Marvin gave us a good march of not less than seventeen miles, at first over very rough ice, then over larger and more level floes, with a good deal of young ice between.

At the end of this march, on the evening of the 19th, while the Eskimos were building the igloos, I outlined to the remaining members of my party, Bartlett, Marvin, Borup, and Henson, the program which I should endeavor to follow from that time on. At the end of the next march (which would be five marches from where MacMillan and the doctor turned back) Borup would return with three Eskimos, twenty dogs, and one sledge, leaving the main party — twelve men, ten sledges, and eighty dogs. Five marches farther on Marvin would return with two Eskimos, twenty dogs, and one sledge, leaving the main party with nine men, seven sledges, and sixty dogs. Five marches farther

on Bartlett would return with two Eskimos, twenty
dogs, and one sledge, leaving the main party six men,
forty dogs, and five sledges.

I hoped that with good weather, and the ice no worse
than that which we had already encountered, Borup
might get beyond 85°, Marvin beyond 86°, and Bartlett beyond 87°. At the end of each five-march section I should send back the poorest dogs, the least
effective Eskimos, and the worst damaged sledges.

As will appear, this program was carried out without a hitch, and the farthest of each division was even
better than I had hoped. At this camp the supplies,
equipment, and personal gear of Borup and his Eskimos were left for them to pick up on their way home,
thus avoiding the transportation of some two hundred
and fifty pounds out and back over the next march.

The 19th was a brilliant day of yellow sunlight.
The season was now so far advanced that the sun,
circling as always in this latitude around and around
the heavens, was above the horizon nearly half the
time, and during the other half there was almost no
darkness — only a gray twilight.

The temperature this day was in the minus fifties,
as evidenced by the frozen brandy and the steam-
enshrouded dogs; but bubbles in all my spirit ther-
mometers prevented a definite temperature reading.
These bubbles were caused by the separation of the
column, owing to the jolting of the thermometer with
our constant stumbling over the rough ice of the polar
sea. The bubbles might be removed at night in camp,
but this required some time, and the accurate noting
of temperatures during our six or seven weeks' march

to the Pole and back did not seem sufficiently vital to our enterprise to make me rectify the thermometer every night. When I was not too tired, I got the bubbles out.

Again Marvin, who was still pioneering the trail, gave us a fair march of fifteen miles or more, at first over heavy and much-raftered ice, then over floes of greater size and more level surface. But the reader must understand that what we regard as a level surface on the polar ice might be considered decidedly rough going anywhere else.

The end of this march put us between 85° 7' and 85° 30', or about the latitude of our "Storm Camp" of three years before; but we were twenty-three days ahead of that date, and in the matter of equipment, supplies, and general condition of men and dogs there was no comparison. Bartlett's estimate of our position at this camp was 85° 30', Marvin's 85° 25', and my own 85° 20'. The actual position, as figured back later from the point where we were first able, by reason of the increasing altitude of the sun, to take an observation for latitude, was 85° 23'.

In the morning Bartlett again took charge of the pioneer division, starting early with two Eskimos, sixteen dogs, and two sledges. Borup, a little later, with three Eskimos, sixteen dogs, and one sledge, started on his return to the land.

I regretted that circumstances made it expedient to send Borup back from here in command of the second supporting party. This young Yale athlete was a valuable member of the expedition. His whole heart was in the work, and he had hustled his heavy sledge along and driven his dogs with almost the skill of an Eskimo, in a way that commanded the admiration of the whole party and would have made his father's eyes glisten could he have seen. But with all his enthusiasm for this kind of work, he was still inexperienced in the many treacheries of the ice; and I was not willing to subject him to any further risks. He had also, like MacMillan, frosted one of his heels.

It was a serious disappointment to Borup that he was obliged to turn back; but he had reason to feel proud of his work — even as I was proud of him. He had carried the Yale colors close up to eighty-five and a half degrees, and had borne them over as many miles of polar ice as Nansen had covered in his entire journey from his ship to his "farthest north."

I can still see Borup's eager and bright young face, slightly clouded with regret, as he turned away at last and disappeared with his Eskimos and steaming dogs among the ice hummocks of the back trail.

A few minutes after Borup went south, Henson with two Eskimos, three sledges, and twenty-four dogs began to follow Bartlett's trail to the north. Marvin and myself, with four Eskimos, five sledges, and forty dogs, were to remain in camp twelve hours longer in order to give Bartlett one march the start of us. With the departure of Borup's supporting party, the main expedition comprised twelve men, ten sledges, and eighty dogs.

From this camp on, each division comprised three men instead of four; but I did not reduce the division daily allowance of tea, milk, and alcohol. This meant a slightly greater individual consumption of these supplies, but so long as we kept up the present rate of speed I considered it justified. With the increasing appetite caused by the continuous work, three men were easily able to consume four men's tea rations. The daily allowance of pemmican and biscuit I could not increase. Three men in an igloo were also more comfortable than four, and the smaller igloos just about balanced in time and energy the lesser number of men that were left to build them.

We had now resumed the program of advance party and main party, which had been interrupted during the last two marches. The now continuous daylight permitted a modification of the previous arrangement so as to bring the two parties in touch every twenty-four hours. The main party remained in camp for about twelve hours after the departure of the advance. The advance party made its march, camped, and turned in. When the main party had covered the march made by the advance party and arrived at their igloos, the advance party broke out and started on while the main party occupied their igloos and turned in for sleep.

Thus I was in touch with Bartlett and his division every twenty-four hours, to make any changes in the loads that seemed advisable, and to encourage the men if necessary. At this stage in our journey Henson's party traveled with Bartlett's pioneer party, and Marvin and his men traveled with mine.

This arrangement kept the parties closer together, relieved the pioneers of all apprehension, and reduced by fifty per cent. the chance of separation of the parties by the opening of a lead.

Occasionally I found it advisable to transfer an

Eskimo from one division to another. Sometimes, as has been seen, these odd people are rather difficult to manage; and if Bartlett or any other member of the expedition did not like a certain Eskimo, or had trouble in managing him, I would take that Eskimo into my own division, giving the other party one of my Eskimos, because I could get along with any of them. In other words, I gave the other men their preferences, taking myself the men who were left. Of course, when I came to make up my division for the final dash, I took my favorites among the most efficient of the Eskimos.

At the next camp Marvin made a sounding and to our surprise reached bottom at only three hundred and ten fathoms, but in the process of reeling up the wire it separated, and the lead and some of the wire were lost.

Soon after midnight we got under way, Marvin taking a sledge, and after a short march — only some ten miles — we reached Bartlett's camp. He had been delayed by the breaking of one of his sledges, and I found one of his men and Henson's party still there repairing the sledge. Bartlett himself had gone on, and Henson and the other men got away soon after our arrival.

Marvin made another sounding of seven hundred fathoms and no bottom, unfortunately losing two pickaxes (which had been used in place of a lead) and more of the wire in hauling it up. Then we turned in. It was a fine day, with clear, brilliant sunlight, a fine breeze from the north, and temperature in the minus forties.

The next march, on the 22d, was a fair one of not less than fifteen miles. The going was at first tortuous, over rough, heavy ice, which taxed the sledges, dogs, and drivers to the utmost; then we struck a direct line across large and level floes. At the end of this march I found that Bartlett and one of his men had already left; but Henson and his party were in their igloo. Ooqueah, of Bartlett's party, whose sledge had broken down the day before, was also in camp. I turned Marvin's sledge over to Ooqueah, so that Bartlett should have no further hindrance in his work of pioneering, and started him and Henson's party off. The damaged sledge I turned over to Marvin, giving him a light load. We were not without our difficulties at this period of the journey, but our plan was working smoothly and we were all hopeful and in excellent spirits.

CHAPTER XXVII

GOOD BY TO MARVIN

UP to this time no observations had been taken. The altitude of the sun had been so low as to make observations unreliable. Moreover, we were traveling at a good clip, and the mean estimate of Bartlett, Marvin, and myself, based on our previous ice experience, was sufficient for dead reckoning. Now, a clear, calm day, with the temperature not lower than minus forty, made a checking of our dead reckoning seem desirable. So I had the Eskimos build a wind shelter of snow, in order that Marvin might take a meridian altitude for latitude. I intended that Marvin should take all the observations up to his farthest, and Bartlett all beyond that to his farthest. This was partly to save my eyes, but principally to have independent observations with which to check our advance.

The mercury of the artificial horizon was thoroughly warmed in the igloo; a semi-circular wind-guard of snow blocks two tiers high was put up, opening to the south; a musk-ox skin was laid upon the snow inside this; my special instrument box was placed at the south end and firmly bedded into the snow in a level position; the artificial horizon trough, especially devised for this kind of work, was placed on top and the mercury poured into it until it was

REPAIRING SLEDGES IN CAMP

MARVIN TAKING AN OBSERVATION IN A SNOW SHELTER

even full, when it was covered with the glass horizon roof.

Marvin, then lying full length upon his face, with his head to the south and both elbows resting upon the snow, was able to hold the sextant steady enough to get his contact of the sun's limb in the very narrow strip of the artificial horizon which was available. A pencil and open note-book under the right hand offered the means of noting the altitudes as they were obtained.

The result of Marvin's observations gave our position as approximately 85° 48′ north latitude, figuring the correction for refraction only to a temperature of minus 10 F., the lowest temperature for which we had tables. It was from this point that, reckoning twenty-five miles for our last two marches, we calculated the position of Camp 19, where Borup turned back, as being 85° 23′, as against our respective dead reckoning estimates of 85° 20′, 85° 25′, and 85° 30′. This observation showed that we had thus far averaged eleven and a half minutes of latitude *made good* for each actual march. Included in these marches had been four short ones resulting from causes the recurrence of which I believed I could prevent in future. I was confident that if we were not interrupted by open water, against which no calculations and no power of man can prevail, we could steadily increase this average from this time on.

The next march was made in a temperature of minus thirty and a misty atmosphere which was evidently caused by open water in the neighborhood. About five miles from camp we just succeeded by the liveliest work in getting four of our five sledges across an opening lead. Getting the last sledge over caused a delay of a few hours, as we had to cut an ice raft with pick-axes to ferry the sledge, dogs, and Eskimo driver across. This impromptu ferry-boat was cut on our side and was moved across the lead by means of two coils of rope fastened together and stretching from side to side. When the cake was ready, two of my Eskimos got on it, we threw the line across to the Eskimo on the other side, the Eskimos on the ice raft took hold of the rope, the Eskimos on either shore held the ends, and the raft was pulled over. Then the dogs and sledge and the three Eskimos took their place on the ice cake, and we hauled them over to our side. While we were engaged in this business we saw a seal disporting himself in the open water of the lead.

At the end of the next march, which was about fifteen miles, and which put us across the 86th parallel, we reached Bartlett's next camp, where we found Henson and his party in their igloo. I got them out and under way at once, sending by one of them a brief note of encouragement to Bartlett, telling him that his last camp was beyond 86°, that he would probably sleep that night beyond the Norwegian record, and urging him to speed us up for all he was worth.

In this march there was some pretty heavy going. Part of the way was over small old floes, which had been broken up by many seasons of unceasing conflict with the winds and tides. Enclosing these more or less level floes were heavy pressure ridges over which we and the dogs were obliged to climb. Often the driver of a heavily loaded sledge would be forced to lift it by main strength over some obstruction. Those who have pictured us sitting comfortably on our sledges, riding over hundreds of miles of ice smooth as a skating pond, should have seen us lifting and tugging at our five-hundred-pound sledges, adding our own strength to that of our dogs.

The day was hazy, and the air was full of frost, which, clinging to our eyelashes, almost cemented them together. Sometimes, in opening my mouth to shout an order to the Eskimos, a sudden twinge would cut short my words — my mustache having frozen to my stubble beard.

This fifteen mile march put us beyond the Norwegian record (86° 13′ 6″; see Nansen's "Farthest North," Vol. 2, page 170) and fifteen days ahead of that record. My leading sledge found both Bartlett and Henson in camp; but they were off again, pioneering the trail, before I, bringing up the rear as usual, came in. Egingwah's sledge had been damaged during this march, and as our loads could now be carried on four sledges, owing to what we had eaten along the way, we broke up Marvin's damaged sledge and used the material in it for repairing the other four. As Marvin and two Eskimos were to turn back from the next camp, I left here his supplies for the return and part of his equipment, in order to save unnecessary transportation out and back. The time employed in mending the sledges and shifting the loads cut into our hours of sleep, and after a short rest of three hours we were again under way, with four sledges and teams of ten dogs each.

The next march was a good one. Bartlett had responded like a thoroughbred to my urging. Favored by good going, he reeled off full twenty miles, notwithstanding a snow-storm part of the time, which made it hard to see. The temperature, which varied from 16° to 30° below zero, indicated that there was more or less open water to the west, from which direction the wind came. During this march we crossed several leads covered with young ice, treacherous under the recently fallen snow. Along the course of one of these leads we saw the fresh track of a polar bear going west, over two hundred miles from land.

At half-past ten on the morning of the 25th I came upon Bartlett and Henson with their men, all in camp, in accordance with my instructions to wait for me at the end of their fifth march. I turned them all out, and every one jumped in to repair the sledges, redistribute the loads, weed out the least efficient dogs, and rearrange the Eskimos in the remaining divisions.

While this work was going on, Marvin, favored by clear weather, took another meridian observation for latitude and obtained 86° 38′. This placed us, as I expected, beyond the Italian record, and showed that in our last three marches we had covered a distance of fifty minutes of latitude, an average of sixteen and two-thirds miles per march. We were thirty-two days ahead of the Italian record in time.

I was doubly glad of the result of the observations, not only for the sake of Marvin, whose services had been invaluable and who deserved the privilege of claiming a higher northing than Nansen and Abruzzi, but also for the honor of Cornell University, to the faculty of which he belonged, and two of whose alumni and patrons had been generous contributors to the

Peary Arctic Club. I had hoped that Marvin would be able to make a sounding at his farthest north, but there was no young ice near the camp through which a hole could be made.

About four o'clock in the afternoon Bartlett, with Ooqueah and Karko, two sledges, and eighteen dogs, got away for the advance. Bartlett started off with the determination to bag the 88th parallel in the next five marches (after which he was to turn back), and I sincerely hoped that he would be able to reel off the miles to that point, as he certainly deserved such a record.

Later I learned that he had intended to cover twenty-five or thirty miles in his first march, which he would have done had conditions not been against him. Though tired with the long march and the day's work in camp, after a short sleep the night before, I was not able to turn in for several hours after Bartlett got away. There were numerous details which required personal attention. There were letters to write and orders for Marvin to take back, together with his instructions for his projected trip to Cape Jesup.

The next morning, Friday, March 26, I rapped the whole party up at five o'clock, after a good sleep all round. As soon as we had eaten our usual breakfast of pemmican, biscuit, and tea, Henson, Ootah, and Keshingwah, with three sledges and twenty-five dogs, got away on Bartlett's trail.

Marvin, with Kudlooktoo and "Harrigan," one sledge, and seventeen dogs, started south at half-past nine in the morning.

No shadow of apprehension for the future hung over that parting. It was a clear, crisp morning, the sunlight glittered on the ice and snow, the dogs were alert and active after their long sleep, the air blew cold and fresh from the polar void, and Marvin himself, though reluctant to turn back, was filled with exultation that he had carried the Cornell colors to a point beyond the farthest north of Nansen and Abruzzi, and that, with the exception of Bartlett and myself, he alone of all white men had entered that exclusive region which stretches beyond 86° 34' north latitude.

I shall always be glad that Marvin marched with me during those last few days. As we tramped along together we had discussed the plans for his trip to Cape Jesup, and his line of soundings from there northward; and as he turned back to the land his mind was glowing with hope for the future — the future which he was destined never to know. My last words to him were:

"Be careful of the leads, my boy!"

So we shook hands and parted in that desolate white waste, and Marvin set his face southward toward his death, and I turned again northward toward the Pole.

CHAPTER XXVIII

WE BREAK ALL RECORDS

BY an odd coincidence, soon after Marvin left us on his fatal journey from 86° 38' back to land, the sun was obscured and a dull, lead-colored haze spread over all the sky. This grayness, in contrast to the dead white surface of the ice and snow and the strangely diffused quality of the light, gave an indescribable effect. It was a shadowless light and one in which it was impossible to see for any considerable distance.

That shadowless light is not unusual on the ice-fields of the polar sea; but this was the first occasion on which we had encountered it since leaving the land. One looking for the most perfect illustration of the arctic inferno would find it in that gray light. A more ghastly atmosphere could not have been imagined even by Dante himself — sky and ice seeming utterly wan and unreal.

Notwithstanding the fact that I had now passed the "farthest north" of all my predecessors and was approaching my own best record, with my eight companions, sixty dogs, and seven fully loaded sledges in far better condition than I had even dared to hope, the strange and melancholy light in which we traveled on this day of parting from Marvin gave me an indescribably uneasy feeling. Man in his egotism, from the most primitive ages to our own, has always imagined a sympathetic relationship between nature and the events and feelings of human life. So — in the light of later events — admitting that I felt a peculiar awe in contemplating the ghastly grayness of that day, I am expressing only an ineradicable instinct of the race to which I belong.

The first three-quarters of the march after Marvin turned back, on March 26, the trail was fortunately in a straight line, over large level snow-covered floes of varying height, surrounded by medium-rough old rafters of ice; and the last quarter was almost entirely over young ice averaging about one foot thick, broken and raftered, presenting a rugged and trying surface to travel over in the uncertain light. Without Bartlett's trail to follow, the march would have been even more difficult.

Near the end of the day we were again deflected to the west some distance by an open lead. Whenever the temperature rose as high as minus 15°, where it had stood at the beginning of the day, we were sure of encountering open water. But just before we reached the camp of Bartlett's pioneer division, the gray haze in which we had traveled all day lifted, and the sun came out clear and brilliant. The temperature had also dropped to minus 20°. Bartlett was just starting out again when I arrived, and we agreed that we had made a good fifteen miles in the last march.

The next day, March 27, was a brilliant dazzling day of arctic sunshine, the sky a glittering blue, and the ice a glittering white, which, but for the smoked goggles worn by every member of the party, would certainly have given some of us an attack of snow blindness. From the time when the reappearing sun of the arctic spring got well above the horizon, these goggles had been worn continuously.

The temperature during this march dropped from minus 30° to minus 40°, there was a biting northeasterly breeze, and the dogs traveled forward in their own white cloud of steam. On the polar ice we gladly hail the extreme cold, as higher temperatures and light snow always mean open water, danger, and delay. Of course, such minor incidents as frosted and bleeding cheeks and noses we reckon as part of the great game. Frosted heels and toes are far more serious, because they lessen a man's ability to travel, and traveling is what we are there for. Mere pain and inconvenience are inevitable, but, on the whole, inconsiderable.

This march was by far the hardest for some days. At first there was a continuation of the broken and raftered ice, sharp and jagged, that at times seemed almost to cut through our sealskin kamiks and hare-skin stockings, to pierce our feet. Then we struck heavy rubble ice covered with deep snow, through which we had literally to plow our way, lifting and steadying the sledges until our muscles ached.

During the day we saw the tracks of two foxes in this remote and icy wilderness, nearly two hundred and forty nautical miles beyond the northern coast of Grant Land.

Finally we came upon Bartlett's camp in a maze of small pieces of very heavy old floes raftered in every direction. He had been in his igloo but a short time, and his men and dogs were tired out and temporarily discouraged by the heart-racking work of making a road.

I told him to take a good long sleep before getting under way again; and while my men were building the igloos, I lightened the loads of Bartlett's sledges about one hundred pounds, to put them in better trim for pioneering in this rough going. The added weight would be less burdensome on our own sledges than on his. Notwithstanding the crazy road over which we had traveled, this march netted us twelve good miles toward the goal.

We were now across the 87th parallel and into the region of perpetual daylight, as the sun had not set during the last march. The knowledge that we had crossed the 87th parallel with men and dogs in good condition, and plenty of supplies upon the sledges, sent me to sleep that night with a light heart. Only about six miles beyond this point, at 87° 6', I had been obliged to turn back nearly three years before, with exhausted dogs, depleted supplies, and a heavy and discouraged heart. It seemed to me then that the story of my life was told and that the word failure was stamped across it.

Now, three years older, with three more years of the inevitable wear and tear of this inexorable game behind me, I stood again beyond the 87th parallel still reaching forward to that goal which had beckoned to me for so many years. Even now, on reaching my highest record with every prospect good, I dared not build too much on the chances of the white and treacherous ice which stretched one hundred and eighty nautical miles northward between me and the end. I

had believed for years that this thing could be done
and that it was my destiny to do it, but I always
reminded myself that many a man had felt thus about
some dearly wished achievement, only to fail in the
end.

When I awoke the following day, March 28, the sky
was brilliantly clear; but ahead of us there was a thick,
smoky, ominous haze drifting low over the ice, and a
bitter northeast wind, which, in the orthography of the
Arctic, plainly spelled open water. Did this mean
failure again? No man could say. Bartlett had,
of course, left camp and taken to the trail again·long
before I and the men of my division were awake.
This was in accordance with my general plan, previously outlined, that the pioneer division should be traveling while the main division slept, and *vice versa*, so
that the two divisions might be in communication
every day.

After traveling at a good rate for six hours along
Bartlett's trail, we came upon his camp beside a
wide lead, with a dense, black, watery sky to the northwest, north, and northeast, and beneath it the smoky
fog which we had been facing all day long. In order
not to disturb Bartlett, we camped a hundred yards
distant, put up our igloos as quietly as possible, and
turned in, after our usual supper of pemmican, biscuit,
and tea. We had made some twelve miles over much
better going than that of the last few marches and on
a nearly direct line over large floes and young ice.

I was just dropping off to sleep when I heard the
ice creaking and groaning close by the igloo, but as
the commotion was not excessive, nor of long duration,

I attributed it to the pressure from the closing of the lead which was just ahead of us; and after satisfying myself that my mittens were where I could get them instantly, in an emergency, I rolled over on my bed of deerskins and settled myself to sleep. I was just drowsing again when I heard some one yelling excitedly outside.

Leaping to my feet and looking through the peep-hole of our igloo, I was startled to see a broad lead of black water between our two igloos and Bartlett's, the nearer edge of water being close to our entrance; and on the opposite side of the lead stood one of Bartlett's men yelling and gesticulating with all the abandon of an excited and thoroughly frightened Eskimo.

Awakening my men, I kicked our snow door into fragments and was outside in a moment. The break in the ice had occurred within a foot of the fastening of one of my dog teams, the team escaping by just those few inches from being dragged into the water. Another team had just escaped being buried under a pressure ridge, the movement of the ice having providentially stopped after burying the bight which held their traces to the ice. Bartlett's igloo was moving east on the ice raft which had broken off, and beyond it, as far as the belching fog from the lead would let us see, there was nothing but black water. It looked as if the ice raft which carried Bartlett's division would impinge against our side a little farther on, and I shouted to his men to break camp and hitch up their dogs in a hurry, in readiness to rush across to us should the opportunity present itself.

Then I turned to consider our own position. Our two igloos, Henson's and mine, were on a small piece of old floe, separated by a crack and a low pressure ridge, a few yards away, from a large floe lying to the west of us. It was clear that it would take very little strain or pressure to detach us and set us afloat also like Bartlett's division.

I routed Henson and his men out of their igloo, gave orders to everybody to pack and hitch up immediately, and, while this was being done, leveled a path across the crack to the big floe at the west of us. This was done with a pickax, leveling the ice down into the crack, so as to make a continuous surface over which the sledges could pass. As soon as the loads were across and we were safe on the floe, we all went to the edge of the lead and stood ready to assist Bartlett's men in rushing their sledges across the moment their ice raft should touch our side.

Slowly the raft drifted nearer and nearer, until the side of it crunched against the floe. The two edges being fairly even, the raft lay alongside us as a boat lies against a wharf, and we had no trouble in getting Bartlett's men and sledges across and onto the floe with us.

Though there is always a possibility that a lead may open directly across a floe as large as this one, we could not waste our sleeping hours in sitting up to watch for it. Our former igloos being lost to us, there was nothing to do but to build another set and turn in immediately. It goes without saying that this extra work was not particularly agreeable. That night we slept with our mittens on, ready at a moment's notice for anything that might happen. Had a new lead formed directly across the sleeping platform of our igloo, precipitating us into the icy water, we should not have been surprised after the first shock of the cold bath, but should have clambered out, scraping the water off our fur garments, and made ready for the next move on the part of our treacherous antagonist — the ice.

Notwithstanding the extra fatigue and the precarious position of our camp, this last march had put us well beyond my record of three years before, probably 87° 12′, so that I went to sleep with the satisfaction of having at last beaten my own record, no matter what the morrow might bring forth.

The following day, March 29, was not a happy one for us. Though we were all tired enough to rest, we did not enjoy picnicking beside this arctic Phlegethon, which, hour after hour, to the north, northeast, and northwest, seemed to belch black smoke like a prairie fire. So dense was this cloud caused by the condensation of the vapor and the reflection in it of the black water below that we could not see the other shore of the lead — if, indeed, it had a northern shore. As far as the evidence of our senses went, we might be encamped on the edge of that open polar sea which myth-makers have imagined as forever barring the way of man to the northern end of the earth's axis. It was heart-breaking, but there was nothing to do but wait. After breakfast we overhauled the sledges and made a few repairs, dried out some of our garments over the little oil lamps which we carried for that purpose, and Bartlett made a sounding of 1,260 fathoms, but found no bottom. He did not let all the line go out, fearing there might be a defect in the wire which would lose us more of it, as we were desirous of keeping all that we had for a sounding at our "farthest north," which we hoped would be at the Pole itself. I had only one sounding lead now left, and I would not let Bartlett risk it at this point, but had him use a pair of sledge shoes (brought along for this very purpose from the last broken up sledge) to carry the line down.

When our watches told us that it was bedtime — for we were now in the period of perpetual sunlight — we again turned into the igloos which had been hurriedly built after our exciting experience the night before. A low murmur as of distant surf was issuing from the blackness ahead of us, and steadily growing in volume. To the inexperienced it might have seemed an ominous sound, but to us it was a cheering thing because we knew it meant the narrowing, and perhaps the closing, of the stretch of open water that barred our way. So we slept happily in our frosty huts that "night."

CHAPTER XXIX

OUR hopes were soon realized, for at one o'clock in the morning, March 30, when I awoke and looked at my watch, the murmur from the closing lead had increased to a hoarse roar, punctuated with groans and with reports like those of rifles, dying away to the east and west like the sounds from a mighty firing line. Looking through the peephole, I saw that the black curtain had thinned so that I could see through it to another similar, though blacker, curtain behind, indicating still another lead further on.

At eight o'clock in the morning the temperature was down to minus 30°, with a bitter northwest breeze. The grinding and groaning of the ice had ceased, and the smoke and haze had disappeared, as is usual when a lead closes up or freezes over. We rushed across before the ice should open again. All this day we traveled together, Bartlett's division, Henson's, and mine, constantly crossing narrow lanes of young ice, which had only recently been open water. During this march we had to cross a lake of young ice some six or seven miles across — so thin that the ice buckled under us as we rushed on at full speed for the other side. We did our best to make up for the previous day's delay, and when we finally camped on a heavy old floe we had made a good twenty miles.

CROSSING A LARGE LAKE OF YOUNG ICE, NORTH OF 87°

("As Level as a Floor" for Six or Seven Miles. In Places This Ice Was so Thin That It Buckled Under the Sledges and Drivers)

CAMP AT 85° 48′ NORTH, MARCH 22, 1909

A MOMENTARY HALT IN THE LEE OF A BIG HUMMOCK NORTH OF 88°

The entire region through which we had come during the last four marches was full of unpleasant possibilities for the future. Only too well we knew that violent winds for even a few hours would set the ice all abroad in every direction. Crossing such a zone on a journey north is only half the problem, for there is always the return to be figured on. Though the motto of the Arctic must be, "Sufficient unto the day is the evil thereof," we ardently hoped there might not be violent winds until we were south of this zone again on the return.

The next march was to be Bartlett's last, and he let himself out to do his best. The going was fairly good, but the weather was thick. There was a strong northerly wind blowing full in our faces, bitter and insistent, and the temperature was in the minus thirties. But this northerly wind, though hard to struggle against, was better than an easterly or westerly one, either of which would have set us adrift in open water, while, as it was, the wind was closing up every lead behind us and thus making things easier for Bartlett's supporting party on its return. True, the wind pressure was forcing to the south the ice over which we traveled, and thus losing us miles of distance; but the advantage of frozen leads was more than compensation for this loss.

So good was Bartlett's pace during the last half of the march that if I stopped an instant for any purpose I had to jump on a sledge or run, to catch up, and during the last few miles I walked beside Bartlett in advance. He was very sober and anxious to go further; but the program was for him to go back from here in command of the fourth supporting party, and we did not have supplies enough for an increase in the main party. The food which he and his two Eskimos and dog teams would have consumed between this point and the Pole, on the upward and return journeys, might mean that we would all starve before we could reach the land again.

Had it been clear we should undoubtedly have covered twenty-five miles in this march; but it is difficult to break a trail in thick weather as rapidly as in clear, and this day netted us only twenty miles. We knew that if we were not on or close to the 88th parallel at the end of this march, it would be because the northern winds of the past two days had set the ice south, crushing up the young ice in the leads between us and the land.

The sun came out just as we were preparing to camp, and it looked as if we should have clear weather the next day for Bartlett's meridian observations at his "farthest north."

When our igloos were built, I told the two Eskimos, Keshingwah and Karko, that they were to go back with the captain the next day; so they could get their clothes as dry as possible, as they probably would not have time to dry them on the forced march home. Bartlett was to return with these two Eskimos, one sledge, and eighteen dogs.

After about four hours' sleep, I turned everyone out at five o'clock in the morning. The wind had blown violently from the north all night, and still continued.

After breakfast Bartlett started to walk five or

six miles to the north in order to make sure of reaching the 88th parallel. On his return he was to take a meridian observation to determine our position. While he was gone I culled the best dogs from his teams, replacing them with the poorer dogs from the teams of the main party. The dogs were on the whole in very good condition, far better than on any of my previous expeditions. I had been throwing the brunt of the dragging on the poorest dogs, those that I judged were going to fail, so as to keep the best dogs fresh for the final spurt.

My theory was to work the supporting parties to the limit, in order to keep the main party fresh; and those men who I expected from the beginning would form the main party at the last had things made as easy as possible for them all the way up. Ootah, Henson and Egingwah were in this group. Whenever I could do so I had eased their loads for them, giving them the best dogs, and keeping the poorest dogs with the teams of those Eskimos who I knew were going back. It was a part of the deliberate plan to work the supporting parties as hard as possible, in order to keep the main party fresh up to the farthest possible point.

From the beginning there were certain Eskimos who, I knew, barring some unforeseen accident, would go to the Pole with me. There were others who were assigned not to go anywhere near there, and others who were available for either course. If any accidents occurred to those men whom I had originally chosen, I planned to fill their places with the next best ones who were all willing to go.

On Bartlett's return the Eskimos built the usual

wind shelter already described, and Bartlett took a latitude observation, getting 87° 46′ 49″.

Bartlett was naturally much disappointed to find that even with his five-mile northward march of the morning he was still short of the 88th parallel. Our latitude was the direct result of the northerly wind of the last two days, which had crowded the ice southward as we traveled over it northward. We had traveled fully twelve miles more than his observation showed in the last five marches, but had lost them by the crushing up of the young ice in our rear and the closing of the leads.

Bartlett took the observations here, as had Marvin five camps back partly to save my eyes and partly to have independent observations by different members of the expedition. When the calculations were completed, two copies were made, one for Bartlett and one for me, and he got ready to start south on the back trail in command of my fourth supporting party, with his two Eskimos, one sledge, and eighteen dogs.

I felt a keen regret as I saw the captain's broad shoulders grow smaller in the distance and finally disappear behind the ice hummocks of the white and glittering expanse toward the south. But it was no time for reverie, and I turned abruptly away and gave my attention to the work which was before me. I had no anxiety about Bartlett. I knew that I should see him again at the ship. My work was still ahead, not in the rear. Bartlett had been invaluable to me, and circumstances had thrust upon him the brunt of the pioneering instead of its being divided among several, as I had originally planned.

Though he was naturally disappointed at not having reached the 88th parallel, he had every reason to be proud, not only of his work in general, but that he had surpassed the Italian record by a degree and a quarter. I had given him the post of honor in command of my last supporting party for three reasons: first, because of his magnificent handling of the *Roosevelt;* second, because he had cheerfully and gladly stood between me and every possible minor annoyance from the start of the expedition to that day; third, because it seemed to me right that, in view of the noble work of Great Britain in arctic exploration, a British subject should, next to an American, be able to say that he had stood nearest the North Pole.

With the departure of Bartlett, the main party now consisted of my own division and Henson's. My men were Egingwah and Seegloo; Henson's men were Ootah and Ooqueah. We had five sledges and forty dogs, the pick of one hundred and forty with which we had left the ship. With these we were ready now for the final lap of the journey.

We were now one hundred and thirty-three nautical miles from the Pole. Pacing back and forth in the lee of the pressure ridge near which our igloos were built, I made out my program. Every nerve must be strained to make five marches of at least twenty-five miles each, crowding these marches in such a way as to bring us to the end of the fifth march by noon, to permit an immediate latitude observation. Weather and leads permitting, I believed that I could do this. From the improving character of the ice, and in view of the recent northerly winds, I hoped that I should have no serious trouble with the going.

If for any reason I fell short of these proposed distances, I had two methods in reserve for making up the deficit. One was to double the last march — that is, make a good march, have tea and a hearty lunch, rest the dogs a little, and then go on again, without sleep. The other was, at the conclusion of my fifth march, to push on with one light sledge, a double team of dogs, and one or two of the party, leaving the rest in camp. Even should the going be worse than was then anticipated, eight marches like the three from 85° 48′ to 86° 38′, or six similar to our last one, would do the trick.

Underlying all these calculations was the ever-present knowledge that a twenty-fours' gale would open leads of water which might be impassable, and that all these plans would be negatived.

As I paced to and fro, making out my plans, I remembered that three years ago that day we had crossed the "big lead" on our way north, April 1, 1906. A comparison of conditions now and then filled me with hope for the future.

This was the time for which I had reserved all my energies, the time for which I had worked for twenty-two years, for which I had lived the simple life and trained myself as for a race. In spite of my years, I felt fit for the demands of the coming days and was eager to be on the trail. As for my party, my equipment, and my supplies, they were perfect beyond my most sanguine dreams of earlier years. My party might be regarded as an ideal which had now come to

BARTLETT AND HIS PARTY READY TO START BACK FROM 87° 47′ NORTH, APRIL 1, 1909

CUTTING BLOCKS OF SNOW FOR IGLOOS AT NEXT TO LAST CAMP, 89° 25' NORTH

(At This Camp It Was Difficult to Find Enough Snow for the Igloos)

realization — as loyal and responsive to my will as the fingers of my right hand.

My four Eskimos carried the technic of dogs, sledges, ice, and cold as their racial heritage. Henson and Ootah had been my companions at the farthest point on the expedition three years before. Egingwah and Seegloo had been in Clark's division, which had such a narrow escape at that time, having been obliged for several days to subsist upon their sealskin boots, all their other food being gone.

And the fifth was young Ooqueah, who had never before served in any expedition; but who was, if possible, even more willing and eager than the others to go with me wherever I should elect. For he was always thinking of the great treasures which I had promised each of the men who should go to the farthest point with me — whale-boat, rifle, shotgun, ammunition, knives, et cetera — wealth beyond the wildest dreams of Eskimos, which should win for him the daughter of old Ikwa of Cape York, on whom he had set his heart.

All these men had a blind confidence that I would somehow get them back to land. But I recognized fully that all the impetus of the party centered in me. Whatever pace I set, the others would make good; but if I played out, they would stop like a car with a punctured tire. I had no fault to find with the conditions, and I faced them with confidence.

CHAPTER XXX

THE FINAL SPURT BEGUN

AT this time it may be appropriate to say a word regarding my reasons for selecting Henson as my fellow traveler to the Pole itself. In this selection I acted exactly as I have done on all my expeditions for the last fifteen years. He has in those years always been with me at my point farthest north. Moreover, Henson was the best man I had with me for this kind of work, with the exception of the Eskimos, who, with their racial inheritance of ice technic and their ability to handle sledges and dogs, were more necessary to me, as members of my own individual party, than any white man could have been. Of course they could not lead, but they could follow and drive dogs better than any white man.

Henson, with his years of arctic experience, was almost as skilful at this work as an Eskimo. He could handle dogs and sledges. He was a part of the traveling machine. Had I taken another member of the expedition also, he would have been a passenger, necessitating the carrying of extra rations and other impedimenta. It would have amounted to an additional load on the sledges, while the taking of Henson was in the interest of economy of weight.

The second reason was that while Henson was more useful to me than any other member of my expedition when it came to traveling with my last party over the polar ice, he would not have been so competent as the white members of the expedition in getting himself and his party back to the land. If Henson had been sent back with one of the supporting parties from a distance far out on the ice, and if he had encountered conditions similar to those which we had to face on the return journey in 1906, he and his party would never have reached the land. While faithful to me, and when *with me* more effective in covering distance with a sledge than any of the others, he had not, as a racial inheritance, the daring and initiative of Bartlett, or Marvin, MacMillan, or Borup. I owed it to him not to subject him to dangers and responsibilities which he was temperamentally unfit to face.

As to the dogs, most of them were powerful males, as hard as iron, in good condition, but without an ounce of superfluous fat; and, by reason of the care which I had taken of them up to this point, they were all in good spirits, like the men. The sledges, which were being repaired that day, were also in good condition. My food and fuel supplies were ample for forty days, and by the gradual utilization of the dogs themselves for reserve food, might be made to last for fifty days if it came to a pinch.

As the Eskimos worked away at repairing the sledges while we rested there on the first day of April, they stopped from time to time to eat some of the boiled dog which the surplus numbers in Bartlett's returning team had enabled them to have. They had killed one of the poorest dogs and boiled it, using the splinters of an extra broken sledge for fuel under their cooker. It was a change for them from the pemmican diet. It was fresh meat, it was hot, and they seemed thoroughly to enjoy it. But though I remembered many times when from sheer starvation I had been glad to eat dog meat raw, I did not feel inclined to join in the feast of my dusky friends.

A little after midnight, on the morning of April 2, after a few hours of sound, warm, and refreshing sleep, and a hearty breakfast, I started to lift the trail to the north, leaving the others to pack, hitch up, and follow. As I climbed the pressure ridge back of our igloo, I took up another hole in my belt, the third since I left the land — thirty-two days before. Every man and dog of us was as lean and flat-bellied as a board, and as hard.

Up to this time I had intentionally kept in the rear, to straighten out any little hitch or to encourage a man with a broken sledge, and to see that everything was in good marching order. Now I took my proper place in the lead. Though I held myself in check, I felt the keenest exhilaration, and even exultation, as I climbed over the pressure ridge and breasted the keen air sweeping over the mighty ice, pure and straight from the Pole itself.

These feelings were not in any way dampened when I plunged off the pressure ridge into water mid-thigh deep, where the pressure had forced down the edge of the floe north of us and had allowed the water to flow in under the surface snow. My boots and trousers were tight, so that no water could get inside, and as the water froze on the fur of my trousers I scraped it off with the blade of the ice lance which I carried, and was no worse for my involuntary morning plunge. I thought of my unused bath tub on the *Roosevelt*, three hundred and thirty nautical miles to the south, and smiled.

It was a fine marching morning, clear and sunlit, with a temperature of minus 25°, and the wind of the past few days had subsided to a gentle breeze. The going was the best we had had since leaving the land. The floes were large and old, hard and level, with patches of sapphire blue ice (the pools of the preceding summer). While the pressure ridges surrounding them were stupendous, some of them fifty feet high, they were not especially hard to negotiate, either through some gap or up the gradual slope of a huge drift of snow. The brilliant sunlight, the good going save for the pressure ridges, the consciousness that we were now well started on the last lap of our journey, and the joy of again being in the lead affected me like wine. The years seemed to drop from me, and I felt as I had felt in those days fifteen years before, when I headed my little party across the great ice-cap of Greenland, leaving twenty and twenty-five miles behind my snowshoes day after day, and on a spurt stretching it to thirty or forty.

Perhaps a man always thinks of the very beginning of his work when he feels it is nearing its end. The appearance of the ice-fields to the north this day, large and level, the brilliant blue of the sky, the biting character of the wind — everything excepting the surface of the ice, which on the great cap is absolutely dead level with a straight line for a horizon — reminded me of those marches of the long ago.

The most marked difference was the shadows, which on the ice-cap are absent entirely, but on the polar ice, where the great pressure ridges stand out in bold relief, are deep and dark. Then, too, there are on the polar ice those little patches of sapphire blue already mentioned, made from the water pools of the preceding summer. On the Greenland ice-cap years ago I had been spurred on by the necessity of reaching the musk-oxen of Independence Bay before my supplies gave out. Now I was spurred on by the necessity of making my goal, if possible, before the round face of the coming full moon should stir the tides with unrest and open a network of leads across our path.

After some hours the sledges caught up with me. The dogs were so active that morning, after their day's rest, that I was frequently obliged to sit on a sledge for a few minutes or else run to keep up with them, which I did not care to do just yet. Our course was nearly, as the crow flies, due north, across floe after floe, pressure ridge after pressure ridge, headed straight for some hummock or pinnacle of ice which I had lined in with my compass.

In this way we traveled for ten hours without stopping, covering, I felt sure, thirty miles, though, to be conservative, I called it twenty-five. My Eskimos said that we had come as far as from the *Roosevelt* to Porter Bay, which by our winter route scales thirty-five miles on the chart. Anyway, we were well over the 88th parallel, in a region where no human being had ever been before. And whatever distance we

made, we were likely to retain it now that the wind
had ceased to blow from the north. It was even possible that with the release of the wind pressure the ice
might rebound more or less and return us some of the
hard-earned miles which it had stolen from us during
the previous three days.

Near the end of the march I came upon a lead which
was just opening. It was ten yards wide directly in
front of me, but a few hundred yards to the east was
an apparently practicable crossing where the single
crack was divided into several. I signaled to the
sledges to hurry; then, running to the place, I had time
to pick a road across the moving ice cakes and return
to help the teams across before the lead widened so
as to be impassable. This passage was effected by my
jumping from one cake to another, picking the way,
and making sure that the cake would not tilt under the
weight of the dogs and the sledge, returning to the
former cake where the dogs were, encouraging the dogs
ahead while the driver steered the sledge across from
cake to cake, and threw his weight from one side to
the other so that it could not overturn. We got the
sledges across several cracks so wide that while the
dogs had no trouble in jumping, the men had to be
pretty active in order to follow the long sledges. Fortunately the sledges were of the new Peary type,
twelve feet long. Had they been of the old Eskimo
type, seven feet long, we might have had to use ropes
and pull them across hand over hand on an ice cake.

It is always hard to make the dogs leap a widening
crack, though some of the best dog drivers can do it
instantly, using the whip and the voice. A poor dog

driver would be likely to get everything into the water in the attempt. It is sometimes necessary to go ahead of the dogs, holding the hand low and shaking it as though it contained some dainty morsel of food, thus inspiring them with courage for the leap.

Perhaps a mile beyond this, the breaking of the ice at the edge of a narrow lead as I landed from a jump sent me into the water nearly to my hips; but as the water did not come above the waistband of my trousers, which were water-tight, it was soon scraped and beaten off before it had time to freeze.

This lead was not wide enough to bother the sledges.

As we stopped to make our camp near a huge pressure ridge, the sun, which was gradually getting higher, seemed almost to have some warmth. While we were building our igloos, we could see, by the water clouds lying to the east and southeast of us some miles distant, that a wide lead was opening in that direction. The approaching full moon was evidently getting in its work.

As we had traveled on, the moon had circled round and round the heavens opposite the sun, a disk of silver opposite a disk of gold. Looking at its pallid and spectral face, from which the brighter light of the sun had stolen the color, it seemed hard to realize that its presence there had power to stir the great ice-fields around us with restlessness — power even now, when we were so near our goal, to interrupt our pathway with an impassable lead.

The moon had been our friend during the long winter, giving us light to hunt by for a week or two each month.   Now it seemed no longer a friend, but a dangerous presence to be regarded with fear.   Its power, which had before been beneficent, was now malevolent and incalculably potent for evil.

When we awoke early in the morning of April 3, after a few hours' sleep, we found the weather still clear and calm.   There were some broad heavy pressure ridges in the beginning of this march, and we had to use pickaxes quite freely.   This delayed us a little, but as soon as we struck the level old floes we tried to make up for lost time.   As the daylight was now continuous we could travel as long as we pleased and sleep as little as we must.   We hustled along for ten hours again, as we had before, making only twenty miles, because of the early delay with the pickaxes and another brief delay at a narrow lead.   We were now half-way to the 89th parallel, and I had been obliged to take up another hole in my belt.

Some gigantic rafters were seen during this march, but they were not in our path.   All day long we had heard the ice grinding and groaning on all sides of us, but no motion was visible to our eyes.   Either the ice was slacking back into equilibrium, sagging northward after its release from the wind pressure, or else it was feeling the influence of the spring tides of the full moon.   On, on we pushed, and I am not ashamed to confess that my pulse beat high, for the breath of success seemed already in my nostrils.

CHAPTER XXXI

WITH every passing day even the Eskimos were becoming more eager and interested, notwithstanding the fatigue of the long marches. As we stopped to make camp, they would climb to some pinnacle of ice and strain their eyes to the north, wondering if the Pole was in sight, for they were now certain that we should get there this time.

We slept only a few hours the next night, hitting the trail again a little before midnight between the 3d and 4th of April. The weather and the going were even better than the day before. The surface of the ice, except as interrupted by infrequent pressure ridges, was as level as the glacial fringe from Hecla to Cape Columbia, and harder. I rejoiced at the thought that if the weather held good I should be able to get in my five marches before noon of the 6th.

Again we traveled for ten hours straight ahead, the dogs often on the trot and occasionally on the run, and in those ten hours we reeled off at least twenty-five miles. I had a slight accident that day, a sledge runner having passed over the side of my right foot as I stumbled while running beside a team; but the hurt was not severe enough to keep me from traveling.

Near the end of the day we crossed a lead about one

hundred yards wide, on young ice so thin that, as I ran ahead to guide the dogs, I was obliged to slide my feet and travel wide, bear style, in order to distribute my weight, while the men let the sledges and dogs come over by themselves, gliding across where they could.   The last two men came over on all fours.

I watched them from the other side with my heart in my mouth — watched the ice bending under the weight of the sledges and the men. As one of the sledges neared the north side, a runner cut clear through the ice, and I expected every moment that the whole thing, dogs and all, would go through the ice and down to the bottom.   But it did not.

This dash reminded me of that day, nearly three years before, when in order to save our lives we had taken desperate chances in recrossing the "Big Lead" on ice similar to this — ice that buckled under us and through which my toe cut several times as I slid my long snowshoes over it. A man who should wait for the ice to be really safe would stand small chance of getting far in these latitudes. Traveling on the polar ice, one takes all kinds of chances. Often a man has the choice between the possibility of drowning by going on or starving to death by standing still, and challenges fate with the briefer and less painful chance.

That night we were all pretty tired, but satisfied with our progress so far. We were almost inside of the 89th parallel, and I wrote in my diary: "Give me three more days of this weather!" The temperature at the beginning of the march had been minus 40°. That night I put all the poorest dogs in one team and began to eliminate and feed them to the others, as it became necessary.

We stopped for only a short sleep, and early in the evening of the same day, the 4th, we struck on again. The temperature was then minus 35°, the going was the same, but the sledges always haul more easily when the temperature rises, and the dogs were on the trot much of the time. Toward the end of the march we came upon a lead running north and south, and as the young ice was thick enough to support the teams, we traveled on it for two hours, the dogs galloping along and reeling off the miles in a way that delighted my heart. The light air which had blown from the south during the first few hours of the march veered to the east and grew keener as the hours wore on.

I had not dared to hope for such progress as we were making. Still the biting cold would have been impossible to face by anyone not fortified by an inflexible purpose. The bitter wind burned our faces so that they cracked, and long after we got into camp each day they pained us so that we could hardly go to sleep. The Eskimos complained much, and at every camp fixed their fur clothing about their faces, waists, knees, and wrists. They also complained of their noses, which I had never known them to do before. The air was as keen and bitter as frozen steel.

At the next camp I had another of the dogs killed. It was now exactly six weeks since we left the *Roosevelt*, and I felt as if the goal were in sight. I intended the next day, weather and ice permitting, to make a long march, "boil the kettle" midway, and then go

on again without sleep, trying to make up the five miles
which we had lost on the 3d of April.

During the daily march my mind and body were
too busy with the problem of covering as many miles
of distance as possible to permit me to enjoy the
beauty of the frozen wilderness through which we
tramped. But at the end of the day's march, while
the igloos were being built, I usually had a few minutes
in which to look about me and to realize the picturesque-
ness of our situation — we, the only living things
in a trackless, colorless, inhospitable desert of ice.
Nothing but the hostile ice, and far more hostile icy
water, lay between our remote place on the world's
map and the utmost tips of the lands of Mother Earth.

I knew of course that there was always a *possibility* that we might still end our lives up there, and
that our conquest of the unknown spaces and silences
of the polar void might remain forever unknown to the
world which we had left behind. But it was hard to
realize this. That hope which is said to spring eternal
in the human breast always buoyed me up with the
belief that, as a matter of course, we should be able
to return along the white road by which we had come.

Sometimes I would climb to the top of a pinnacle
of ice to the north of our camp and strain my eyes
into the whiteness which lay beyond, trying to imagine
myself already at the Pole. We had come so far,
and the capricious ice had placed so few obstructions
in our path, that now I dared to loose my fancy,
to entertain the image which my will had heretofore
forbidden to my imagination — the image of ourselves
at the goal.

We had been very fortunate with the leads so far, but I was in constant and increasing dread lest we should encounter an impassable one toward the very end. With every successive march, my fear of such impassable leads had increased. At every pressure ridge I found myself hurrying breathlessly forward, fearing there might be a lead just beyond it, and when I arrived at the summit I would catch my breath with relief — only to find myself hurrying on in the same way at the next ridge.

At our camp on the 5th of April I gave the party a little more sleep than at the previous ones, as we were all pretty well played out and in need of rest. I took a latitude sight, and this indicated our position to be 89° 25', or thirty-five miles from the Pole; but I determined to make the next camp in time for a noon observation, if the sun should be visible.

Before midnight on the 5th we were again on the trail. The weather was overcast, and there was the same gray and shadowless light as on the march after Marvin had turned back. The sky was a colorless pall gradually deepening to almost black at the horizon, and the ice was a ghastly and chalky white, like that of the Greenland ice-cap — just the colors which an imaginative artist would paint as a polar ice-scape. How different it seemed from the glittering fields, canopied with blue and lit by the sun and full moon, over which we had been traveling for the last four days.

The going was even better than before. There was hardly any snow on the hard granular surface of the old floes, and the sapphire blue lakes were larger than ever. The temperature had risen to minus 15°,

THE HALT FOR LUNCH IN LAST FORCED MARCH, 89° 25' TO 89° 57', SHOWING ALCOHOL STOVES IN
SNOW SHELTER

Left to Right: Henson, Egingwah, Ootah, Seegloo, Ooqueah

CAMP MORRIS K. JESUP, 89° 57′, APRIL 6 AND 7, 1909

which, reducing the friction of the sledges, gave the dogs the appearance of having caught the high spirits of the party. Some of them even tossed their heads and barked and yelped as they traveled.

Notwithstanding the grayness of the day, and the melancholy aspect of the surrounding world, by some strange shift of feeling the fear of the leads had fallen from me completely. I now felt that success was certain, and, notwithstanding the physical exhaustion of the forced marches of the last five days, I went tirelessly on and on, the Eskimos following almost automatically, though I knew that they must feel the weariness which my excited brain made me incapable of feeling.

When we had covered, as I estimated, a good fifteen miles, we halted, made tea, ate lunch, and rested the dogs. Then we went on for another estimated fifteen miles. In twelve hours' actual traveling time we made thirty miles. Many laymen have wondered why we were able to travel faster after the sending back of each of the supporting parties, especially after the last one. To any man experienced in the handling of troops this will need no explanation. The larger the party and the greater the number of sledges, the greater is the chance of breakages or delay for one reason or another. A large party cannot be forced as rapidly as a small party.

Take a regiment, for instance. The regiment could not make as good an average daily march for a number of forced marches as could a picked company of that regiment. The picked company could not make as good an average march for a number of forced marches as could a picked file of men from that particular company; and this file could not make the same average for a certain number of forced marches that the fastest traveler in the whole regiment could make.

So that, with my party reduced to five picked men, every man, dog, and sledge under my individual eye, myself in the lead, and all recognizing that the moment had now come to let ourselves out for all there was in us, we naturally bettered our previous speed.

When Bartlett left us the sledges had been practically rebuilt, all the best dogs were in our pack, and we all understood that we must attain our object and get back as quickly as we possibly could. The weather was in our favor. The average march for the whole journey from the land to the Pole was over fifteen miles. We had repeatedly made marches of twenty miles. Our average for five marches from the point where the last supporting party turned back was about twenty-six miles.

CHAPTER XXXII

WE REACH THE POLE

THE last march northward ended at ten o'clock on the forenoon of April 6. I had now made the five marches planned from the point at which Bartlett turned back, and my reckoning showed that we were in the immediate neighborhood of the goal of all our striving. After the usual arrangements for going into camp, at approximate local noon, of the Columbia meridian, I made the first observation at our polar camp. It indicated our position as 89° 57'.

We were now at the end of the last long march of the upward journey. Yet with the Pole actually in sight I was too weary to take the last few steps. The accumulated weariness of all those days and nights of forced marches and insufficient sleep, constant peril and anxiety, seemed to roll across me all at once. I was actually too exhausted to realize at the moment that my life's purpose had been achieved. As soon as our igloos had been completed and we had eaten our dinner and double-rationed the dogs, I turned in for a few hours of absolutely necessary sleep, Henson and the Eskimos having unloaded the sledges and got them in readiness for such repairs as were necessary. But, weary though I was, I could not sleep long. It was, therefore, only a few hours later when I woke. The first thing I did after awaking was to write these

words in my diary: "The Pole at last. The prize of
three centuries. My dream and goal for twenty years.
Mine at last! I cannot bring myself to realize it. It
seems all so simple and commonplace."

Everything was in readiness for an observation[1] at

[1] The instruments used in taking observations for latitude may be either a
sextant and an artificial horizon, or a small theodolite. Both these instruments
were taken on the sledge journey; but the theodolite was not used, owing to the
low altitude of the sun. Had the expedition been delayed on the return until May
or June, the theodolite would then have been of value in determining position and
variation of the compass.

The method of taking meridian observations with a sextant and an artificial
horizon on a polar sledge journey is as follows: if there is any wind, a semicircular
wind-guard of snow blocks, two tiers high, is put up, opening to the south. If
there is no wind, this is not necessary.

The instrument box is firmly bedded in the snow, which is packed down to a
firm bearing and snow is packed around the box. Then something, usually a
skin, is thrown over the snow, partly to prevent any possible warmth from the sun
melting the snow and shifting the bearing of the box; partly to protect the eyes
of the observer from the intense reflected glare of light from the snow.

The mercury trough of the artificial horizon is placed on top of the level box,
and the mercury, which has been thoroughly warmed in the igloo, is poured into
the trough until it is full. In the case of the special wooden trough devised and
used on the last expedition, it was possible to bring the surface of the mercury
level with the edges of the trough, thus enabling us to read angles very close to
the horizon.

The mercury trough is covered with what is called the roof — a metal framework carrying two pieces of very accurately ground glass, set inclined, like the
opposite sides of the roof of a house. The object of this roof is to prevent any
slightest breath of wind disturbing the surface of the mercury and so distorting
the sun's image in it, and also to keep out any fine snow or frost crystals that
may be in the atmosphere. In placing the trough and the roof on the top of the
instrument box, the trough is placed so that its longer diameter will be directed
toward the sun.

A skin is then thrown down on the snow close to the box and north of it,
and the observer lies down flat on his stomach on this, with his head to the south,
and head and sextant close to the artificial horizon. He rests both elbows on the
snow, holding the sextant firmly in both hands, and moving his head and the
instrument until the image or part of the image of the sun is seen reflected on
the surface of the mercury.

The principle on which the latitude of the observer is obtained from the altitude of the sun at noon is very simple. It is this: that the latitude of the observer

THE RECONNOITERING PARTY AT THE POLE

(On the Sledge are Merely the Instruments, a Tin of Pemmican and a Skin or Two.   (Note the Firm Character of the Surface Ice.   Snow Shoes
Were not Required Here)

THE DOUBLE TEAM OF DOGS USED WITH THE RECONNOITERING SLEDGE AT THE POLE, SHOWING THEIR
ALERTNESS AND GOOD CONDITION

(Each Dog had Received Nearly Double the Standard Ration of One Pound of Pemmican Per Day)

6 P.M., Columbia meridian time, in case the sky should be clear, but at that hour it was, unfortunately, still overcast. But as there were indications that it would clear before long, two of the Eskimos and myself made ready a light sledge carrying only the instruments, a tin of pemmican, and one or two skins; and drawn by a double team of dogs, we pushed on an estimated distance of ten miles. While we traveled, the sky cleared, and at the end of the journey, I was able to get a satisfactory series of observations at Columbia meridian midnight. These observations indicated that our position was then beyond the Pole.

Nearly everything in the circumstances which then surrounded us seemed too strange to be thoroughly realized; but one of the strangest of those circumstances seemed to me to be the fact that, in a march of only a few hours, I had passed from the western to the eastern hemisphere and had verified my position at the summit of the world. It was hard to realize that, in the first miles of this brief march, we had been traveling due north, while, on the last few miles of the same march, we had been traveling south, although we had all the time been traveling precisely in the same direction. It would be difficult to imagine a better illustration of the fact that most things are relative. Again,

---

is equal to the distance of the center of the sun from the zenith, plus the declination of the sun for that day and hour.

The declination of the sun for any place at any hour may be obtained from tables prepared for that purpose, which give the declination for noon of every day on the Greenwich meridian, and the hourly change in the declination.

Such tables for the months of February, March, April, May, June, and July, together with the ordinary tables for refraction to minus 10° Fahrenheit, I had with me on pages torn from the "Nautical Almanac and Navigator."

please consider the uncommon circumstance that, in order to return to our camp, it now became necessary to turn and go north again for a few miles and then to go directly south, all the time traveling in the same direction.

As we passed back along that trail which none had ever seen before or would ever see again, certain reflections intruded themselves which, I think, may fairly be called unique. East, west, and north had disappeared for us. Only one direction remained and that was south. Every breeze which could possibly blow upon us, no matter from what point of the horizon, must be a south wind. Where we were, one day and one night constituted a year, a hundred such days and nights constituted a century. Had we stood in that spot during the six months of the arctic winter night, we should have seen every star of the northern hemisphere circling the sky at the same distance from the horizon, with Polaris (the North Star) practically in the zenith.

All during our march back to camp the sun was swinging around in its ever-moving circle. At six o'clock on the morning of April 7, having again arrived at Camp Jesup, I took another series of observations. These indicated our position as being four or five miles from the Pole, towards Bering Strait. Therefore, with a double team of dogs and a light sledge, I traveled directly towards the sun an estimated distance of eight miles. Again I returned to the camp in time for a final and completely satisfactory series of observations on April 7 at noon, Columbia meridian time. These observations gave results essentially the same

PEARY WITH CHRONOMETER, SEXTANT AND ARTIFICIAL HORIZON
AT THE POLE

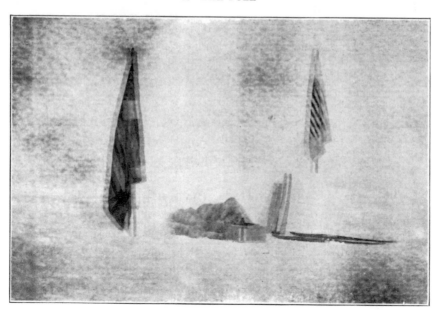

PEARY TAKING AN OBSERVATION AT THE POLE, WITH ARTIFICIAL
HORIZON, IN A SNOW SHELTER
Photos by Henson, April 7

PEARY'S IGLOO AT CAMP MORRIS K. JESUP, APRIL 6, 1909;
The Most Northerly Human Habitation in the World. In the Background Flies
Peary's North Polar Flag Which He Had Carried for Fifteen Years

as those made at the same spot twenty-four hours before.

I had now taken in all thirteen single, or six and one-half double, altitudes of the sun, at two different stations, in three different directions, at four different times. All were under satisfactory conditions, except for the first single altitude on the sixth. The temperature during these observations had been from minus 11° Fahrenheit to minus 30° Fahrenheit, with clear sky and calm weather (except as already noted for the single observation on the sixth). I give here a facsimile of a typical set of these observations. (See the two following pages.)

In traversing the ice in these various directions as I had done, I had allowed approximately ten miles for possible errors in my observations, and at some moment during these marches and counter-marches, I had passed over or very near the point[1] where north and south and east and west blend into one.

[1] Ignorance and misconception of all polar matters seem so widespread and comprehensive that it appears advisable to introduce here a few a b c paragraphs. Anyone interested can supplement these by reading the introductory parts of any good elementary school geography or astronomy.

The North Pole (that is, the geographical pole as distinguished from the magnetic pole, and this appears to be the first and most general stumbling block of the ignorant) is simply the point where that imaginary line known as the earth's axis — that is, the line on which the earth revolves in its daily motion — intersects the earth's surface.

Some of the recent sober discussions as to the size of the North Pole, whether it was as big as a quarter, or a hat, or a township, have been intensely ludicrous.

Precisely speaking, the North Pole is simply a mathematical point, and therefore, in accordance with the mathematical definition of a point, it has neither length, breadth, nor thickness.

If the question is asked, how closely can the Pole be determined (this is the point which has muddled some of the ignorant wiseacres), the answer will be:

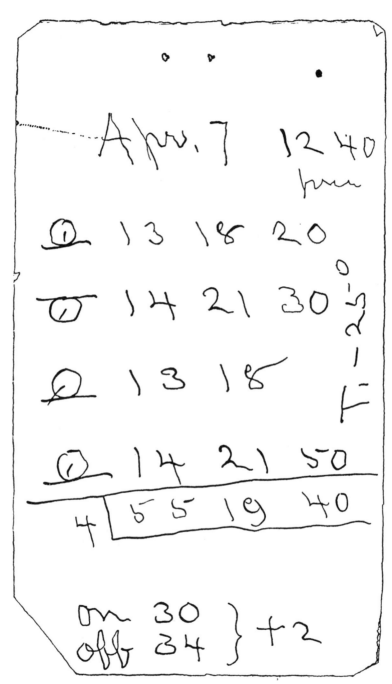

FACSIMILE OF OBSERVATIONS AT CAMP MORRIS JESUP, APRIL 7, 1909

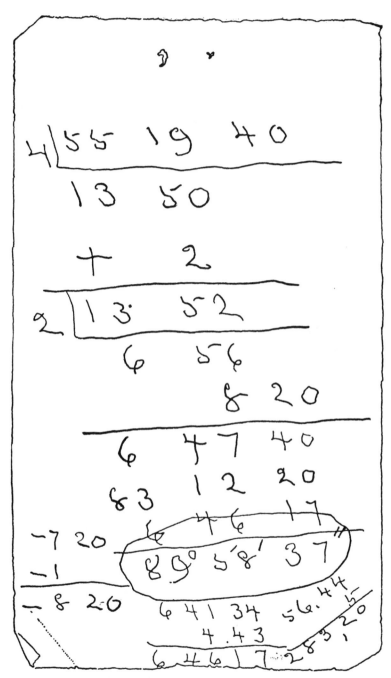

FACSIMILE OF OBSERVATIONS AT CAMP MORRIS JESUP, APRIL 7, 1909

Of course there were some more or less informal ceremonies connected with our arrival at our difficult destination, but they were not of a very elaborate character. We planted five flags at the top of the world. The first one was a silk American flag which Mrs. Peary gave me fifteen years ago. That flag has done more traveling in high latitudes than any other ever made.

That depends upon the character of the instruments used, the ability of the observer using them, and the number of observations taken.

If there were land at the Pole, and powerful instruments of great precision, such as are used in the world's great observatories, were mounted there on suitable foundations and used by practised observers for repeated observations extending over years, then it would be possible to determine the position of the Pole with great precision.

With ordinary field instruments, transit, theodolite, or sextant, an extended series of observations by an expert observer should permit the determination of the Pole within entirely satisfactory limits, but not with the same precision as by the first method.

A single observation at sea with sextant and the natural horizon, as usually taken by the master of a ship, is assumed under ordinary satisfactory conditions to give the observer's position within about a mile.

In regard to the difficulties of taking observations in the arctic regions, I have found a tendency on the part of experts who, however, have not had practical experience in the arctic regions themselves, to overestimate and exaggerate the difficulties and drawbacks of making these observations due to the cold.

My personal experience has been that, to an experienced observer, dressed in furs and taking observations in calm weather, in temperatures not exceeding say 40° below zero Fahrenheit, the difficulties of the work resulting from cold alone are not serious. The amount and character of errors due to the effect of cold upon the instrument might perhaps be a subject for discussion, and for distinct differences of opinion.

My personal experience has been that my most serious trouble was with the eyes.

To eyes which have been subjected to brilliant and unremitting daylight for days and weeks, and to the strain of continually setting a course with the compass, and traveling towards a fixed point in such light, the taking of a series of observations is usually a nightmare; and the strain of focusing, of getting precise contact of the sun's images, and of reading the vernier, all in the blinding light of which only those who have taken observations in bright sunlight on an un-broken snow expanse in the arctic regions can form any conception, usually leaves the eyes bloodshot and smarting for hours afterwards.

MEMBERS OF THE PARTY CHEERING THE STARS AND STRIPES AT THE
POLE, APRIL 7, 1909
From Left to Right; Ooqueah, Ootah, Henson, Egingwah and Seegloo

RETURNING TO CAMP WITH THE FLAGS, APRIL 7, 1909

THE FOUR NORTH POLE ESKIMOS:
From Left to Right: Ootah, Ooqueah, Seegloo, Egingwah

I carried it wrapped about my body on every one of my expeditions northward after it came into my possession, and I left a fragment of it at each of my successive "farthest norths": Cape Morris K. Jesup, the northernmost point of land in the known world; Cape Thomas Hubbard, the northernmost known point of Jesup Land, west of Grant Land; Cape Columbia, the northernmost point of North American lands; and my farthest north in 1906, latitude 87° 6' in the ice of the polar sea. By the time it actually reached the Pole, therefore, it was somewhat worn and discolored.

A broad diagonal section of this ensign would now mark the farthest goal of earth — the place where I and my dusky companions stood.

It was also considered appropriate to raise the colors of the Delta Kappa Epsilon fraternity, in which I was initiated a member while an undergraduate

---

The continued series of observations in the vicinity of the Pole, noted above, left me with eyes that were, for two or three days, useless for anything requiring careful vision, and had it been necessary for me to set a course during the first two or three days of our return I should have found it extremely trying.

Snow goggles, as worn by us continually during the march, while helping, do not entirely relieve the eyes from strain, and during a series of observations the eyes become extremely tired and at times uncertain.

Various authorities will give different estimates of the probable error in observations taken at the Pole. I am personally inclined to think that an allowance of five miles is an equitable one.

No one, except those entirely ignorant of such matters, has imagined for a moment that I was able to determine with my instruments the precise position of the Pole, but after having determined its position approximately, then setting an arbitrary allowance of about ten miles for possible errors of the instruments and myself as observer, and then crossing and recrossing that ten mile area in various directions, no one except the most ignorant will have any doubt but what, at some time, I had passed close to the precise point, and had, perhaps, actually passed over it.

student at Bowdoin College, the "World's Ensign of Liberty and Peace," with its red, white, and blue in a field of white, the Navy League flag, and the Red Cross flag.

After I had planted the American flag in the ice, I told Henson to time the Eskimos for three rousing cheers, which they gave with the greatest enthusiasm. Thereupon, I shook hands with each member of the party — surely a sufficiently unceremonious affair to meet with the approval of the most democratic. The Eskimos were childishly delighted with our success. While, of course, they did not realize its importance fully, or its world-wide significance, they did understand that it meant the final achievement of a task upon which they had seen me engaged for many years.

Then, in a space between the ice blocks of a pressure ridge, I deposited a glass bottle containing a diagonal strip of my flag and records of which the following is a copy:

90 N. Lat., North Pole,
April 6, 1909.

Arrived here to-day, 27 marches from C. Columbia.

I have with me 5 men, Matthew Henson, colored, Ootah, Egingwah, Seegloo, and Ookeah, Eskimos; 5 sledges and 38 dogs. My ship, the S. S. *Roosevelt*, is in winter quarters at C. Sheridan, 90 miles east of Columbia.

The expedition under my command which has succeeded in reaching the Pole is under the auspices of the Peary Arctic Club of New York City, and has been fitted out and sent north by the members and friends of the club for the purpose of securing this geographical prize, if possible, for the honor and prestige of the United States of America.

The officers of the club are Thomas H. Hubbard, of New York, President; Zenas Crane, of Mass., Vice-president; Herbert L. Bridgman, of New York, Secretary and Treasurer.

I start back for Cape Columbia to-morrow.

ROBERT E. PEARY,
United States Navy.

90 N. LAT., NORTH POLE,
April 6, 1909.

I have to-day hoisted the national ensign of the United States of America at this place, which my observations indicate to be the North Polar axis of the earth, and have formally taken possession of the entire region, and adjacent, for and in the name of the President of the United States of America.

I leave this record and United States flag in possession.

ROBERT E. PEARY,
United States Navy.

If it were possible for a man to arrive at 90° north latitude without being utterly exhausted, body and brain, he would doubtless enjoy a series of unique sensations and reflections. But the attainment of the Pole was the culmination of days and weeks of forced marches, physical discomfort, insufficient sleep, and racking anxiety. It is a wise provision of nature that the human consciousness can grasp only such

degree of intense feeling as the brain can endure, and
the grim guardians of earth's remotest spot will accept
no man as guest until he has been tried and tested by
the severest ordeal.

Perhaps it ought not to have been so, but when I
knew for a certainty that we had reached the goal,
there was not a thing in the world I wanted but sleep.
But after I had a few hours of it, there succeeded
a condition of mental exaltation which made further
rest impossible. For more than a score of years
that point on the earth's surface had been the object of my every effort. To its attainment my whole
being, physical, mental, and moral, had been dedicated.
Many times my own life and the lives of those with
me had been risked. My own material and forces
and those of my friends had been devoted to this
object. This journey was my eighth into the arctic
wilderness. In that wilderness I had spent nearly
twelve years out of the twenty-three between my
thirtieth and my fifty-third year, and the intervening
time spent in civilized communities during that period
had been mainly occupied with preparations for
returning to the wilderness. The determination to
reach the Pole had become so much a part of my being
that, strange as it may seem, I long ago ceased to think
of myself save as an instrument for the attainment
of that end. To the layman this may seem strange,
but an inventor can understand it, or an artist, or
anyone who has devoted himself for years upon years
to the service of an idea.

But though my mind was busy at intervals during
those thirty hours spent at the Pole with the exhilarating

EGINGWAH SEARCHING THE HORIZON FOR LAND

PEARY SEARCHING THE HORIZON FOR LAND
From Top of Pressure Ridge Back of Igloos at Camp Jesup

LOOKING TOWARD CAPE CHELYUSKIN

LOOKING TOWARD SPITZBERGEN

LOOKING TOWARD CAPE COLUMBIA

LOOKING TOWARD BERING STRAIT

(The Four Directions from the Pole)

thought that my dream had come true, there was one recollection of other times that, now and then, intruded itself with startling distinctness. It was the recollection of a day three years before, April 21, 1906, when after making a fight with ice, open water, and storms, the expedition which I commanded had been forced to turn back from 87° 6' north latitude because our supply of food would carry us no further. And the contrast between the terrible depression of that day and the exaltation of the present moment was not the least pleasant feature of our brief stay at the Pole. During the dark moments of that return journey in 1906, I had told myself that I was only one in a long list of arctic explorers, dating back through the centuries, all the way from Henry Hudson to the Duke of the Abruzzi, and including Franklin, Kane, and Melville — a long list of valiant men who had striven and failed. I told myself that I had only succeeded, at the price of the best years of my life, in adding a few links to the chain that led from the parallels of civilization towards the polar center, but that, after all, at the end the only word I had to write was failure.

But now, while quartering the ice in various directions from our camp, I tried to realize that, after twenty-three years of struggles and discouragement, I had at last succeeded in placing the flag of my country at the goal of the world's desire. It is not easy to write about such a thing, but I knew that we were going back to civilization with the last of the great adventure stories — a story the world had been waiting to hear for nearly four hundred years, a story which was to be told at last under the folds of the Stars and Stripes, the flag that during a lonely and isolated life had come to be for me the symbol of home and everything I loved — and might never see again.

The thirty hours at the Pole, what with my marchings and countermarchings, together with the observations and records, were pretty well crowded. I found time, however, to write to Mrs. Peary on a United States postal card which I had found on the ship during the winter. It had been my custom at various important stages of the journey northward to write such a note in order that, if anything serious happened to me, these brief communications might ultimately reach her at the hands of survivors. This was the card, which later reached Mrs. Peary at Sydney:—

"90 NORTH LATITUDE, April 7th.
"*My dear Jo,*
"I have won out at last. Have been here a day. I start for home and you in an hour. Love to the "kidsies."

"BERT."

In the afternoon of the 7th, after flying our flags and taking our photographs, we went into our igloos and tried to sleep a little, before starting south again.

I could not sleep and my two Eskimos, Seegloo and Egingwah, who occupied the igloo with me, seemed equally restless. They turned from side to side, and when they were quiet I could tell from their uneven breathing that they were not asleep. Though they had not been specially excited the day before when I told them that we had reached the goal, yet they also seemed to be under the same exhilarating influence which made sleep impossible for me.

Finally I rose, and telling my men and the three men in the other igloo, who were equally wakeful, that we would try to make our last camp, some thirty miles to the south, before we slept, I gave orders to hitch up the dogs and be off. It seemed unwise to waste such perfect traveling weather in tossing about on the sleeping platforms of our igloos.

Neither Henson nor the Eskimos required any urging to take to the trail again. They were naturally anxious to get back to the land as soon as possible — now that our work was done. And about four o'clock on the afternoon of the 7th of April we turned our backs upon the camp at the North Pole.

Though intensely conscious of what I was leaving, I did not wait for any lingering farewell of my life's goal. The event of human beings standing at the hitherto inaccessible summit of the earth was accomplished, and my work now lay to the south, where four hundred and thirteen nautical miles of ice-floes and possibly open leads still lay between us and the north coast of Grant Land. One backward glance I gave — then turned my face toward the south and toward the future.

CHAPTER XXXIII

WE turned our backs upon the Pole at about four o'clock of the afternoon of April 7. Some effort has been made to give an adequate impression of the joy with which that remote spot had been reached, but however much pleasure we experienced upon reaching it, I left it with only that tinge of sadness that sometimes flashes over one at the thought, "This scene my eyes will never see again."

Our pleasure at being once more upon the homeward trail was somewhat lessened by a distinct feeling of anxiety with regard to the task that still lay before us. All the plans for the expedition were formulated quite as much with an eye toward a safe return from the Pole as toward the task of reaching it. The North Pole expedition has some relation to the problem of flying: a good many people have found that, while it was not so very difficult to fly, the difficulties of alighting in safety were more considerable.

It will be remembered, doubtless, that the greatest dangers of the expedition of 1905–06 were encountered not upon the upward journey, but in the course of our return from our farthest north over the polar ice, for it was then that we encountered the implacable "Big Lead," whose perils so nearly encompassed the destruction of the entire party. And it will be further

ATTEMPTED SOUNDING, APRIL 7, 1909

ACTUAL SOUNDING, FIVE MILES SOUTH OF THE POLE, APRIL 7, 1909, 1500 FATHOMS (9000 FT.)

NO BOTTOM

remembered that even after the "Big Lead" was safely
crossed and we had barely managed to stagger ashore
upon the inhospitable edge of northernmost Greenland
we escaped starvation only by the narrowest possible
margin.

Memories of this narrow escape were, therefore, in
the minds of every member of our little party as we
turned our backs upon the North Pole, and I dare
say that every one of us wondered whether a similar
experience were in store for us. We had found the
Pole. Should we return to tell the story? Before
we hit the trail I had a brief talk with the men of the
party and made them understand that it was essential
that we should reach the land before the next spring
tides. To this end every nerve must be strained.
From now on it was to be a case of "big travel," little
sleep, and hustle every minute. My plan was to try
to make double marches on the entire return journey;
that is to say, to start out, cover one northward march,
make tea and eat luncheon, then cover another march,
then sleep a few hours, and push on again. As a
matter of fact, we did not fall much short of accomplishing this program. To be accurate, day in and day
out we covered five northward marches in three return
marches. Every day we gained on the return lessened
the chances of the trail being destroyed by high winds
shifting the ice. There was one region just above the
87th parallel, a region about fifty-seven miles wide,
which gave me a great deal of concern until we had
passed it. Twelve hours of strong wind blowing
from any quarter excepting the north would have
turned that region into an open sea. I breathed

a sigh of relief when we left the 87th parallel behind.

It will be recalled, perhaps, that though the expedition of 1905-06 started for the Pole from the northern shore of Grant Land, just as did this last expedition, the former expedition returned by a different route, reaching land again on the Greenland coast. This result was caused by the fact that strong winds carried the ice upon which we traveled far to the eastward of our upward course. This time, however, we met with no such misfortune. For the most part we found the trail renewed by our supporting parties easily recognizable and in most cases in good condition. Moreover there was an abundance of food both for men and for dogs, and so far as equipment went we were stripped as if for racing. Nor must the stimulating effects of the party's high spirits be forgotten. Everything, in short, was in our favor. We crowded on all speed for the first five miles of our return journey. Then we came to a narrow crack which was filled with recent ice, which furnished a chance to try for a sounding, a thing that had not been feasible at the Pole itself on account of the thickness of the ice. Here, however, we were able to chop through the ice until we struck water. Our sounding apparatus gave us 1500 fathoms of water with no bottom. As the Eskimos were reeling in, the wire parted and both the lead and wire went to the bottom. With the loss of the lead and wire, the reel became useless, and was thrown away, lightening Ooqueah's sledge by eighteen pounds. The first camp, at 89° 25', was reached in good time, and the march would have been a pleasant one for me but for my eyes burning from the strain of the continued observations of the previous hours.

After a few hours' sleep we hurried on again, Eskimos and dogs on the *qui vive*.

At this camp I began the system followed throughout the return march, of feeding the dogs according to the distance covered; that is, double rationing them when we covered two marches. I was able to do this, on account of the reserve supply of food which I had in my dogs themselves, in the event of our being seriously delayed by open leads.

At the next camp we made tea and ate our lunch in the igloos, rested the dogs, and then pushed on again. The weather was fine, though there were apparently indications of a coming change. It took all of our will power to reach the next igloos, but we did it, and were asleep almost before we had finished our supper. Without these igloos to look forward to and work for, we should not have made this march.

Friday, April 9, was a wild day. All day long the wind blew strong from the north-northeast, increasing finally to a gale, while the thermometer hung between 18° and 22° below zero. All the leads that we had passed here on the upward journey were greatly widened and new ones had been formed. We struck one just north of the 88th parallel which was at least a mile wide, but fortunately it was all covered with practicable young ice. It was not a reassuring day. For the last half of this march the ice was raftering all about us and beneath our very feet under the pressure of the howling gale. Fortunately we were traveling nearly before the wind, for it would have been impossible to move and follow a trail with the gale in our faces. As it was, the dogs scudded along before the wind much of the time on the gallop. Under the impact of the storm the ice was evidently crushing southward and bearing us with it. I was strongly reminded of the wild gale in which we regained "storm camp" on our return march in 1906. Luckily there was no lateral movement of the ice, or we should have had serious trouble. When we camped that night, at 87° 47', I wrote in my diary: "From here to the Pole and back has been a glorious sprint with a savage finish. Its results are due to hard work, little sleep, much experience, first class equipment, and good fortune as regards weather and open water."

During the night the gale moderated and gradually died away, leaving the air very thick. All hands found the light extremely trying to the eyes. It was almost impossible for us to see the trail. Though the temperature was only 10° below zero, we covered only Bartlett's last march that day. We did not attempt to do more because the dogs were feeling the effects of the recent high speed and it was desired to have them in the best possible condition for the next day, when I expected some trouble with the young ice we were sure to meet. At this spot certain eliminations which we were compelled to make among the dogs left us a total of thirty-five.

Sunday, April 11, proved a brilliant day, the sun breaking through the clouds soon after we left camp. The air was nearly calm, the sun seemed almost hot, and its glare was intense. If it had not been for our

CROSSING A LEAD ON AN ICE-CAKE AS A FERRY-BOAT

smoked goggles we should have suffered from snow-
blindness. Despite the expectation of trouble with
which we began this march, we were agreeably disappointed. On the upward journey, all this region
had been covered with young ice, and we thought
it reasonable to expect open water here, or at the best
that the trail would have been obliterated; but there
had not been enough movement of the ice to break
the trail. So far there had been no lateral — east and
west — movement of the ice. This was the great, fortunate, natural feature of the home trip, and the
principal reason why we had so little trouble. We
stopped for lunch at the "lead" igloos, and as we
finished our meal the ice opened behind us. We had
crossed just in time. Here we noticed some fox
tracks that had just been made. The animal was
probably disturbed by our approach. These are the
most northerly animal tracks ever seen.

Inspirited by our good fortune, we pressed on again,
completing two marches, and when we camped were
very near the 87th parallel. The entry that I made in
my diary that night is perhaps worth quoting: "Hope
to reach the Marvin return igloo to-morrow. I shall be
glad when we get there onto the big ice again. This
region here was open water as late as February and
early March and is now covered with young ice which
is extremely unreliable as a means of return. A few
hours of a brisk wind, east, west, or south, would make
this entire region open water for from fifty to sixty
miles north and south and an unknown extent east
and west. Only calm weather or a northerly wind
keeps it practicable."

A double march brought us to Camp Abruzzi, 86° 38', named in honor of the farthest north of the Duke of the Abruzzi. The trail was faulted in several places, but we picked it up each time without much difficulty. The following day was a bitterly disagreeable one. On this march we had in our faces a fresh southwest wind that, ever and again, spat snow that stung like needles and searched every opening in our clothing. But we were so delighted that we were across the young ice that these things seemed like trifles. The end of this march was at "Camp Nansen," named in honor of Nansen's "Farthest North."

This return journey was apparently destined to be full of contrasts, for the next day was one of brilliant sunlight and perfect calm. Despite the good weather the dogs seemed almost lifeless. It was impossible to get them to move faster than a walk, light though the loads were. Henson and the Eskimos also appeared to be a bit stale, so that it seemed wise to make a single march here instead of the usual double march.

After a good sleep we started to put in another double march and then we began to feel the effects of the wind. Even before we broke camp the ice began to crack and groan all about the igloo. Close by the camp a lead opened as we set out, and in order to get across it we were obliged to use an ice-cake ferry.

Between there and the next camp, at 85° 48', we found three igloos where Marvin and Bartlett had been delayed by wide leads, now frozen over. My Eskimos identified these igloos by recognizing in their construction the handiwork of men in the parties of Bartlett and Marvin. The Eskimos can nearly

SWINGING AN ICE-CAKE ACROSS A LEAD TO FORM AN IMPROMPTU BRIDGE

PASSING OVER THE BRIDGE

always tell who built an igloo. Though they are all constructed on one general principle, there are always peculiarities of individual workmanship which are readily recognized by these experienced children of the North.

During the first march of the day we found the trail badly faulted, the ice breaking up in all directions under the pressure of the wind, and some of the way we were on the run, the dogs jumping from one piece of ice to another. During the second march we saw a recent bear track, probably made by the same animal whose track we had seen on the upward journey. All along here were numerous cracks and narrow leads, but we were able to cross them without any great delay. There was one lead a mile wide which had formed since the upward trip, and the young ice over it was now breaking up.

Perhaps we took chances here, perhaps not. One thing was in our favor: our sledges were much lighter than on the upward journey, and we could now "rush" them across thin ice that would not have held them a moment then. In any event we got no thrill or irregularity of the pulse from the incident. It came as a matter of course, a part of the day's work.

As we left the camp where we had stopped for lunch, a dense, black, threatening bank of clouds came up from the south and we looked for a gale, but the wind fell and we arrived at the next camp, where Marvin had made a 700-fathom sounding and lost wire and pickaxes, in calm and brilliant sunlight after a march of eighteen hours. We were now approximately one hundred and forty-six miles from land.

We were coming down the North Pole hill in fine shape now and another double march, April 16–17, brought us to our eleventh upward camp at 85° 8′, one hundred and twenty-one miles from Cape Columbia. On this march we crossed seven leads, which, with the repeated faulting of the trail, lengthened our march once more to eighteen hours. Sunday, April 18, found us still hurrying along over the trail made by Marvin and Bartlett. They had lost the main trail, but this made little difference to us except as to time. We were able to make longer marches when on the main trail because there we camped in the igloos already built on the upward journey instead of having to build fresh ones for ourselves. This was another eighteen-hour march. It had a calm and warm beginning, but, so far as I was concerned, an extremely uncomfortable finish. During the day my clothes had become damp with perspiration. Moreover, as our long marches and short sleeps had brought us round to the calendar day, we were facing the sun, and this, with the southwest wind, burned my face so badly that it was little short of agonizing. But I consoled myself with the reflection that we were now less than a hundred miles from land. I tried to forget my stinging flesh in looking at the land clouds which we could see from this camp. There is no mistaking these clouds, which are permanent and formed of the condensation of the moisture from the land in the upper strata of the atmosphere. To-morrow, we knew, we might even be able to see the land itself. Meantime the dogs had again become utterly lifeless. Three of them had played out entirely. Extra rations were fed to them and we made a longer stop in this camp, partly on their account and partly to bring us around again to "night" marching, with the sun at our backs.

During the next march from Sunday to Monday, April 18th to 19th, there was a continuation of the fine weather and we were still coming along on my proposed schedule. Our longer sleep of the night before had heartened both ourselves and the dogs, and with renewed energy we took to the trail again about one o'clock in the afternoon. At a quarter past two we passed Bartlett's igloo on the north side of an enormous lead which had formed since we went up. We were a little over two hours crossing this lead.

It was not until eleven that night when we again picked up the main trail, in Henson's first pioneer march. When, traveling well in advance of the sledges I picked it up and signaled to my men that I had found it, they nearly went crazy with delight. The region over which we had just come had been an open sea at the last full moon, and a brisk wind from any direction excepting the north would make it the same again; or the raftering from a north wind would make it a ragged surface of broken plate glass.

It may seem strange to the reader that in this monotonous waste of ice we could distinguish between the various sections of our upward marches and recognize them on return. But, as I have said, my Eskimos know who built or even who has occupied an igloo, with the same instinct by which migratory birds recognize their old nests of the preceding year; and I have traveled these arctic wastes so long and lived so long with these instinctive children of Nature that my sense of location is almost as keen as their own.

At midnight we came upon pieces of a sledge which Egingwah had abandoned on the way up, and at three o'clock in the morning of the 19th we reached the MacMillan-Goodsell return igloos. We had covered Henson's three pioneer marches in fifteen and one-half hours of travel.

Another dog played out that day and was shot, leaving me with thirty. At the end of this march we could see the mountains of Grant Land in the far distance to the south, and the sight thrilled us. It was like a vision of the shores of the home land to sea-worn mariners.

Again, the next day, we made a double march. Starting late in the afternoon we reached the sixth outward camp, "boiled the kettle," and had a light lunch; then plunged on again until early in the morning of the 20th, when we reached the fifth outward camp.

So far we had seemed to bear a charm which protected us from all difficulties and dangers. While Bartlett and Marvin and, as I found out later, Borup had been delayed by open leads, at no single lead had we been delayed more than a couple of hours. Sometimes the ice had been firm enough to carry us across; sometimes we had made a short detour; sometimes we halted for the lead to close; sometimes we used an ice-cake as an improvised ferry: but whatever the mode of our crossing, we had crossed without serious difficulty.

It had seemed as if the guardian genius of the polar waste, having at last been vanquished by man, had accepted defeat and withdrawn from the contest.

SOUNDING

BREAKING CAMP. PUSHING THE SLEDGES UP TO THE TIRED DOGS

LAST CAMP ON THE ICE ON THE RETURN

BACK ON THE "GLACIAL FRINGE"
(Land Ice of Grant Land Near Cape Columbia, April 23, 1909)

Now, however, we were getting within the baleful sphere of influence of the "Big Lead," and in the fifth igloos from Columbia (the first ones north of the lead) I passed an intensely uncomfortable night, suffering from a variety of disagreeable symptoms which I diagnosed as those of quinsy.   On this march we had brought the land up very rapidly so that I had some consolation for my discomfort.   In three or four days at the, most, barring accident, our feet would again press land.   Despite my aching throat and no sleep, I took much comfort from this welcome thought.

CHAPTER XXXIV

BACK TO LAND AGAIN

WE had now reached the neighborhood of the "Big Lead" which had held us in check so many days on the upward journey and which had nearly cost the lives of my entire party in 1906. I anticipated trouble, therefore, in the march of April 20–21, and I was not disappointed. Although the "Big Lead" was frozen over we found that Bartlett on his return had lost the main trail here and did not find it again. For the rest of the ice journey, therefore, we were compelled to follow the single trail made by Bartlett instead of our well beaten outward trail. I could not complain. We had kept the beaten road back to within some fifty miles of the land.

For me this was the most uncomfortable march of the entire trip. It was made following a sleepless night in a cold igloo. For all that my clothes were wet with perspiration, my jaw and head throbbed and burned incessantly, though toward the end of the march I began to feel the effects of the quinine I had taken, and not long after we reached the captain's igloo the worst of the symptoms had departed. But it was hard drilling that day, and our troubles were in no way lessened by the fact that the dogs seemed utterly without energy or spirit.

314

The beautiful weather which had accompanied us for several days still continued on the next day. It was really a surprising stretch of splendid weather. We marched six hours, then stopped for luncheon, and then drilled along for six hours more. Repeatedly we passed fresh tracks of bear and hare, together with numerous fox tracks. Save for these, the march was uneventful, with the exception of two narrow leads which we crossed over thin young ice. All that day the sun was hot and blinding to an almost intolerable degree. It would have been practically impossible to travel with the sun in our faces, so fierce were its rays. Yet all this day the temperature ranged between 18° and 30° below zero.

The last day's journey before we reached shore began at 5 P.M. in that same brilliant, clear, calm weather. A short distance from camp we encountered an impracticable lead which the captain's trail crossed. In one fruitless attempt to pass it we got one of our teams in the water. Ultimately the lead swung to the east, and we found the captain's trail, took it up, and worked around the end of the lead.

Only a short distance further on we got our first glimpse of the edge of the glacial fringe ahead of us and stopped our march long enough to take some photographs. Before midnight that night the whole party had reached the glacial fringe of Grant Land. We had now left the ice of the polar sea and were practically on *terra firma*. When the last sledge came to the almost vertical edge of the glacier's fringe I thought my Eskimos had gone crazy. They yelled and called and danced until they fell from utter exhaustion. As Ootah sank down on his sledge he remarked in Eskimo: "The devil is asleep or having trouble with his wife or we should never have come back so easily." We stopped long enough for a leisurely luncheon with tea *ad libitum* and then pressed on until Cape Columbia was reached.

It was almost exactly six o'clock on the morning of April 23 when we reached the igloo of "Crane City" at Cape Columbia and the work was done. Here I wrote these words in my diary:

"My life work is accomplished. The thing which it was intended from the beginning that I should do, the thing which I believed could be done, and that I could do, I have done. I have got the North Pole out of my system after twenty-three years of effort, hard work, disappointments, hardships, privations, more or less suffering, and some risks. I have won the last great geographical prize, the North Pole, for the credit of the United States. This work is the finish, the cap and climax of nearly four hundred years of effort, loss of life, and expenditure of fortunes by the civilized nations of the world, and it has been accomplished in a way that is thoroughly American. I am content."

Our return from the Pole was accomplished in sixteen marches, and the entire journey from land to the Pole and back again occupied fifty-three days, or forty-three marches. It had been, as a result of our experience and perfected clothing and equipment, an amazingly comfortable return as compared with previous ones, but a little difference in the weather would have given us a different story to tell. There was no one in our party who was not delighted to have passed the treacherous lead and those wide expanses of young thin ice where a gale would have put an open sea between us and the land and rendered our safe return hazardous, to say the least.

In all probability no member of that little party will ever forget our sleep at Cape Columbia. We slept gloriously for practically two days, our brief waking intervals being occupied exclusively with eating and with drying our clothes.

Then for the ship. Our dogs, like ourselves, had not been hungry when we arrived, but simply lifeless with fatigue. They were different animals now, and the better ones among them stepped out with tightly curled tails and uplifted heads, their iron legs treading the snow with piston-like regularity and their black muzzles every now and then sniffing the welcome scent of the land.

We reached Cape Hecla in one march of forty-five miles and the *Roosevelt* in another of equal length. My heart thrilled as, rounding the point of the cape, I saw the little black ship lying there in its icy berth with sturdy nose pointing straight to the Pole.

And I thought of that other time three years before when, dragging our gaunt bodies round Cape Rawson on our way from the Greenland coast, I thought the *Roosevelt's* slender spars piercing the brilliant arctic sunlight as fair a sight as ever I had seen. As we approached the ship I saw Bartlett going over the rail. He came out along the ice-foot to meet me, and something in his face told me he had bad news even before he spoke.

"Have you heard about poor Marvin?" he asked.

"No," I answered.

Then he told me that Marvin had been drowned at the "Big Lead," coming back to Cape Columbia. The news staggered me, killing all the joy I had felt at the sight of the ship and her captain. It was indeed a bitter flavor in the cup of our success. It was hard to realize at first that the man who had worked at my side through so many weary months under conditions of peril and privation, to whose efforts and example so much of the success of the expedition had been due, would never stand beside me again. The manner of his death even will never be precisely known. No human eye was upon him when he broke through the treacherous young ice that had but recently closed over a streak of open water. He was the only white man in the supporting party of which he was in command and with which he was returning to the land at the time he met his death. As was customary, on breaking camp he had gone out ahead of the Eskimos, leaving the natives to break camp, harness the dogs, and follow. When he came to the "Big Lead," the recent ice of which was safe and secure at the edges, it is probable that, hurrying on, he did not notice the gradual thinning of the ice toward the center of the lead until it was too late and he was in the water. The Eskimos were too far in the rear to hear his calls for help, and in that ice-cold water the end must have come very quickly. He who had never shrunk from loneliness in the performance of his duty had at last met death alone.

Coming along over the trail in his footsteps, the

APPROACHING THE PEAKS OF CAPE COLUMBIA OVER THE SURFACE OF
THE "GLACIAL FRINGE"

CRANE CITY AT CAPE COLUMBIA, ON THE RETURN

EGINGWAH BEFORE STARTING
ON THE SLEDGE TRIP

EGINGWAH AFTER THE RE-
TURN FROM THE TRIP

OOTAII BEFORE STARTING ON
THE SLEDGE TRIP

OOTAH AFTER THE RETURN
FROM THE SLEDGE TRIP

(The Portraits at the Left Were Made by Flashlight on the *Roosevelt* Before the Journey.
Those on the Right Were Taken Immediately After the Return)

Eskimos of his party came to the spot where the broken ice gave them the first hint of the accident. One of the Eskimos said that the back of Marvin's fur jacket was still visible at the top of the water, while the condition of the ice at the edge seemed to indicate that Marvin had made repeated efforts to drag himself from the water, but that the ice was so thin that it had crumbled and broken beneath his weight, plunging him again into the icy water. He must have been dead some time before the Eskimos came up. It was, of course, impossible for them to rescue the body, since there was no way of their getting near it. Of course they knew what had happened to Marvin; but with childish superstition peculiar to their race they camped there for a while on the possibility that he might come back. But after a time, when he did not come back, Koodlooktoo and "Harrigan" became frightened. They realized that Marvin was really drowned and they were in dread of his spirit. So they threw from the sledge everything they could find belonging to him, that the spirit, if it came back that way, might find these personal belongings and not pursue the men. Then they hurried for the land as fast as they could go.

Quiet in manner, wiry in build, clear of eye, with an atmosphere of earnestness about him, Ross G. Marvin had been an invaluable member of the expedition. Through the long hot weeks preceding the sailing of the *Roosevelt*, he worked indefatigably looking after the assembling and delivery of the countless essential items of our outfit, until he, Bartlett, and myself were nearly exhausted. On the northern voyage he was always willing and ready, whether for taking an observation on deck or stowing cargo in the hold. When the Eskimos came aboard, his good humor, his quiet directness, and his physical competence gained him at once their friendship and respect. From the very first he was able to manage these odd people with uncommon success.

Later, when face to face with the stern problems of life and work in the arctic regions, he met them quietly, uncomplainingly, and with a steady, level persistence that could have but one result, and I soon came to know Ross Marvin as a man who would accomplish the task assigned to him, whatever it might be. The tidal and meteorological observations of the expedition were his particular charge, while, during the long dark winter night, his mathematical training enabled him to be of great assistance in working out problems of march formation, transportation and supplies, and arrangements of the supporting parties. In the spring sledge campaign of 1906 he commanded a separate division. When the great storm swept the polar sea and scattered my parties hopelessly in a chaos of shattered ice, Marvin's division, like my own farther north, was driven eastward and came down upon the Greenland coast, whence he brought his men safely back to the ship. From this expedition he returned trained in arctic details and thoroughly conversant with the underlying principles of all successful work in northern regions, so that when he went north with us in 1908, he went as a veteran who could absolutely be depended upon in an emergency.

The bones of Ross G. Marvin lie farther north than those of any other human being. On the northern shore of Grant Land we erected a cairn of stones, and upon its summit we placed a rude tablet inscribed: "In Memory of Ross G. Marvin of Cornell University, Aged 34. Drowned April 10, 1909, forty-five miles north of C. Columbia, returning from 86° 38′ N. Lat." This cenotaph looks from that bleak shore northward toward the spot where Marvin met his death. His name heads that glorious roll-call of arctic heroes among whom are Willoughby, Franklin, Sontag, Hall, Lockwood, and others who died in the field, and it must be some consolation to those who grieve for him that his name is inseparably connected with the winning of that last great trophy for which, through nearly four centuries, men of every civilized nation have suffered and struggled and died.

The Eskimos of whom Marvin was in command at the time he lost his life fortunately overlooked, in throwing Marvin's things upon the ice, a little canvas packet on the upstanders of the sledge containing a few of his notes, among them what is probably the last thing he ever wrote. It is so typical of the man's intelligent devotion to his duty that it is here appended as he wrote it. It will be seen that it was written on the very day that I last saw him alive, that day upon which he turned back to the south from his farthest north.

"March 25, 1909. This is to certify that I turned back from this point with the third supporting party, Commander Peary advancing with nine men in the party, seven sledges with the standard loads, and sixty dogs. Men and dogs are in first class condition. The captain, with the fourth and last supporting party, expects to turn back at the end of five more marches. Determined our latitude by observations on March 22, and again to-day, March 25. A copy of the observations and computations is herewith enclosed. Results of observations were as follows: Latitude at noon, March 22, 85° 48′ north. Latitude at noon, March 25, 86° 38′ north. Distance made good in three marches, fifty minutes of latitude, an average of sixteen and two-thirds nautical miles per march. The weather is fine, going good and improving each day.

"Ross G. Marvin,

"*College of Civil Engineering,*
   Cornell University."

With a sad heart I went to my cabin on the *Roosevelt*. Notwithstanding the good fortune with which we had accomplished the return, the death of Marvin emphasized the danger to which we had all been subjected, for there was not one of us but had been in the water of a lead at some time during the journey.

Despite the mental depression that resulted from this terrible news about poor Marvin, for twenty-four hours after my return I felt physically as fit as ever and ready to hit the trail again if necessary. But at the end of twenty-four hours the reaction came, and it came with a bump. It was, of course, the inevitable result of complete change of diet and atmosphere, and the substitution of inaction in place of incessant effort. I had no energy or ambition for anything. Scarcely could I stop sleeping long enough to eat, or eating long enough to sleep. My ravenous appetite was not the result of hunger or short rations, for we had all had plenty to eat on the return from the Pole. It was merely because none of the ship's food seemed to have the satisfying effect of pemmican, and I could not seem to hold enough to satisfy my appetite. However, I knew better than to gorge myself and compromised by eating not much at a time, but at frequent intervals.

Oddly enough, this time there was no swelling of the feet or ankles and in three or four days we all began to feel like ourselves. Anyone who looks at the contrasted pictures of the Eskimos, taken before and after the sledge trip, will realize, perhaps, something of the physical strain of a journey to the Pole and back, and will read into the day-by-day narrative of our progress all the details of soul-racking labor and exhaustion which at the time we had been obliged stoically to consider as a part of the day's work, in order to win our goal.

One of the first things done after reaching the ship and bringing our sleep up to date was to reward the Eskimos who had served us so faithfully. They were all fitted out with rifles, shotguns, cartridges, shells, reloading tools, hatchets, knives, and so on, and they behaved like so many children who had just received a boundless supply of toys. Among the things I have given them at various times, none are more important than the telescopes, which enable them to distinguish game in the distance. The four who stood with me at the Pole were to receive whale-boats, tents, and other treasures when I dropped them at their home settlements along the Greenland coast on the southward journey of the *Roosevelt*.

PERMANENT MONUMENT ERECTED AT CAPE COLUMBIA TO MARK POINT
OF DEPARTURE AND RETURN OF NORTH POLE SLEDGE PARTY

MEMORIAL ERECTED TO THE MEMORY OF
PROFESSOR ROSS G. MARVIN, AT
CAPE SHERIDAN

PEARY CAIRN AT CAPE MORRIS K. JESUP,
AS PHOTOGRAPHED BY MACMILLAN
AND BORUP

CHAPTER XXXV

LAST DAYS AT CAPE SHERIDAN

IT is not long now to the end of the story. On returning to the *Roosevelt* I learned that MacMillan and the doctor had reached the ship March 21, Borup on April 11, the Eskimo survivors of Marvin's party April 17, and Bartlett on April 24. MacMillan and Borup had started for the Greenland coast, before my return, to deposit caches for me, in the event that I should be obliged by the drifting of the ice to come back that way, as in 1906. (Borup, on his return to the land, had deposited a cache for me at Cape Fanshawe Martin, on the Grant Land coast, some eighty miles west from Cape Columbia, thus providing for a drift in either direction.)

Borup also, with the aid of the Eskimos, built at Cape Columbia a permanent monument, consisting of a pile of stones formed round the base of a guide-post made of sledge planks, with four arms pointing true north, south, east, and west — the whole supported and guyed by numerous strands of heavy sounding wire. On each arm is a copper plate, with an inscription punched in it. On the eastern arm is, "Cape Morris K. Jesup, May 16, 1900, 275 miles;" on the southern arm is, "Cape Columbia, June 6, 1906;" on the western arm is, "Cape Thomas H. Hubbard, July 1, 1906, 225 miles;" on the northern arm, "North

Pole, April 6, 1909, 413 miles." Below these arms, in a frame covered with glass to protect it from the weather, is a record containing the following:

PEARY ARCTIC CLUB NORTH POLE EXPEDITION, 1908

S. S. Roosevelt,
June 12th, 1909.

This monument marks the point of departure and return of the sledge expedition of the Peary Arctic Club, which in the spring of 1909 attained the North Pole.

The members of the expedition taking part in the sledge work were Peary, Bartlett, Goodsell, Marvin,[1] MacMillan, Borup, Henson.

The various sledge divisions left here February 28th and March 1st, and returned from March 18th to April 23rd.

The Club's Steamer *Roosevelt* wintered at C. Sheridan, 73 miles east of here.

R. E. PEARY, U. S. N.

Commander, R. E. Peary, U. S. N., Comdg. Expedition.
Captain R. A. Bartlett, Master of *Roosevelt.*
Chief Engr. George A. Wardwell.
Surgeon J. W. Goodsell.
Prof. Ross G. Marvin, Assistant.
Prof. D. B. McMillan,   "
    George Borup,   "
    M. A. Henson,   "
Charles Percy, Steward.
Mate Thomas Gushue.
Bosun John Connors.
Seaman John Coadey.
   "   John Barnes.
   "   Dennis Murphy.
   "   George Percy.
2nd Engr. Banks Scott.
Fireman James Bently.
    Patrick Joyce.
    Patrick Skeans.
    John Wiseman.

[1] Drowned April 10th, returning from 86° 38' N. Lat.

On the 18th MacMillan and Borup with five Eskimos and six sledges had departed for the Greenland coast to establish depots of supplies in case my party should be obliged to make its landing there as in 1906, and also to make tidal readings at Cape Morris Jesup. I, therefore, at once started two Eskimos off for Greenland with a sounding apparatus and a letter informing MacMillan and Borup of our final success. It had been the plan to have Bartlett make a line of ten or five mile soundings from Columbia to Camp No. 8 to bring out the cross section of the continental shelf and the deep channel along it, and Bartlett had got his equipment ready for this purpose. However, I decided not to send him for the reason that he was not in the best physical condition, his feet and ankles being considerably swollen, while he was, moreover, afflicted with a number of Job's comforters. My own physical condition, however, remained perfect during the rest of our stay in the north, with the exception of a bad tooth from which I suffered more or less torture during a space of three weeks.

This was the first time in all my arctic expeditions that I had been at headquarters through May and June. Hitherto there had always seemed to be something more to be done in the field; but now the principal work was completed, and it remained only to arrange the results. In the meantime the energies of the Eskimos were largely employed in short journeys in the neighborhood, most of them for the purpose of visiting the various supply depots established between the ship and Cape Columbia and removing their unused supplies to the ship. Between them these various small expeditions did some interesting work. Most of this supplementary work in the field was accomplished by other members of the expedition, but I had plenty of work on board the *Roosevelt*. Along about the 10th of May we began to get genuine spring weather. On that day Bartlett and myself began spring housecleaning. We overhauled the cabins, cleared out the dark corners, and dried out everything that needed it, the quarter-deck being littered with all kinds of miscellaneous articles the whole day. On the same day spring work on the ship was also begun, the winter coverings being taken off the *Roosevelt's* stack and ventilators, and preparations being made for work on the engines.

A few days later a beautiful white fox came to the ship and attempted to get on board. One of the Eskimos killed him. The creature behaved in an extraordinary manner, acting, in fact, just like the Eskimo dogs when those creatures run amuck. The Eskimos say that in the Whale Sound region foxes often seem to go mad in the same way and sometimes attempt to break into the igloos. This affliction from which arctic dogs and foxes suffer, while apparently a form of madness, does not seem to have any relation to rabies since it does not appear to be contagious or infectious.

The spring weather, though unmistakably the real thing, was fickle on the whole. On Sunday, May 16, for example, the sun was hot and the temperature high, and the snow all about us was disappearing almost like magic, pools of water forming about the ship; but the next day we had a stiff southwest gale with considerable wet snow. On the whole, it was a very disagreeable day.

On the 18th the engineer's force began work on the boilers in earnest. Four days later two Eskimos returned from MacMillan, whom they had left at Cape Morris Jesup on the Greenland coast. They brought notes from him giving some details of his work there. On the 31st MacMillan and Borup

themselves arrived from Greenland, having made
the return trip from Cape Morris Jesup, a distance of
270 miles, in eight marches, an average of 34 miles
per march.   MacMillan reported that he got as far
as 84° 17' north of Cape Jesup, had made a sounding
which showed a depth of 90 fathoms, and had obtained
ten days' tidal observations.   They brought in as
many of the skins and as much of the meat as the
sledges could carry of 52 musk-oxen which they had
killed.

Early in June, Borup and MacMillan continued
their work; MacMillan making tidal observations at
Fort Conger; and Borup erecting at Cape Columbia
the monument which has been already described.

MacMillan while taking tidal observations at Fort
Conger on Lady Franklin Bay, to connect our work at
Capes Sheridan, Columbia, Bryant, and Jesup with
the observation of the Lady Franklin Bay expedition
of 1881–83, found still some remains of the supplies
of the disastrous Greely expedition of 1881–84.   They
included canned vegetables, potatoes, hominy, rhubarb,
pemmican, tea, and coffee.   Strange to say, after the
lapse of a quarter of a century, many of these supplies
were still in good condition, and some of them were
eaten with relish by various members of our party.

One of the finds was a text book which had belonged
to Lieutenant Kislingbury, who lost his life with the
Greely party.   Upon its flyleaf it bore this inscription:
"To my dear father, from his affectionate son, Harry
Kislingbury. May God be with you and return
you safely to us."   Greely's old coat was also found
lying on the ground.   This also was in good con-

dition and I believe that MacMillan wore it for some days.

All hands were now beginning to look forward to the time when the *Roosevelt* should again turn her nose toward the south and home. Following our own housecleaning, the Eskimos had one on June 12. Every movable article was taken out of their quarters, and the walls, ceilings, and floors were scrubbed, disinfected, and whitewashed. Other signs of returning summer were observed on all sides. The surface of the ice-floe was going blue, the delta of the river was quite bare, and the patches of bare ground ashore were growing larger almost hourly. Even the *Roosevelt* seemed to feel the change and gradually began to right herself from the pronounced list which she had taken under the press of the ice in the early winter. On June 16 we had the first of the summer rains, though the next morning all the pools of water were frozen over. On the same day Borup captured a live musk calf near Clements Markham Inlet. He managed to get his unique captive back to the ship alive, but the little creature died the next evening, though the steward nursed him carefully in an effort to save his life.

On the summer solstice, June 22, midnoon of the arctic summer and the longest day of the year, it snowed all night; but a week later the weather seemed almost tropical, and we all suffered from the heat, strange though it seems to say it. The glimpses of open water off Cape Sheridan were increasing in frequency and size, and on July 2 we could see a considerable lake just off the point of this cape. The

4th of July as we observed it would have pleased the advocates of "a quiet Fourth." What with the recent death of Marvin and the fact that the day was Sunday, nothing out of the ordinary routine was done except to dress the ship with flags, and there was scarcely enough wind even to display our bunting. Three years ago that very day the *Roosevelt* got away from her winter quarters at almost the same spot in a strong southerly gale; but the experience on that occasion convinced me that it would be best to hang on in our present position just as late in July as possible, and thus give the ice in Robeson and Kennedy Channels more time to break up.

It almost seemed as if the *Roosevelt* shared with us our anticipation of a speedy return, for she continued gradually to regain an even keel, and within four or five days she had automatically completed this operation. On the 8th we put out the eight-inch hawser and made the ship fast, bow and stern, in order to hold her in position in case she should be subjected to any pressure before we were ready to depart. On the same day we began in real earnest to make ready for the homeward departure. The work began with the taking on' of coal, which, it will be remembered, had been transferred to shore along with quantities of other supplies when we went into winter quarters, in order to make provisions against the loss of the ship by fire, or ice pressure, or what not, in the course of the winter. The process of getting the ship ready for her homeward voyage does not require detailed description. Suffice it to say that it furnished the entire party with hard work and plenty of it for fully ten days.

At the expiration of that period Bartlett reported the ship ready to sail. Observation of conditions off shore revealed the fact that Robeson Channel was practicable for navigation. Our work was done, success had crowned our efforts, the ship was ready, we were all fit, and on July 18, with only the tragic memory of the lost lamented Marvin to lessen our high spirits, the *Roosevelt* pulled slowly out from the cape and turned her nose again to the south.

Off Cape Union the *Roosevelt* was intentionally forced out into the ice to fight a way down the center of the channel in accordance with my deliberate program.

For a ship of the *Roosevelt's* class, this is the best and quickest return route — far preferable to hugging the shore.

The voyage to Battle Harbor was comparatively uneventful. It involved, of course, as does any journey in those waters, even under favorable conditions, unceasing watchfulness and skill in ice navigation, but the trip was without pronounced adventure. On August 8 the *Roosevelt* emerged from the ice and passed Cape Sabine, and the value of experience and the new departure of forcing the ship down the center of the channel instead of along shore will be appreciated from the fact that we were now thirty-nine days ahead of our 1906 record on the occasion of our previous return from Cape Sheridan, although we had left Cape Sheridan considerably later than before. The voyage from Cape Sheridan to Cape Sabine had been made in fifty-three days, less time than in 1906.

We stopped at Cape Saumarez, the Nerke of the

Eskimos, and a boat's crew went ashore. It was there I first heard of the movements of Dr. Frederick Cook during the previous year while absent from Anoratok. We arrived at Etah on the 17th of August. There I learned further details as to the movements of Dr. Cook during his sojourn in that region.

At Etah we picked up Harry Whitney, who had spent the winter in that neighborhood in arctic hunting. Here, also, we killed some seventy-odd walrus for the Eskimos, whom we distributed at their homes whence we had taken them in the previous summer.

They were all as children, yet they had served us well. They had, at times, tried our tempers and taxed our patience; but after all they had been faithful and efficient. Moreover, it must not be forgotten that I had known every member of the tribe for nearly a quarter of a century, until I had come to regard them with a kindly and personal interest, which any man must feel with regard to the members of any inferior race who had been accustomed to respect and depend upon him during the greater part of his adult life. We left them all better supplied with the simple necessities of arctic life than they had ever been before, while those who had participated in the sledge journey and the winter and spring work on the northern shore of Grant Land were really so enriched by our gifts that they assumed the importance and standing of arctic millionaires. I knew, of course, that in all probability I should never see them again. This feeling was tempered with the knowledge of success; but it was not without keen regret that I looked my last upon these strange and faithful people who had meant so much to me.

We cleared from Cape York on August 26, and on September 5 we steamed into Indian Harbor. Here the first despatch that went over the wires was to Mrs. Peary: "*Have made good at last. I have the Pole. Am well. Love,*" followed in rapid succession by one from Bartlett to his mother; and, among others, one to H. L. Bridgman, secretary of the Peary Arctic Club: "*Sun,*" a cipher meaning, "Pole reached. *Roosevelt* safe."

Three days later the *Roosevelt* reached Battle Harbor. On September 13 the ocean-going tug *Douglas H. Thomas* arrived from Sydney, C. B., a distance of four hundred and seventy-five miles, bringing Regan and Jefferds, representatives of the Associated Press, whom I greeted by saying, "This is a new record in newspaper enterprise, and I appreciate the compliment." Three days later the Canadian Government cable steamer, *Tyrian,* in command of Captain Dickson, arrived, bringing twenty-three special correspondents who had been hurried north as soon as our first despatches had reached New York, and on the 21st of September, as the *Roosevelt* was approaching the little town of Sydney, Cape Breton, we saw a beautiful sea-going yacht approaching us. It was the *Sheelah,* whose owner, Mr. James Ross, was bringing Mrs. Peary and our children up to meet me. Further down the bay we met a whole flotilla of boats, gay with bunting and musical with greetings. As we neared the city, the entire water-front was alive with people. The little town to which I had returned so many times unsuccessful gave us a royal welcome as the *Roosevelt* came back to her once more, flying at her mastheads, besides the Stars and Stripes and the ensign of our Canadian hosts and cousins, a flag which never before had entered any port in history, the North Pole flag.

Little more remains to be said.

The victory was due to experience; to the courage, endurance, and devotion of the members of the expedition, who put all there was in them into the work; and to the unswerving faith and loyalty of the officers, members, and friends of the Peary Arctic Club, who furnished the sinews of war, without which nothing could have been accomplished.

APPENDIX I

SUMMARY OF BATHYMETRICAL, TIDAL, AND METEOROLOGICAL OBSERVATIONS[1]

BY R. A. HARRIS,
Coast and Geodetic Survey, Washington, D.C.

SOUNDINGS. — Previous to the expeditions of Peary, little was known concerning the depths of that portion of the Arctic Ocean which lies north of Greenland and Grant Land. In 1876 Markham and Parr at a point nearly north of Cape Joseph Henry, in latitude 83° $20\frac{1}{2}'$, and longitude 63° W., found a depth of 72 fathoms. In 1882 Lockwood and Brainard at a point lying northerly from Cape May, in latitude about 82° 38' N., and longitude about $51\frac{1}{4}$° W., sounded to a depth of 133 fathoms without touching bottom.

The motion of the polar pack was inferred by Lockwood from the existence of a tidal crack extending from Cape May to Beaumont Island. Peary's journeys along the northern coast of Greenland in 1900, and upon the Arctic ice in 1902 and 1906, firmly established the motion suspected by Lockwood. In April of the years 1902 and 1906 he found an eastward drifting of the ice due to westerly or northwesterly winds. Moreover, along the line of separation between two ice-fields the northern field had a greater eastward motion than had the field to the south of the

[1] Transmitted by O. H. TITTMANN, Superintendent, Coast and Geodetic Survey.

line. These facts, together with the water sky observed to the north of Cape Morris Jesup in 1900, strongly indicated the existence of deep water between Greenland and the North Pole.

Though few in number, the soundings taken in 1909 between Cape Columbia and the Pole are of great interest to geographers.

The accompanying diagram shows the results obtained.

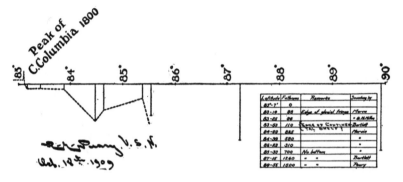

These soundings prove the existence of a continental shelf covered by about 100 fathoms of water and whose edge, north of Cape Columbia, lies about 46 sea miles from the shore. In latitude 84° 29′ the depth was found to be 825 fathoms, while in latitude 85° 23′ it was found to be only 310 fathoms. This diminution in depth is a fact of considerable interest in reference to the possible existence of land to the westward.

The three soundings taken between the point of comparatively shallow water and the Pole failed to reach bottom. The one made within five sea miles of the Pole proved the depth there to be at least 1500 fathoms. This is not at variance with the northernmost sounding taken by the *Fram*, at a point north of Franz Josef Land and in latitude about 85° 20', viz., 1640 fathoms and no bottom.

TIDES.—Tidal observations upon the arctic coasts of Grant Land and Greenland were carried out under instructions from the Coast and Geodetic Survey, this Bureau having been ordered by President Roosevelt through the Secretary of Commerce and Labor to have such work undertaken.

The object was to secure observations along the northern coasts of Grant Land and Greenland at a sufficient number of places for determining the tides in this region; it being the belief that such observations might throw light upon the possible existence of a "considerable land mass in the unknown area of the Arctic Ocean."

Systematic tidal and meteorological observations were carried on day and night at Cape Sheridan, Point Aldrich (near Cape Columbia), Cape Bryant, Cape Morris Jesup, and Fort Conger — the periods of time covered at these stations being about 231, 29, 28, 10, and 15 days, respectively.[1]

The tides were observed upon vertical staves or poles held in position by means of stones placed around them at the bottom of the shallow water along the coast. At Cape Sheridan, Point Aldrich, and Cape Bryant igloos were built over the tide staves. These being heated, usually by means of oil-stoves, the observers were enabled to maintain open well-holes with comparative ease.

[1] These observations were made by Marvin and MacMillan, assisted by Borup, seaman Barnes, and fireman Wiseman.—R.E.P.

In order to secure fixed data of reference, permanent bench marks were established on the land, not far from the igloos or tide staves.

The ice-covering of the water nearly obliterated all wind waves which generally impair the accuracy of staff readings made in open bodies of water. The measurement of the height upon staff of the surface of the water, as the surface rose and fell in the well-holes, was carried on with great precision, a fact which the plottings of the observations have well brought out. The observations were taken hourly; and during a large percentage of the time these were supplemented by observations taken more frequently, often at intervals of ten minutes each.

The chronometer used in connection with tidal work was compared with true Greenwich time at New York before and after the cruise to the Arctic. The comparisons showed that during this period of 461 days the average daily gain of the chronometer was 2.2 seconds.

The mean lunitidal intervals and the mean ranges of tide, together with the approximate geographical positions of the stations, are as follows:

Station	Latitude		Longitude		HW Interval		LW Interval		Mean Rise and Fall
	°	′	°	′	h	m	h	m	Feet
Cape Sheridan...........	82	27	61	21	10	31	4	14	1.76
Point Aldrich	83	07	69	44	7	58	1	50	0.84
Cape Bryant............	82	21	55	30	0	03	6	22	1.07
C. Morris Jesup	83	40	33	35	10	49	4	33	0.38
Fort Conger	81	44	64	44	11	35	5	15	4.06
Fort Conger[1]	81	44	64	44	11	33	5	20	4.28

[1] Results from Greely's observations, 1881–83, covering a period of nearly two years.

The harmonic constants for these places will be given in a paper on Arctic Tides about to be issued by the Coast and Geodetic Survey.

As indicated by its name, a "lunitidal interval" is the time elapsing between the passage of the moon across the meridian of the place or station and the occurrence of high or low water. If two stations have the same longitude, then the difference between the lunitidal intervals for the two stations denotes the difference in the times of occurrence of the tides. If they have not the same longitude, then the intervals must be converted into lunar hours (1 lunar hour = 1.035 solar hours) and increased by the west longitude of the stations expressed in hours. The result will be the tidal hours of the stations expressed in Greenwich lunar time. The difference between the tidal hours for two stations will be the difference in the time of occurrence of the tides expressed in lunar hours.

One of the most important results brought out from the tidal observations of the expedition is the fact that high water occurs two hours earlier (in absolute time) at Cape Columbia than at Cape Sheridan. The Cape Columbia tides are even earlier than the tides along the northern coast of the Spitzbergen Islands. These facts prove that the tide at Cape Columbia comes from the west. It is the Baffin Bay tide transmitted, first, northwesterly through the eastern portion of the Arctic Archipelago to the Arctic Ocean, and then easterly along the northern coast of Grant Land to Cape Columbia. That the tide wave should be felt after a passage of this kind, instead of practically disap-

pearing after entering the Arctic Ocean, is one
argument for the existence of a waterway of limited
width to the northwest of Grant Land. This suggests
that Crocker Land, first seen by Peary on June 24,
1906, from an altitude of about 2000 feet, may form
a portion of the northern boundary of this channel or
waterway.

The tides along the northern coast of Greenland
are due mainly to the large rise-and-fall occurring at
the head of Baffin Bay. The Arctic Ocean being of
itself a nearly tideless body so far as semidaily tides
are concerned, it follows that the time of tide varies
but little as one goes through Smith Sound, Kane
Basin, Kennedy Channel, and Robeson Channel; in
other words there exists a stationary oscillation in this
waterway. The northeasterly trend of the shore line
of Peary Land beyond Robeson Channel and the
deflecting force due to the earth's rotation tend to preserve, far to the northeastward and partly in the form
of a free wave of transmission, the disturbance resulting from the stationary oscillation in the straits. The
tide observations indicate that this disturbance is felt
as far as Cape Morris Jesup, where the semidaily range
of tide is only 0.38 foot. At Cape Bryant, northeast
of Robeson Channel, the range is 1.07 feet. These
values, taken in connection with the Robeson Channel
disturbance, indicate that the time of tide along the
coast of Peary Land becomes later as one travels eastward from Cape Bryant.

Owing to the comparatively short distance between
Cape Bryant and Cape Morris Jesup, it is probable
that at the latter point the crest of the wave trans-

mitted from the southwest will appear to arrive much earlier than will the crest of the wave passing between Spitzbergen Islands and Greenland. In this way the small size of the semidaily tide at Cape Morris Jesup, as well as its time of occurrence, can be partially explained.

A no-tide point doubtless exists in Lincoln Sea, off Peary Land.

The semidiurnal tidal forces vanish at the Pole and are very small over the entire Arctic Ocean. As a consequence the semidiurnal portion of the tide wave in these regions is almost wholly derived from the tides in the Atlantic Ocean. The diurnal forces attain a maximum at the Pole and produce sensible tides in the deeper waters of the Arctic Ocean. Such tides are essentially equilibrium tides for this nearly enclosed body of water. The diurnal portion of the Baffin Bay tide produces the diurnal portion of the tide in Smith Sound, Kane Basin, and Kennedy Channel. In passing from Fort Conger to the Arctic Ocean one could reasonably expect to find a great change in the time of occurrence of the diurnal tide in going a comparatively short distance; in other words the change in the tidal hour for the diurnal wave would probably be considerable where the Baffin Bay tide joins the arctic tide.

Peary's observations show that such is the case. They show that the diurnal tide at Cape Bryant, Cape Sheridan, Point Aldrich, and Cape Morris Jesup follows that at Fort Conger by respective intervals of $3\frac{1}{2}$, 5, 6, and 8 hours. They also show that in going northward from Fort Conger to Point Aldrich the ratio of the two principal diurnal constituents approximates more and more nearly to the theoretical ratio; that is, to the ratio between the two corresponding tidal forces. This is what one would expect to find in passing from a region possessing diurnal tides derived from the irregular tides of Baffin Bay to a region where the equilibrium diurnal tides of the Arctic become important.

The range and time of occurrence of the diurnal tide at Point Aldrich do not differ greatly from their equilibrium values based upon the assumption of a deep polar basin extending from Grant Land and the Arctic Archipelago to the marginal waters off the portion of the coast of Siberia lying east of the New Siberian Islands. But De Long's party observed tides at Bennett Island in 1881. From these observations it is seen that the diurnal tide has a much smaller range than would be permissible under the hypothesis of deep water in the portion of the Arctic Basin just referred to. The diurnal tides at Pitlekaj, Point Barrow, and Flaxman Island are, as noted below, also too small to permit of this hypothesis. The smallness of the diurnal tide in the cases cited can probably be explained on no other assumption than that of obstructing land masses extending over a considerable portion of the unknown region of the Arctic Ocean.

No further attempt will be made here to prove the necessity for a tract of land, an archipelago, or an area of very shallow water situated between the present Arctic Archipelago and Siberia. A brief discussion of this question, together with a tidal map of the Arctic Regions, will be found in a paper about to be issued by the Coast and Geodetic Survey and which has been already referred to.   A few pertinent facts may, however, be mentioned.

(1) At Point Barrow, Alaska, the flood stream comes from the west and not from the north, as the hypothesis of an extensive, deep polar basin implies.

(2) The semidaily range of tide at Bennett Island is 2.5 feet, while it is only 0.4 foot at Point Barrow and 0.5 foot at Flaxman Island, Alaska.   This indicates that obstructing land masses lie between the deep basin or channel traversed by the *Fram* and the northern coast of Alaska.

(3) The observed tidal hours and ranges of tide show that the semidaily tide is not propagated from the Greenland Sea to the Alaskan coast directly across a deep and uninterrupted polar basin.

(4) The observed ranges of the diurnal tides at Teplitz Bay, Franz Josef Land; at Pitlekaj, northeastern Siberia; and at Point Barrow and Flaxman Island have less than one-half of their theoretical equilibrium values based upon the assumption of an uninterrupted and deep polar basin.

In addition to these facts are the following items which have a bearing upon the shape and size of this unknown land:

The westerly drifting of the *Jeannette*.

The westerly drifting north of Alaska observed by Mikkelsen and Leffingwell.

The existence of Crocker Land.

The shoaling indicated by a sounding of 310 fathoms taken in Lat. 85° 23′ N.

The eastward progression of the tide wave along the northern coast of Grant Land as shown by observations at Point Aldrich, Cape Sheridan, and Cape Bryant.

The great age of the ice found in Beaufort Sea.

Items of some importance in this connection, but which cannot be regarded as established facts are:

The probable westerly courses taken by casks set adrift off Point Barrow and off Cape Bathurst, the one recovered on the northeastern coast of Iceland, the other on the northern coast of Norway;

The question suggested by Harrison whether or not enough ice escapes from the Arctic to account for the quantity which must be formed there if one were to adopt the assumption of an unobstructed polar basin.

Taking various facts into consideration, it would seem that an obstruction (land, islands, or shoals) containing nearly half a million square statute miles probably exists. That one corner lies north of Bennett Island; another, north of Point Barrow; another, near Banks Land and Prince Patrick Island; and another, at or near Crocker Land.

METEOROLOGY. — Regular hourly observations of the thermometer and barometer were carried on day and night by the tide observers.

A brief résumé of the results obtained is given below, together with a few taken from the Report of the Proceedings of the U. S. Expedition to Lady Franklin Bay by Lieutenant (now General) A. W. Greely.

TEMPERATURES

Cape Sheridan				Fort Conger [1]
	Maximum	Minimum	Mean	Mean
	°	°	°	°
November 14–30	− 7	− 39	− 23.96	
December, 1908	− 5	− 53	− 29.22	− 28.10
January, 1909	− 6	− 49	− 30.61	− 38.24
February, 1909	− 7	− 49	− 31.71	− 40.13
March, 1909	+ 13	− 52	− 20.87	− 28.10
April, 1909...................	+ 13	− 37	− 15.63	− 13.55
May, 1909	+ 46	− 15	+ 18.00	+ 14.08
June, 1909...................	+ 52	+ 15	+ 31.51	+ 32.65
November 17–December 13, 1908.	− 7	− 39	− 25.75	
January 16–February 12, 1909 ...	− 21	− 48	− 35.48	
May 17–May 22, 1909..........	+ 37	+ 12	+ 22.97	
June 11–June 25, 1909..........	+ 50	+ 25	+ 34.17	

TEMPERATURES

Station	Date	Maximum	Minimum	Mean
		°	°	°
Point Aldrich near Cape Columbia	Nov. 17–Dec. 13, 1908	− 14	− 46	− 31.96
Cape Bryant..........	Jan. 16–Feb. 12, 1909	− 12	− 55	− 36.68
Cape Morris Jesup	May 17–May 22, 1909	+ 35	+ 16	+ 27.92
Fort Conger	June 11–June 25, 1909	+ 54	+ 28	+ 34.44
Fort Conger [1]	June 11–June 25, 1882	+ 44.4	+ 26.7	+ 34.883
Fort Conger [2]	June 11–June 25, 1883	+ 39.6	+ 26.4	+ 33.393

From these values we see that from November 17 to December 13, 1908, the average temperature at Point Aldrich was 6.21 degrees lower than the temperature at Cape Sheridan for the same period; that from January 16 to February 12, 1909, the average tempera-

[1] Observations made in 1875–76 and 1881–83. Greely's Report, Vol. II, p. 230.
[2] Greely's Report, Vol. II, pp. 196, 197, 220, 221. Hourly readings used.

ture at Cape Bryant was 1.20 degrees lower than that at Cape Sheridan; that from May 17 to May 22, 1909, the average temperature at Cape Morris Jesup was 4.95 degrees higher than that at Cape Sheridan; and that from June 11 to June 25, 1909, the average temperature at Fort Conger was practically the same as that at Cape Sheridan during this period.

BAROMETER READINGS (UNCORRECTED)

Station	Date	Maximum	Minimum	Mean	Mean
		°	°	°	° Fort Conger[1]
Cape Sheridan ...	Nov. 13–30, 1908	30.42	28.96	29.899	
	Dec., 1908...........	30.27	29.28	29.749	29.922
	Jan., 1909	30.42	29.18	29.752	29.796
	Feb., 1909..........	30.59	29.03	29.772	29.672
	March, 1909	30.89	29.69	30.282	29.893
	April, 1909	30.58	29.20	29.991	30.099
	May, 1909	30.60	29.39	30.105	30.066
	June, 1909	30.21	29.37	29.804	29.878
	Nov. 17–Dec. 13, 1908	30.42	29.26	29.866	
	Jan. 16–Feb. 4, 1909..	30.40	29.18	29.691	
	May 14–May 22, 1909	30.52	30.04	30.304	
	June 11–June 25, 1909	30.10	29.47	29.834	
Point Aldrich	Nov. 17–Dec. 13, 1908	30.51	29.35	29.998	
Cape Bryant.....	Jan. 16–Feb. 4, 1909..	30.10	29.83	29.976	
Cape Morris Jesup	May 14–May 22, 1909	30.70	30.24	30.469	
Fort Conger	June 11–June 25, 1909	30.19	29.74	30.013	
Fort Conger[2].....	June 11–June 25, 1882	30.129	29.416	29.817	
Fort Conger[2].....	June 11–June 25, 1883	30.218	29.590	29.949	

The above tabulation shows that during the month the average fluctuation of the barometer at Cape Sheridan amounts to 1.2 inches, being greatest in February and least in June.

[1] Observations made in 1881–83. Greely's Report, Vol. II, p. 166.

[2] Greely's Report, Vol. II, pp. 122, 123, 146, 147. Hourly readings are reduced to sea level.

An inspection of the monthly means shows that the barometer at Cape Sheridan is lowest for the months of December and January, or about January 1st, and highest about April 1st, the range of the fluctuation being about 0.5 inch. These results agree well with those obtained by Greely at Fort Conger and illustrated by a diagram upon p. 166, Vol. II, of his Report.

From a tabulation made according to hours of the day, but not given here, there is seen to be a diurnal fluctuation at Cape Sheridan amounting to a little more than $\frac{1}{100}$ of an inch. The minima of this fluctuation are fairly well defined from November to April and occur at about 2 o'clock both A.M. and P.M.

After leaving Etah, August 17, 1908, on the voyage northward until July 12, 1909, thermograms covering $5\frac{1}{2}$ months and barograms covering nine months of this interval were obtained from self-recording instruments. These are records in addition to the direct hourly readings of the thermometer and barometer made by the tide observers and from which the above results have been deduced.

APPENDIX II

Facsimiles of Original Observations by Marvin, Bart-lett, and Peary and of Original Certificates by Marvin and Bartlett, respectively, during the Sledge Journey to the Pole.

[NOTE. — The originals were all made in pencil in notebooks. The engravings in line printed in this appendix are reproductions in slightly reduced size of tracings carefully made of the original manuscripts. The enclosing line in each case indicates the edges of the leaf on which the original work was written.

The size of this leaf is, with practical uniformity throughout the series, 4 x 6¾ inches. The facsimiles of Peary's observations of April 7, 1909, (*q. v.*) on pages 292 and 293 have been similarly made but are in the exact size of the originals. *The Publishers.*]

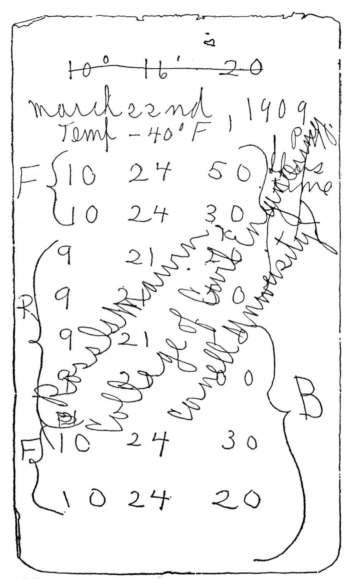

I. (a) FACSIMILE, SLIGHTLY REDUCED IN SIZE, OF MARVIN'S
OBSERVATIONS OF MARCH 22, 1909

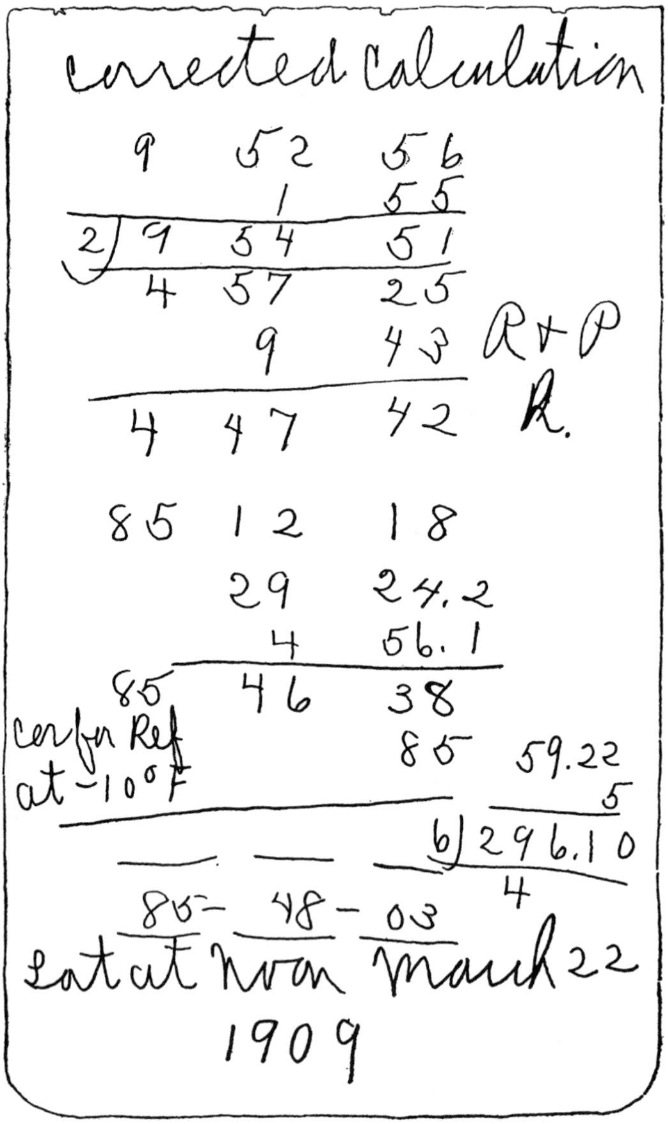

corrected Calculation

9   52   56
       1   55
2) 9 54   51
   4 57   25
         9 43 R+P
                R.
   4 47   42

85   12   18
     29   24.2
      4   56. 1
85   46   38
cor for Ref
at -10°F   85   59.22
                       5
               6) 296.10
                      4
   85- 48- 03
Lat at Noon March 22
        1909

I. (b) FACSIMILE, SLIGHTLY REDUCED IN SIZE, OF MARVIN'S
    OBSERVATIONS OF MARCH 22, 1909

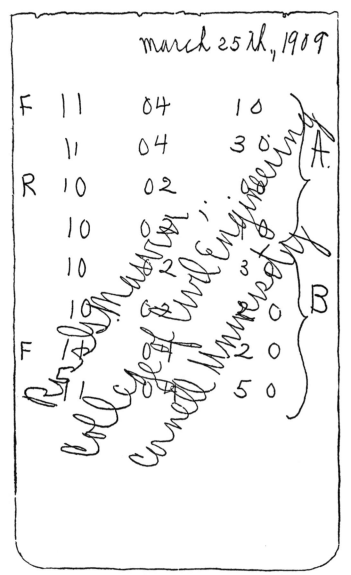

II. (a) FACSIMILE, SLIGHTLY REDUCED IN SIZE, OF MARVIN'S
OBSERVATIONS OF MARCH 25, 1909

```
11      0 4      1 0
11      o 4      3 8
11      0 4      2 0
11      0 4      5 0
10      0 2      0 0
10      0 2      1 0
10      0 2      3 0
10      0 2      2 0
        2 6      5 8
        2 4 0
        2 6 6


10      3 3      2 1
         2       4 4    y. C.
2) 1 0   3 6      1 5
   5     1 8      0 7
           9      1 5
   5  -  0 8  -  5 2

   8 4  -  5 1  -  0 8
```

II. (b) FACSIMILE, SLIGHTLY REDUCED IN SIZE, OF MARVIN'S
OBSERVATIONS OF MARCH 25, 1909

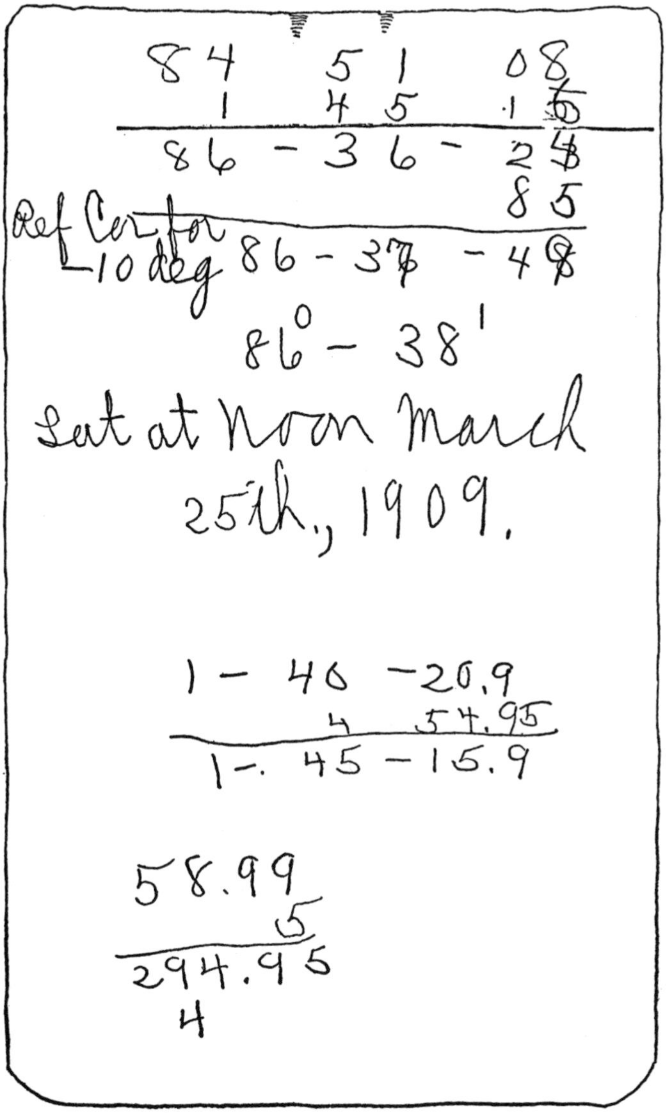

$$84 \quad 5\,1 \quad 0\,8$$
$$1 \quad 4\,5 \quad \cdot 1\,5$$
$$\overline{86 - 36 - 2\,4}$$
$$8\,5$$

Ref Cen for
$$-10 \deg \quad 86 - 37 - 4\,8$$
$$86° - 38'$$

Sat at Noon March 25th., 1909.

$$1 - 46 - 20.9$$
$$4 \quad 54.95$$
$$\overline{1 -. \ 45 - 15.9}$$

$$58.99$$
$$5$$
$$\overline{294.95}$$
$$4$$

march 25th., 1909.

This is to certify that I turn back from this point with the 3 rd supporting party Commander Peary advancing with nine men in the party seven sledges with the standard loads, and 6 0 dogs, men and dogs all in first class condition. The Captain with the 4 th and last supporting party expects to turn back at the end of five more marches determined our latitude by observation on

III. (a) FACSIMILE, SLIGHTLY REDUCED IN SIZE, OF MAR-
VIN'S CERTIFICATE OF MARCH 25, 1909

March 22nd and again today, March 25th. A copy of the observations and computations is herewith enclosed. Results of observations were as follows.

Lat at Noon March 22nd
85° 48' North

Lat at Noon March 25th
86° 38' North

Distance made good in three marches 50 minutes of latitude, an average of 16 2/3 nautical miles per march.

III. (b) FACSIMILE, SLIGHTLY REDUCED IN SIZE, OF MARVIN'S CERTIFICATE OF MARCH 25, 1909

The weather is fine, going good and improving each day.
signed,
RsslsMarvin,
College of Civil Engineering
Cornell University

III. (c) FACSIMILE, SLIGHTLY REDUCED IN SIZE, OF MAR-
VIN'S CERTIFICATE OF MARCH 25, 1909

obs Alt 13 9 00
P8 + 4 00
13 13 · 00
Refrak + P − 3 · 55
13 9 05
Smud + 16 · 02
13 · 25 · 07
Ther Cor + 10 − 33
2 (13 24 34
Jast 6 42 17
90 7
83 17 · 43
4 29 · 06
Lat-in 87 46 49 N
at-Noon
April 1/09

A dif 57 · 91
5
2 8/9 · 55
4 · 50

Ap decl 4 · 24 · 16 · 1
4 : 50
True decl 4 · 29 06

Robert A. Bartlett
Master, SS. "Roosevelt"

IV. FACSIMILE, SLIGHTLY REDUCED IN SIZE, OF BARTLETT'S
OBSERVATIONS OF APRIL 1, 1909

Arctic Ocean, April. 1. 09.

I have today personally determined our latitude to be by sextant observations;—

Lat in 87. 46. 49 N

I return from here in command of the 4th. Supporting Party.

I leave Commander Peary with 5 men, 5 sledges with full loads, And 40 picked dogs.

Men & dogs are in good condition, the going fair, the weather good

At the same average as our

v. (a) FACSIMILE, SLIGHTLY REDUCED IN SIZE, OF BART-
LETT'S CERTIFICATE OF APRIL 1, 1909

last eight marches Commander Peary should reach the Pole in eight days

Robert A. Bartlett, Master, S. S. "Roosevelt."

v. (b) FACSIMILE, SLIGHTLY REDUCED IN SIZE, OF BART-
LETT'S CERTIFICATE OF APRIL 1, 1909

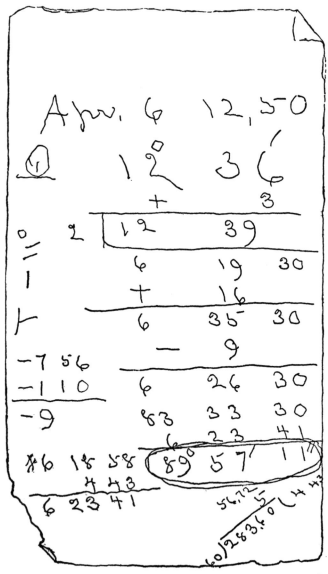

VI. FACSIMILE, SLIGHTLY REDUCED IN SIZE, OF PEARY'S
OBSERVATIONS OF APRIL 6, 1909

APPENDIX III

Report of the sub-commitee of the National Geographic Society on Peary's Records, and Some of the Honors Awarded for the Attainment of the Pole.

The Board of Managers of the National Geographic Society at a meeting held at Hubbard Memorial Hall, November 4, 1909, received the following report:

"The sub-committee to which was referred the task of examining the records of Commander Peary in evidence of his having reached the North Pole, beg to report that they have completed their task.

"Commander Peary has submitted to his sub-committee his original journal and record of observations, together with all his instruments and apparatus, and certain of the most important of the scientific results of his expedition. These have been carefully examined by your sub-committee, and they are unanimously of the opinion that Commander Peary reached the North Pole on April 6, 1909.

"They also feel warranted in stating that the organization, planning, and management of the expedition, its complete success, and its scientific results, reflect the greatest credit on the ability of Commander Robert E. Peary, and render him worthy

363

of the highest honors that the National Geographic Society can bestow upon him."

(*Signed*) HENRY GANNETT.[1]

C. M. CHESTER.[2]

O. H. TITTMANN.[3]

The foregoing report was unanimously approved.

Immediately after this action the following resolutions were unanimously adopted:

"*Whereas*, Commander Robert E. Peary has reached the North Pole, the goal sought for centuries; and

"*Whereas*, this is the greatest geographical achievement that this society can have opportunity to honor: Therefore

"*Resolved*, that a special medal be awarded to Commander Peary."

Among the home and foreign honors awarded for the attainment of the pole are the following:

[1] HENRY GANNETT, *chairman of the committee* which reported on Commander Peary's observations, has been chief geographer of the United States Geological Survey since 1882; he is the author of "Manual of Topographic Surveying," "Statistical Atlases of the Tenth and Eleventh Censuses," "Dictionary of Altitudes," "Magnetic Declination in the United States," Stanford's "Compendium of Geography," and of many government reports. Mr. Gannett is vice-president of the National Geographic Society and was one of the founders of the society in 1888.

[2] *Rear-Admiral* COLBY M. CHESTER, *United States Navy*, was graduated from the United States Naval Academy in 1863. He has held practically every important command under the Navy Department, including superintendent of the United States Naval Observatory, commander-in-chief Atlantic Squadron, Superintendent of the United States Naval Academy, Chief Hydrographic Division, United States Navy. Admiral Chester has been known for many years as one of the best and most particular navigators in the service.

[3] O. H. TITTMANN has been Superintendent of the United States Coast and Geodetic Survey since 1900. He is the member for the United States of the Alaskan Boundary Commission and was one of the founders of the National Geographic Society.

THE SPECIAL GREAT GOLD MEDAL OF THE NATIONAL GEOGRAPHIC
SOCIETY OF WASHINGTON
(This medal is four inches in diameter)

THE SPECIAL GREAT GOLD MEDAL OF THE ROYAL GEOGRAPHICAL
SOCIETY OF LONDON. (ACTUAL SIZE)
(Designed by the wife of Captain Robert F. Scott, R. N., Leader of the British South Polar
Expeditions of 1901–1904 and 1910–1912)

The Special Great Gold Medal of the National Geographic Society of Washington.

The Special Gold Medal of the Philadelphia Geographical Society.

The Helen Culver Medal of the Chicago Geographical Society.

The Honorary Degree of Doctor of Laws from Bowdoin College.

The Special Great Gold Medal of the Royal Geographical Society of London.

The Nachtigall Gold Medal of the Imperial German Geographical Society.

The King Humbert Gold Medal of the Royal Italian Geographical Society.

The Hauer Medal of the Imperial Austrian Geographical Society.

The Gold Medal of the Hungarian Geographical Society.

The Gold Medal of the Royal Belgian Geographical Society.

The Gold Medal of the Royal Geographical Society of Antwerp.

[1]A Special Trophy from the Royal Scottish Geographical Society — a replica in silver of the ships used by Hudson, Baffin, and Davis.

The Honorary Degree of Doctor of Laws from the Edinburgh University.

Honorary Membership in the Manchester Geographical Society.

Honorary Membership in the Royal Netherlands Geographical Society of Amsterdam.

---

[1] At Edinburgh, at the conclusion of the address to the Royal Scottish Geographical Society, Lord Balfour of Burleigh presented to Commander Peary a silver model of a ship such as was used by illustrious arctic navigators in the olden times. The ship is a copy of a three-masted vessel in full sail, such as was in use in the latter part of the sixteenth century. The model is a beautiful specimen of the silversmith's art. On one of the sails is engraved the badge of the Royal Scottish Geographical Society, while another bears the inscription in Latin from the pen of Mr. W. B. Blaikie, which, translated, is as follows:

"This model of a ship, such as was used by John Davis, Henry Hudson, and William Baffin, illustrious arctic navigators of the olden time, has been presented by the Royal Scottish Geographical Society as an evidence of its congratulation, admiration, and recognition to Robert Edwin Peary, American citizen, an explorer of the frozen Arctic, not less daring than his daring predecessors, who was the first to attain to that thrice-noble goal so long sought by innumerable bold mariners, the North Pole. Edinburgh, May 24th, 1910."

INDEX

OTHER COOPER SQUARE PRESS TITLES OF INTEREST

MY ATTAINMENT OF THE POLE
Frederick A. Cook
New introduction by Robert M. Bryce
680 pp., 45 b/w illustrations
0-8154-1137-5
$22.95

THE SOUTH POLE
An Account of the Norwegian Antarctic Expedition
in the *Fram*, 1910–1912
Captain Roald Amundsen
Foreword by Fridtjof Nansen
New introduction by Roland Huntford
960 pp., 155 b/w illustrations
0-8154-1127-8
$29.95

THE *KARLUK*'S LAST VOYAGE
An Epic of Death and Survival in the Arctic, 1913–1916
Captain Robert A. Bartlett
New introduction by Edward E. Leslie
378 pp., 23 b/w photos, 3 maps
0-8154-1124-3
$18.95

CARRYING THE FIRE
An Astronaut's Journeys
Michael Collins
Foreword by Charles Lindbergh
512 pp., 32 pp. of b/w photos
0-8154-1028-6
$19.95

THROUGH THE BRAZILIAN WILDERNESS
Theodore Roosevelt
New introduction by H. W. Brands
448 pp., 3 maps
0-8154-1095-6
$19.95

AFRICAN GAME TRAILS
An Account of the African Wanderings of
an American Hunter-Naturalist
Theodore Roosevelt
New introduction by H. W. Brands
600 pp., 210 b/w illustrations
0-8154-1132-4
$22.95

ANTARCTICA
Firsthand Accounts of Exploration and Endurance
Edited by Charles Neider
468 pp.
0-8154-1023-9
$18.95

MAN AGAINST NATURE
Firsthand Accounts of Adventure and Exploration
Edited by Charles Neider
512 pp.
0-8154-1040-9
$18.95

GREAT SHIPWRECKS AND CASTAWAYS
Firsthand Accounts of Disasters at Sea
Edited by Charles Neider
256 pp.
0-8154-1094-8
$16.95

THE FABULOUS INSECTS
Essays by the Foremost Nature Writers
Edited by Charles Neider
288 pp.
0-8154-1100-6
$17.95

Available at bookstores; or call 1-800-462-6420

 Cooper Square Press

150 Fifth Avenue
Suite 911
New York, NY 10011